HIDDEN
CONFLICT IN
ORGANIZATIONS

OTHER RECENT VOLUMES IN THE
SAGE FOCUS EDITIONS

HIDDEN CONFLICT IN ORGANIZATIONS

Uncovering Behind-the-Scenes Disputes

Deborah M. Kolb
Jean M. Bartunek
editors

SAGE Publications
International Educational and Professional Publisher
Newbury Park   London   New Delhi

For information address:

SAGE Publications, Inc.
2455 Teller Road
Newbury Park, California 91320
E-mail: order@sagepub.com

SAGE Publications Ltd.
6 Bonhill Street
London EC2A 4PU
United Kingdom

SAGE Publications India Pvt. Ltd.
M-32 Market
Greater Kailash I
New Delhi 110 048 India

Printed in the United States of America

Library of Congress Cataloging-in-Publication Data

Main entry under title:
Hidden conflict in organizations : uncovering behind-the-scenes
    disputes / Deborah M. Kolb, Jean M. Bartunek, editors.
        p. cm. — (Sage focus editions; v. 141)
    Includes bibliographical references and index.
    ISBN 0-8039-4160-9. —ISBN 0-8039-4161-7 (pbk.)
    1. Interpersonal conflict.   2. Mediation.   3. Conflict management.
4. Organizational sociology.   I. Kolb, Deborah M.   II. Bartunek,
Jean M.
HM136.H43   1992
303.6'9—dc20   91-37721
                                                            CIP

    97 98 99 00 01 10 9 8 7 6 5

Sage Production Editor: Judith L. Hunter

Contents

Preface

This book began behind the scenes of our professional lives at a small restaurant in Boston. Since 1986, the two of us have been meeting almost every month at the same place, eating yuppie salads and soup. Relative strangers at the start, and from different disciplinary traditions, we began talking about the research each of us was planning or conducting in the field. Jean was soon to begin a study in which she and Robin Reid would investigate the processes of a structural change at a school. Deborah's interest in mediation had recently extended into organizations in a search for more emergent forms. As our various projects progressed, we began to make interesting connections. Because of the conflicts at the school, change seemed stymied, and because of the ways emergent mediators worked, they tended to preserve the existing structures in which they intervened. From these discussions, we came to see connections between conflict and a number of dimensions of organizational studies that seemed worthy of further exploration.

Conflict is hardly an understudied phenomenon in organization theory. Causal models and prescriptive formulations proliferate. Most of the concepts advanced in formal studies of conflict, however, did not help us much in making sense of what we found in our field research. Rather, it became clear to us that conflict was embedded in the routine and mundane activities of the work settings and that it was rarely officially acknowledged or managed in the ways most conflict models suggest. From this observation came the first stage of the collaboration that resulted in this book.

In 1988, we organized a very well-attended symposium at the Academy of Management meeting (set that year in Disneyland) that Roy Lewicki chaired. We asked John Van Maanen, Frank Dubinskas, and Calvin Morrill, all ethnographers who had intimate familiarity with organizations, to describe how conflict was manifested and handled in the settings they knew best. Joanne Martin looked at a particular organizational conflict from a feminist perspective. Deborah and Jean and Robin also made presentations. Our hunch proved correct. The symposium made clear how pervasive disputing is in organizations, how it is embedded in the daily routines of work, as well as the multiplicity of ways it is handled behind the organizational scene.

This book includes as authors most of the participants in that symposium. Ray Friedman joined the group by contributing a paper on collective bargaining from a behind-the-scenes perspective. And Linda Putnam became involved in a strange way. She reviewed the book manuscript for Sage and noticed something that had eluded us, that there was a dialectical tension between the way the authors in this book talk about conflict and the dominant ways conflict theorists talk about it. In particular, while most scholarly discussions of conflict are of the public and formal sort, where norms of rationality are the ideal, the conflicts described in this book are more private and informal, occurring in the nooks and crannies of organizations, where they are often handled somewhat nonrationally. We asked her to coauthor the introductory chapter and to use that occasion to develop these ideas.

Many people helped us in direct and indirect ways in formulating the concept of the book and bringing it to publication. Among them are Sally Merry, Susan Silbey, Donald Black, Lotte Bailyn, Jeffrey Rubin, J. William Breslin, Heather Pabrezis, and Blair Sheppard as well as the authors and research participants whose work and activities are reflected here. Cityside Restaurant deserves special mention as the meeting place for our conversations and the development of our ideas. The Kolb family, Jonathan, Sam, and Elizabeth, complained about the work but went to Disneyland anyway. Members of the Religious of the Sacred Heart, Jean's religious community, did not go to Disneyland but provided helpful conversations about the ideas in the book just the same. Harry Briggs has been an extraordinarily helpful editor even in the midst of unexpected delays.

We still meet for our lunch of salad and soup. But now that we know each other better, and have finally finished this book, we just gossip, a good thing to do behind the scenes.

1

Introduction

The Dialectics of Disputing

DEBORAH M. KOLB
LINDA L. PUTNAM

> The picture of the great corporation as a peaceful cooperative of its partic-
> ipants is more than highly improbable, it is extraordinarily fraudulent. It
> depends on a compelling commitment by all parties not to avoid dispute,
> conflict and hostility, but to keep them out of sight. The modern corpora-
> tion is socially a theatre of all the conflicts that might be expected when
> hundreds and thousands of highly charged, exceptionally self-motivated,
> and more than normally, self-serving people work closely together.
>
> Galbraith 1986, 21

Conflict is a persistent fact of organizational life. Situations of conflict
in organizations are not always or even usually the dramatic confrontations that receive most attention and publicity—strikes, walkouts,
firings. Nor is conflict usually bracketed into discrete public forums
where negotiation and designated third parties officially participate
in the resolution of differences. Rather, disputes are embedded in the

AUTHORS' NOTE: This chapter has gone through many revisions over the last few years.
Jean M. Bartunek, Roy J. Lewicki, Sally Merry, Blair Sheppard, Susan Silbey, and John
Van Maanen have each made special contributions at various times.

interactions between members as they go about their daily round of activities. While differences may be publicly aired, the vast majority occur out of sight and in forms other than official negotiation or grievance processing. Therefore the definitions of what constitutes conflict, the variety and sometimes contradictory forms it takes, and the interactions between its forms and processes require a close look at the routine and mundane activities that constitute life in organizations.

Although conflict is a familiar part of our experience in organizations, its value and centrality to considerations about organizations has waxed and waned following the changing winds in managerial ideology and social theory. While important social theorists such as Marx and Weber view group conflict as inevitably the result of social class and organization hierarchy, management theorists who span a number of different traditions define organizational conflict as potentially correctable failures. Conflict theorists, on the other hand, conceive of organizations as an inevitable battleground of differences traceable not to the characteristics of individuals but to the structural and intergroup attributes of organizations (Collins 1975). Conflict according to this perspective is a structural problem that is resolved by managerial intervention to alter reward systems, evaluation and decision-making criteria, reporting relationships, and other mechanisms of organization design (Galbraith 1977).

More recently, within a loosely defined set of theories that might be described as "political," the conflict, and its manifestations, become the concern of a more diverse set of organization members. Conceiving of organizations more as a set of shifting and changing cliques, conflict is not an episodic or problematic phenomenon but a pervasive fact of interaction, and it becomes the essence of organization (Pondy 1989). Organizations are arenas for conflict in which shifting coalitions with different interests and resources vie for influence and control (Pettigrew 1973; March and Olson 1976; Kanter 1977; Pfeffer and Salancik 1978; Bacharach and Lawler 1980).

It is obvious that the consideration of conflict in organizations and the empirical study of the phenomenon are not new. Historically, however, existing work has tended to focus primarily on the sources or reasons for conflict and to suggest the ways in which it supports or detracts from organizational aims and objectives (Pondy 1967; Coser 1956; Gouldner 1954). What people actually do in conflict situations and how the different forms of conflict processing coexist and affect the organizational order have not been of much interest to those who investigate activities in organizations (Collins 1975). Some of the various strains in the study of conflict in organizations will be reviewed in the second section of this introduction.

In parallel developments in legal scholarship, anthropologists and sociologists have sought a dynamic way to study legal processes to compare the varieties of ways conflicts are dealt with short of becoming public and therefore subject to law (Trubek 1980-81).[1] To move away from the study of law and legal institutions as systems of rules and the mechanisms that fostered conformity to them, Laura Nader and others have advocated a focus on disputing behavior, how people who have disagreements with each other deal with them over time and in specific social contexts (Nader 1965).

Disputing behavior can take a variety of forms, some of which are public and therefore subject to a discrete number of procedures. Private conflicts occur when one party does not acknowledge directly to the other a perceived grievance or injury, and so the mode of expression may be avoidance, camouflaged self-help, or toleration. When disagreements are defined as "conflict," they are more likely to be dyadic and the subject of confrontation either through coercion, force, or negotiation (Nader and Todd 1978; Felstiner, Abel, and Sarat 1981; Black 1990). As conflicts become public disputes, others may become actively engaged either as third party dispute resolvers or as partisans and coconspirators (Black and Baumgartner 1983). This dynamic approach to the study of conflict, one that emphasizes meanings, process, and the variety of procedures and relationships, may allow us to discern the lineaments of the kinds of conflict behavior described above. The disputing perspective and its utility for studying conflict in organizations is considered in the third section of this chapter.

A disputing perspective informs the research in this book, but what emerges from the empirical studies is a greater appreciation for some of the understudied dimensions of conflict management. A dialectical approach helps put these findings in perspective. Dialectics is a mode of explanation that takes duality as its focal point (Rawlins 1989). It entails identifying the bipolar opposites that are implicit in the way we study organizational conflict. That is, traditional approaches to the study of disputes in organizations typically center on particular aspects of conflict and ignore the bipolar opposites of these features. For example, studies of organizational conflict usually accent the formal channels through which disputes are processed rather than the informal modes of disagreement (Kolb 1987; Yngvesson 1978). Public arenas of conflict intervention become the domains of inquiry rather than the private realms that enable disputes to go public. Deliberate, logical, and rational approaches to conflict management are treated as superior to such nonrational modes as emotion and intuition. Ways that disputants vent feelings and cope with the nonrational side of conflict are rarely studied.

In this collection, the authors examine the understudied poles of these dualities and the relationships between them that surface in conflict situations. Thus what seems unrelated or ignored is now included as an essential element for understanding conflict processes. Characteristics and implications of this dialectical approach are detailed in the fourth section.

Working in diverse organizational settings, the authors in this book take typical occasions in the lives of organizations and document conflicts that arise and the ways they are understood, managed, and handled. If overt forms of confrontation and negotiation dominate in much existing literature, the penetrating eyes of these analysts are on the less obvious and covert forms of conflict management. What emerges from this work is a new understanding of the ways conflict is lived out in organizations and how organizations are fraught with tensions and contradictions over forms, place, and process. From examination of these contradictions and the dialectical relationships between them comes the possibility of seeing conflict processes within organizations in new ways. The individual chapters of the book are described in the final section of this chapter.

Strands in the Study of Conflict in Organizations

Conflict threads run through much of organization theory. Most acknowledge that conflict as well as harmony mark most social interactions, yet the way the phenomenon is cast, its connection to other features of organizations, and the value attached to it differ depending upon the school of thought that one consults. Even though conflict attracts some attention in organization theory, for the most part, it is a fleeting attention or thread into other frameworks or models (Burrell and Morgan 1979). In the development of hypotheses regarding conflict in organizations, there is virtually no discussion of how disputes are handled and only general connections between the forms of dispute processing and organization structure (Collins 1975; Mintzberg 1979). In the background of the dominant models in organization theory, however, in both its sociological and its managerial wings, there are strands of theory about conflict in organizations that bear on this project. Against this background, a renewed interest in conflict as a defining feature of organizations becomes clearer, and it is in this context that a focus on conflict processes takes on new meaning.

Threads of conflict and its management are woven into early managerial thought in the well-known tenets of classical management and human relations. These works provide a foil for much of what follows them because of their emphases on harmony and cooperation in the workplace as a desired and achievable end. In the works of Taylor and other administrative theorists, conflicts between employees and management are a taken-for-granted feature of organizations. What classical theory advocates is a system of technical analysis and rational administration for the efficient operation of the workplace. Through adherence to principles of classical management and the scientific analysis of jobs, cooperation could be secured. According to Taylor, if everybody adheres to the laws of the situation, there is no place for bargaining and quarrels (as reported in Mouzelis 1967, 83).

While classical theory addresses itself to the controlling function of management, human relations theory is known for its focus on the informal or interpersonal dimensions of leadership. Moving beyond pious pronouncements about the benefits of cooperation, for men such as Elton Mayo and Chester Barnard, achieving cooperation is the very essence of organization. Organizations, according to Barnard, achieve moral purpose only insofar as they are cooperative, and it falls to the executive to instill this moral purpose through the development of shared goals and economic incentives. "Cooperation, not leadership, is the creative process; but leadership is the indispensable fulminator of its forces" (Barnard 1938, 259). In this work written by an executive, descriptions of actual operations are absent. Perrow (1979, 89-90) suggests that omitting the underside of the organization with its conflict, multiple goals, cliques, and nonrational and nonlogical behavior allows Barnard to uphold his vision of the cooperative organization.

Cooperation, in the works of Elton Mayo and the researchers at the Hawthorne plant, is a function of social organization. To induce workers to cooperate with management aims, it falls to the supervisor to adopt a supportive and participatory style of leadership and to enhance communication. While subsequent study has undermined some of these conclusions, the tradition has been a dominant one in organization behavior in most of the work on leadership and motivation. Conflicts of interest between workers and management have no legitimate places in human relations theory. Because cooperation is so highly prized, the role of conflict in achieving cooperation tends to be understudied. Further, by focusing only on individuals and groups, social psychologists emphasize the aspects of interpersonal relations and the misunderstandings that dominate. Indeed, many of the current prescriptive formulations regarding conflict management focus on these interpersonal dynamics (see Pruitt and Rubin 1986; Rahim and Bonoma 1979; Thomas 1976). Minimized in this perspective are the relationships between interpersonal frictions and social conflicts that are rooted in organization and social structures (Mouzelis 1967, 116).

Moving beyond the work group, empirical studies of bureaucracy constitute another thread of conflict in organization theory. Taking off from Weber's formulation of bureaucracy, in which hierarchy, rules, and legitimate, rational-legal authority keep conflict in check, "post-Weberian" scholars carried out a series of case studies whose purpose was to investigate how bureaucratic structures create contradictory conditions that act to modify and undermine aspects of bureaucracy (Blau 1955). In contexts such as a gypsum mine (Gouldner 1965), an employment agency and an investigative bureau (Blau 1955), manufacturing firms (Dalton 1959), and the TVA (Selznick 1949), among others, these authors demonstrate how official conditions affect interpersonal relationships and how these behaviors conflict with, and informally modify, bureaucratic rules. By documenting the patterned ways that members of these different organizations adapt to bureaucratic rules and to the organization's efforts to control them, these writers are, in essence, depicting the ways conflicts between workers and managers or employees and the organization are handled. Further, because the works counterpose bureaucratic functions and dysfunctions, the values traditionally attached to these poles are challenged.

There are a number of themes that emerge from these studies that bear on the work presented here. Rather than seeing organizations as integrated wholes, these studies of the workings of bureaucracy imply considerable conflict of interests between those who manage and those who are at the receiving end, between certain work groups, and between bureaucrats and clients (Gouldner 1954; Blau 1955; Dalton 1959; Crozier 1964). Indeed, these works suggest many of the reasons that conflicts are likely to occur in organizations. The close attention to behavior that marks these case studies begins to demonstrate some of the covert and contradictory ways that conflict is handled. Thus, in the gypsum mine, the workers slow down their pace and the managers in Dalton's firms camouflage their political activity. The interaction between the workers' actions and management's bureaucratic reaction to control the informal activity, and then the union's response, such as a wildcat strike, prefigures the kind of dialectic inquiry that marks the works reported here.

At the same time that these works have connection to this project, there are some significant differences that are important to note. Bureaucracy is the foil for these studies. Their focus is not explicitly on the description and dialectics of conflict, its management, and the consequences of such activity. Instead, the intention is to demonstrate how different variants of bureaucratic functioning may contribute (or not) to organizational stability. In taking this perspective, the multifocal interests that are represented in the descriptions are closed out in the analysis. The analysis clusters around certain specific relationships—line versus staff, professional versus nonprofessional, and workers versus management—but does not explore such issues as how the conflicts as enacted preserve these distinctions and set the stage for future disputes (Mintzberg 1979).

During the 1960s, particularly in management theory, conflict in organizations resurfaced as a major topic of interest (Pondy 1967). Eschewing the small group, cooperative stance of earlier work, scholarship focused on the structural sources of conflict, particularly for conflicts that occurred between various functional departments (Lawrence and Lorsch 1967; Thompson 1967; Walton and Dutton 1969). These works emphasize the organizational necessity for increasing functional specialization and then the inevitable conflict that results from such structural arrangements. What distinguishes this line of inquiry from earlier studies is the explicit focus on a limited range of choices members have in managing conflict and the normative position regarding which modes are to be preferred generally and under specific circumstances. Across functional boundaries, for example, collaboration is to be preferred to competition (Walton and Dutton 1969) and confrontation to smoothing and forcing in most situations, particularly where high stakes are involved (Lawrence and Lorsch 1967; Thomas 1976).

The normative perspective that underlies this strand of work and its focus on formal and institutionalized causes and processes of conflict has been challenged in two major ways by recent work. First, shifts in world markets and the consequent revisions in corporate strategy and structure result in organizations that are characterized less by bureaucracy than by *adhocracy* (Drucker 1988; Peters and Waterman 1982). Organizations are often less hierarchical and leaner and meaner, characterized by the proliferation of task forces, project teams, and product groups. Conflict is built into these organizations and not just into a hierarchy. As Mintzberg (1979, 462) describes it: Adhocracies imply conflict, "where specialists from different professions must work together on multidisciplinary teams, and where, owing to the organic nature of the structure, the political games that result are played without rules." Politics and political models of organizations supplant those that take bureaucracy and formal structures as their point of departure.

Second, the work force in organizations has become increasingly diverse such that society's conflicts are increasingly enacted in the workplace. This has meant that industrial sociologists have expanded their focus beyond the organization. Where traditionally the study of conflict involved represented groups engaged in institutionalized forms of conflict management, such as collective bargaining, now the purview is expanded to include other ways that technology and rule making control the expression of conflict (Burroway 1979; Hill 1981; Clegg 1981). The implications of gender, race, and ethnicity have also changed some of the ways that conflict is conceptualized in organizations (Hearn et al. 1989; Kanter 1977).

Political theories of organization define conflict as inherent in the structure of organizations (Bacharach and Lawler 1980; Kanter 1977; Pettigrew 1973; Pfeffer and Salancik 1978). In the politics of organizations, shifting coalitions (or groups) with different interests and resources try to establish their influence and control within constraints imposed by technology, structures, and cultures (Tichy 1981). The expected relationship between politics and the dynamics of conflict management—specifically, which coalitions are of interest and the forms of disputing employed—take different forms depending on the theory one consults. Decision-making metaphors of the firm emphasize conflicts among members of the ruling coalition. Conflict is resolved through negotiations over goals and sequential attention to decisions (Cyert and March 1963). The structural mechanisms for the partial resolution of the conflicts engendered by these differentiated entities are the subject of well-known prescriptions of specialized roles and the use of team configurations (Galbraith 1977; Lawrence and Lorsch 1967; Miles 1980; Thompson 1967). Within these teams and across units, however, disputes arise and are just as likely to be tolerated and/or handled off-line as they are to be the subject of negotiations (Kunda 1986; Kolb 1989a).

Pluralist versions of organizations focus on interest group coalitions that hold each other in check through a system of countervailing power, akin to a miniature state (Hyman 1978). While relationships between management and workers, at least in unionized firms, have been described as pluralistic (Kerr 1955), more recently the label has been used to describe relationships between groups and units at the same hierarchical level (Morgan 1981). The process most associated with managing conflict in pluralistic entities is negotiation.[2] Those who work in this tradition are concerned with sources of power available to different coalitions, how they are mobilized and used in negotiations, and with what consequences (Bacharach and Lawler 1980; Kanter 1977; Mintzberg 1985; Pfeffer and Salancik 1978). Again, the relationships between organized negotiation and the coexisting and disorganized processes of conflict expression are not considered.

Changing demography and demand for labor have resulted in a work force that is considerably more diverse than the cohort even 10 years ago. As new groups enter the work force and move up in organizations, conflicts rooted in class, gender, race, and ethnicity have become more prominent. Society's conflicts are imported into organizations, and the forms these differences take in organizational settings become, out of necessity, of more concern to scholars and practitioners (Burroway 1979; Kanter 1977; Marshall 1984). These changes challenge some of the central assumptions of pluralism; namely, that interested coalitions are organized and have equal access (if not equal opportunity) to sources of power (Lukes 1974; Hyman 1978). Blacks, women, ethnic minorities, and other interest groups may cluster into support groups, caucuses, or networks but these groups generally lack the kind of voice and clout of organizations such as unions. The political focus shifts therefore to disparities of power in organizations and the way structure and culture defuse certain kinds of political influence and enable some gro.ps to control and dominate others (Braverman 1974; Burrell and Morgan 1979; Burroway 1979; Edwards 1979; Goldman and Van Houten. 1977; Kunda 1986). If the key process for managing conflict is structural in the first strain, and bargaining in the second, it is suppression by those with power and avoidance and toleration by those without it (Black 1990). Those who feel their lack of power often deal with conflict in the few ways that remain open to them and in so doing often reproduce the marginality of their positions (Baumgartner 1988; Crozier 1964; Mechanic 1962; Scott 1985).

In most of the strands of organization theory, especially in its more applied forms, the management of conflict, whether by force or consensus, is defined as central to the smooth or integrated functioning of organizations.[3] Whether conflict is managed through structures and rules (Lawrence and Lorsch 1967), or normative appeals to culture and values (Kunda and Barley 1988; Schein 1985), or by learning more expert negotiation strategies (Bazerman and Neale 1983; Lax and Sebenius 1986), and/or by rites and rituals (Trice 1984; Trice and Beyer 1984), the implications are similar. Effective conflict management, which may include both fostering and preventing conflict (see Brown 1982), leads to higher-performing organizations.

A contrasting perspective highlights the disintegrative tendencies in organizations based on differences in occupations, gender, ethnicity, and culture. These forces pull the organizations in different and autonomous directions and may yield to more disintegration than unity (Edwards 1979; Kunda 1986; Morgan 1981; Weick 1979). Conflict is seen as a perennial feature of organizations, always present in crevices and crannies and just below the surface, bubbling up occasionally as disputes in certain places and enacted in accord with particular conventions and rules. This perspective highlights the increased potential for conflict in organizations at the same time as there are pulls toward integration.

Strains in organizational theorizing about conflict have changed considerably as organizations have become more complicated than the gypsum mine, the old boy's network in manufacturing, the nonprofessional government agencies, and the new quasi-governmental structure in rural Tennessee. What emerges from recent scholarship is a picture of the modern organization as rife with conflict that has its roots in individual, social, organizational, and cultural relationships that overflow existing descriptive and normative typologies of how they are managed

(Pondy 1989). What is needed are different theoretical frameworks and methods to capture the dynamics of conflict in contemporary organizations. The disputing perspective is one such approach.

Disputing in the Workplace

Disputing is the social scientist's way of talking about legal and quasi-legal procedures and institutions. A disputing perspective shifts the focus of inquiry from structures and formal rules to the processes of conflict expression and action. To take a dispute(s) as the unit of analysis is to focus on the behavior of various parties to a conflict as it unfolds over time and to look at the interaction of a conflict and the procedures by which it is processed as the essential ways that issues are made meaningful and resolved (Nader 1965; Sarat 1987). The notion of disputing implies a complex interaction of issues, players, context, and dispute processes as the nexus for understanding how conflicts are managed in different settings.

First, a disputing perspective provides a set of conflict-handling categories. There are only a limited number of ways that people have to deal with differences. The basic forms of conflict management include self-help (force, vengeance), avoidance[4] (withdrawing from the relationship), "lumping it" (tolerating the situation without public comment), negotiation, and the involvement of third parties as mediators, arbitrators, and/or adjudicators (Black 1990; Nader and Todd 1978). While other schemes in the organization field exist, they imply situated behavioral choices such as collaboration and compromise (see Thomas 1976). The basic forms presuppose multiple tracks that are pursued depending on who is involved, how the social drama is orchestrated, and the form dispute resolution takes (Burroway 1979; Yngvesson 1978). There is evidence, for example, that, when complainants feel that a satisfactory outcome has not been achieved, they try again using different tactics and placing blame elsewhere. As grievances accumulate, the aggrieved engage in more defiant acts (Salipante and Fortado 1988). Among managers, there is a noted tendency to treat conflict and potential disputes as problems that can be solved through better decision making or improved communication (March and Simon 1958; Kriesberg 1973). Members have incentives to engage in this "masking" (Kolb 1985) because it allows work to proceed according to customary decision-making rules, which tend to preserve working relationships that more overt forms of disputing might threaten (Yngvesson 1978). By highlighting the multiple forms of dispute processing, it becomes possible to identify some of the forms that are less obvious and public such as avoidance, vengeance, gossip, and other forms of self-help (see Morrill 1991). Further, the fact that these private, nonconfrontational approaches exist helps account for the relative infrequency of publicly articulated grievances that can be dealt with directly through negotiation and third party intervention (Miller and Sarat 1980-81).

Scholarship in disputing has not merely named procedures but has alerted us to the variation among processes and the circumstances that prompt the use of different forms. Existing research suggests that which procedure is employed in a dispute will depend upon the relationships between the parties (Gluckman 1955; Felstiner 1974; Galanter 1974; Yngvesson and Mather 1983), the kind of issues in dispute (Starr and Yngvesson 1975; Silbey and Merry 1987), and the culture in which the procedures are embedded (Nader and Todd 1978; Merry 1987; Greenhouse 1986). Despite the use of similar terms to describe conflict procedures, empirical study suggests that they take different forms in different contexts. Mediation, for example, is practiced in different ways by different practitioners in different settings depending on the problem brought to mediation, the relationship of the parties to each other and the mediator, the institutional location of mediation, and the timing of mediation relative to other procedures (Kolb 1983, 1986; Silbey and Merry 1987).

Within organizations, the study of mediation exemplifies the ways that different processes become blurred. Recently, mediation has been advocated as an effective and fair method for resolving disputes. Studies of mediation in simulated organizational context, for example, suggest that people find it fairer and more satisfactory than other, more controlled forms of intervention (Karambayya and Brett 1989; Lewicki and Sheppard 1985; Sheppard 1983). Despite these desirable attributes, research that is conducted within organizations suggests that managers are not natural mediators (Kolb 1986; Sheppard 1983). There are occasions when managers will mediate disputes, particularly when it is important to maintain a working relationship between the parties. But, to the degree that managers are held accountable for particular decisions, are concerned about precedent, and personalize the bases of disagreement, they are more likely to adopt adjudicative or inquisitorial approaches to conflict management (Lewicki and Sheppard 1985; Sheppard et al. 1990). What these tales from the management field suggest is that conflict management by superiors with subordinates looks more like the exercise of authority than third party facilitation.

Another significant contribution the disputing perspective makes to our understanding of conflict management is the emphasis it places on the interpretive processes that underlie the emergence of disputes and the ways disputes are phrased at different times and places. There is nothing inherent in the notion of a conflict. It is a performance to which different audiences attach meanings, which often change over time (Felstiner, Abel, and Sarat 1981). Depending on the audience and the forum in which it is expressed, the same conflict can be phrased in any number of different ways (Smith 1989). A dispute can be defined in terms of rights that are violated, interests that could be served, or power that is exerted as a matter of choice and custom (Silbey and Sarat 1988; Ury, Brett, and Goldberg 1988). In other words, the issues and problems in disputes have no meaning apart from the context in which they are enacted (Mather and Yngvesson 1980-81; Sarat 1987).

> A dispute is not a static event which simply "happens," but . . . the structure of disputes, quarrels, and offenses includes changes or transformations over time. Transformations occur because participants in the disputing process have different interests in and perspectives on the dispute; participants assert these interests and perspectives in the very process of defining and shaping the object of the dispute. What a dispute is about, whether it is even a dispute or not, and whether it is properly a "legal" dispute, may be central issues for negotiation in the dispute process. (Mather and Yngvesson 1980-81, 776-77)

Thus there is an interaction between conflicts and how they are interpreted and phrased and the ways they are handled. That is, dispute procedures adapt to the kinds of problems, parties, and situations encountered and, in the process, alter and transform the meanings of conflict (Merry and Rochleau 1985; Silbey and Merry 1987).

Finally, scholarship in disputing challenges certain normative assumptions about conflict resolution. Conflicts are rarely resolved but are dealt with and/or processed in ways that rephrase, repress, or redefine them, and so they continue to surface again in different ways (Merry and Silbey 1984; Smith 1989). In other words, the outcomes of most conflicts are other conflicts with only temporary respites in between (Abel 1982). Further, dispute resolution processes influence the structures in which they are embedded. Negotiation and informal third party procedures such as mediation tend to individualize conflict and grievances and so make systemic change less likely (Abel 1982; Kolb 1987). Indeed, absent legal or quasi-legal intervention, these works suggest that power relationships will remain unchanged when disputes are settled by informal means. This occurs because dispute resolution processes tend to take on predictable forms that mobilize power imbalances inherent in existing relationships and institutions (Bachrach and Baratz 1962; Lukes 1974; Galanter 1974; Kolb 1983). Thus conflict management is intimately connected to issues of social control and change.

The study of disputes has not been without its critics. Some argue that a disputing focus displays a bias toward order and harmony because it fails to consider the reasons that people are reluctant to go public with their disputes and engage those in authority (Cain and Kulscar 1982; Engel 1980). Still others suggest that, by extending the concept of dispute to include activities that occur outside the law, disputing has come to encompass much of dyadic interaction (Silbey and Sarat 1988). Kidder (1980-81) observes that dispute studies have become, in essence, micro studies of the management of conflict in which individual perceptions, interpretations, responses, and strategies become the focus of research with little attention to systematic outcomes such as access to justice. From a sociolegal perspective, these critiques may be problematic. In contexts where conflict is seen to be an ongoing feature of organization life, and where it is difficult to demarcate conflict from other forms of social interaction (Turner 1969; Wrong 1979), however, such a perspective focuses attention on the micro management of differences, which is a new and fresh approach to the study of conflict in organizations. As Turner (1957) observes, one of the best ways to study social systems is to locate and isolate those points where conflict is likely to be found and to consider the ways the social dramas are played out (see Kunda 1986).

Contemporary organizations are the settings for many of the current disputes in our society. One might argue that, with changing structures and values in communities, our large organizations constitute the new communities in which people form relationships and social identities (Edwards 1979; Kanter 1977; Kunda 1986). In this view, social conflicts concerning race, gender, class, status, and individualism, among others, are acted out on the organizational stage. Thus organizations in the private and public spheres are natural places to extend our inquiry about disputing, conflict, social control, and law (Silbey and Sarat 1988). There is a major distinction, however, between disputing in the shadow of the law and that which occurs within organizations.[5] Law is not the predominant mode of social control within organizations. Instead, it is bureaucratic procedures and administrative orders and rules, which are necessarily incomplete and partial, that bound action (Thompson 1967). It is certainly true, however, that federal and state law permeates the boundaries of organizations and influences increasingly broader domains of managerial activity (Scott, Nystrom, and Starbuck 1981; Selznick 1970). Labor-management relations, the rights of minorities, the discretion to hire, promote, and fire employees are circumscribed by legislation and court decisions. Partially in response to the increasing legalization of the workplace, organizations have installed complaint systems that are intended to give employees voice in the expression of their grievances (Hirschman 1970; Ewing 1977; Rowe 1987; Westin and Feliu 1988; Ury, Brett, and Goldberg 1988; Ziegenfuss 1988; Edelman 1990). The promise of an open door with the availability of an ombudsman, a peer complaint board, and a multistep grievance procedure are often instituted as means to keep conflicts contained within the organization. In addition to other potential benefits to organizations, these procedures are introduced, in part, to avoid litigation and keep the state out of the organization's human resource management affairs (Westin and Feliu 1988).

These formal dispute resolution systems are closely analogous to some of the adjudicative, arbitral, mediated, and negotiated forms of dispute resolution procedures that exist in communities and have developed as alternatives to litigation (Goldberg, Green, and Sander 1985). The natural study of disputing in organizations might logically, one could argue, focus on the problems and cases that are processed within these formal systems. Indeed, there is a need for this kind of work. Empirical inquiry about organizational complaint procedures has been rather narrow, limited primarily to formal descriptions of procedures (Foulkes 1982; Ewing 1977; Rowe 1987; Westin and Feliu 1988; Ziegenfuss 1988) and some evaluation of satisfaction as well as cost (Ury, Brett, and Goldberg 1988). The few studies that have looked into the way some of these procedures are used show that relatively few disputes find their way into the formal channels and that negative consequences (in terms of performance evaluations and promotions) attend their use (Lewin 1987; Kolb 1987). This is not surprising. Given existing power structures in contemporary organizations and the norms against public claims (in the absence of unions), it is unlikely that these formal channels constitute the only, or even the major, location where conflict and grievances are worked out (Kolb 1987). Thus, to study disputing in organizations, the focus will need to be extended to examine the less public forums in which disputes are processed so that the relationships between private and public domains and the dynamics that mark them can be delineated. What a disputing perspective contributes is the means by which to uncover the dialectics of conflict processes in organizations. Because a disputing perspective bridges public and private domains, it provides a basis for examining the links between bipolar opposites.

A Dialectical Approach to the Study of Organizational Conflict

A dialectical approach is a way of considering the relationship between traditional features of organizational conflict and their opposites. What might appear as a distinct phenomenon can be understood only with reference to its opposite, even when the opposite concept is not visible. For example, what seems unstructured contains the seeds of structure; what is labeled as an individual phenomenon implies the collective as well (Mitroff and Mason 1981). Additionally, the private management of conflict operates within the public arena just as the public scene depends on the private realm.

Bipolar opposites, however, are not merely different than one another; they form a duality in that they mutually exclude and simultaneously include each other. One type of duality that has surfaced frequently in the conflict literature is *cooperation* and *competition*. The relationship between these classic terms provides one example of how two opposing phenomena simultaneously exclude and include each other.

Initially, game theory researchers designed studies to reflect purely competitive or zero-sum situations in which participants sought to maximize their gains and minimize their losses. Then they began to realize that competition in conflict cannot be understood apart from its opposite, cooperation (Gulliver 1979; Lax and Sebenius 1986). Because the parties in conflict rely on each other to achieve their individual goals, they must cooperate to compete. Yet the two parties in conflict see their goals as incompatible or mutually excluding. In effect, each party's reliance on the other to attain an individual goal makes competition include cooperation. Rubin (1983) refers to this duality as a "quintessential illustration of interdependence" that pulls conflict in extreme directions as disputants walk a tightrope between trust and distrust, honesty and dishonesty, and risk of exploitation and risk of escalation.

A dialectical approach looks at the way such bipolar opposites coexist, interact, and evolve in a conflict situation (Putnam 1990; Rawlins 1989). More specifically, a dialectical approach seeks to uncover the nature and type of dualities that exist for given phenomena, the way they surface in a dispute, and how they change and evolve over time (Mitroff and Mason 1981). Hence movement or change is a fundamental property of a dialectical approach. To return to our example, as conflict is enacted, competitive motives and behaviors may gradually drive out cooperative actions such that the competitive pole negates its opposite. Conflict escalation typifies this pattern. In like manner, accommodation may override direct confrontation resulting in an overly cooperative exchange in which neither party reaches his or her objectives. Thus it is possible for one pole in a duality to become dominant and to negate its opposite. Specific to this book, the poles of the public, the formal, and the rational in traditional conflict research dominate the literature and drive out consideration of the private, the informal, and the nonrational aspects of disputes.

The dialectical approach informs the chapters in this book and provides a basis for comparing and contrasting how disputes occur in various organizations. As such, it offers an alternative for uncovering the arenas where disputes are handled and suggests concepts that largely have been ignored by traditional scholarship in conflict management. Many different types of bipolar opposites constitute the nature of disputing. The tensions between cooperation and competition and the links between trust and distrust appear in the conflict literature (Lax and Sebenius 1986; Walton and McKersie 1965). These dualities, however, fit particular types of bureaucratic and systems-related conflicts, namely, those that are managed strategically, formally, and publicly (Pondy 1967; Lawrence and Lorsch 1967). To understand how conflict works offstage

Conflict Arena

Public:	Private:
overt, visible	covert, hidden
authorized	unauthorized
confrontation	avoidance
public norms	situational norms

Social Structure

Formal:	Informal:
official roles	unofficial positions
legal system	normative rules
formal deliberations	gossip, political skirmishes

Conflict Orientation

Rational:	Nonrational:
premeditated	spontaneous
strategic choice	impulsiveness
logical	emotional
prescriptive	situationally adaptive

Figure 1.1. Bipolar Opposites in Conflict Systems

or in the ongoing skirmishes of daily activity, we need to examine alternative bipolar opposites, ones heretofore overlooked by organizational researchers and ones that capture the subtle and less visible aspects of conflict interactions. Three types of bipolar opposites meet this need and provide a framework for this book: *public-private, formal-informal,* and *rational-nonrational.* These three dualities embody other bipolar opposites that make up the nature of conflict systems (see Figure 1.1). These oppositional terms call attention to the arena, the social structure, and the orientation of conflict. Hence they focus on the context in which disputes occur as well as orientations to conflict management.

Theories of organizational conflict (see, for example, Pondy 1967; Thomas 1976) and models of disputing (Nader and Todd 1978) center primarily on public conflicts that are sanctioned, authorized, or labeled as disputes. Conflicts between labor and management, functional departments, and superior-subordinate are public and visible (Kochan 1980; Robbins 1974). The preferred choices for managing these disputes—namely, confrontation—can be observed. *Confrontation* refers to overt discussion of the conflict and underlies such alternatives as negotiation, collaboration, and mutual problem solving (Thomas 1976;

Walton and McKersie 1965). In public conflicts, the norms and procedures for reaching an equitable settlement surface through formally derived laws, written documents, and public norms. For example, collective bargaining and grievance systems are governed by public laws and written contracts (Dunlop 1958; Kochan 1980). Public norms regulate employee rights and responsibilities and disputes between organizations (Brown 1982; Ewing 1977).

Unlike those in the public arena, private disputes occur as covert or hidden conflict, often fused with other activities. Consequently, they are rarely labeled or authorized as disputes (Mechanic 1962). Indeed, they may be read as sabotage and disloyalty (Burroway 1979; Hyman 1978). The preferred modes of conflict management in the private sphere include avoidance, accommodation, tolerance, or "behind-the-scenes" coalition building. Disputants choose to ignore one another or forget about the grievance. They may think they cannot change the system; hence they rely on private grievances as the primary mode of conflict management. In the private arena, norms and rules for appropriate conflict behavior arise from the situation rather than from public standards or bureaucratic rules.

Private forms of conflict management, however, are not independent of public ones. Indeed, private forms of disputing enable public debates, formal negotiations, and grievance hearings to function smoothly. The private chats outside meeting rooms, the coalition building at the lunchroom or on the golf course, and the gossip sessions in the halls make the formal meeting look rational and cooperative.

Formal, like public, conflicts are governed by organizational and social structures. Formal systems institutionalize conflict management. In formal disputes, individuals often have officially sanctioned conflict management roles such as ombudsmen, human resource personnel, negotiators, mediators, and employee relations specialists (Kolb 1987; Rowe 1987). Formal disputes also work within the legal system through official procedures, appropriate topics, and protocols for grievances (Goldberg, Green, and Sander, 1985). In contrast, informal disputes center on the actions and processes of organizational members rather than on the functions of conflict management officials. Rank and position may be treated with less esteem, and norms tend to arise from the organizational culture. For example, informal norms of conflict management might sanction hidden agendas, "bitching," ignoring requests, and other ideographic practices. In the informal setting, everyday practices govern the way issues evolve and the way conflict roles emerge to manage these issues.

An emphasis on the public and formal settings has led to conceiving of conflict management as a rational process. While the domains of public and formal conflict center on the place or locale where conflict occurs, rationality focuses on the orientation to conflict or on the way disputes should be handled. A rational approach to conflict views it as a conscious, premeditated activity guided by individual decision and choice (Raiffa 1982). Rationality captures the preconceived, logical, and systematic side of conflict. This approach underscores the planning of maneuvers and the making of strategic choices in managing disputes (Lax and Sebenius 1986; Robbins 1974). Departures from rationality are handled through prescriptive advice and through effective training (Bazerman and Neale 1983).

A nonrational orientation to conflict stands in opposition to the dominant perspective (Merry and Silbey 1984). This approach accents the unconscious or spontaneous aspects of disputing, ones that are driven by impulse and by the feelings of participants and not simply by their cognition. Emotional reactions such as venting feelings, expressing displeasure, and feeling hurt become means of conflict management rather than irrational displays that hinder logical thinking (Morrill 1991). Nonrational orientations also call attention to different forms of conflict management such as gossip, rituals, and personalized accounts (Trice 1984; Trice and Beyer 1984). Instinct, sensitivity, and situational adaptiveness become the guiding principles for conflict management. Nonrational approaches to conflict are sometimes denigrated as the ones exhibited by disputants who do not know better or who have not learned the appropriate social responses. They are often equated with a feminized, and hence less valued, style of conflict management (Kolb, this volume).

In effect, the dualities of public-private, formal-informal, and rational-nonrational underlie all organizational conflicts. Even though most disputes contain some amount of each of these dualities, traditional conflict theories have attended to only one-half of the poles—the public, formal, and rational aspects of disputes. Our purpose is to explore the understudied poles and show the relationship between these oppositional terms. Obviously, the primacy of particular poles hinges on the way a conflict evolves over time and on the features that begin to define the nature of a dispute.

Relationships between the understudied poles of these dualities and their counterparts introduce issues of power and change. Although power is operative in each aspect of these dualities, the relationship between the formal and informal or the public and private reveals different ways that power and authority function in conflict situations. For example, avoidance and tolerance may keep disputes below the surface and make it more difficult than with public conflicts to change existing structures and systems. By emphasizing how these dualities surface in conflict situations, theorists not only can explore the understudied poles but also can determine how power relationships are altered or reaffirmed through disputes.

To take a dialectical approach to disputes in organizations raises its own set of problems. Specifically, when conflict is viewed through the lens of duality, it is opposition and difference that are emphasized at the expense of similarity. Although the framework (see Figure 1.1) underscores oppositional terms, the chapters in this book take a more eclectic stance. They illustrate commonalities as well as differences in these dual relationships and identify mixed attributes that fall between the public and private spheres, the formal and informal settings, and the rational and nonrational orientations. A second limitation of a dual focus is the tendency to reify oppositional categories and treat them as something more than the social constructions they inevitably are. The chapters in this book attempt to respond to these issues by recognizing the biases of the dialectical approach and rooting the studies of conflict processes in the naturalistic settings in which they occur.

Introduction to the Chapters

Disputes in organizations are not a special class of events. Rather, they are part of the normal undercurrent of the work that goes on in organizations. Those involved express their differences in sometimes blatant or in other more subtle and nuanced ways. Despite the variety of ways in which people deal with their disputes, there has been a pronounced tendency in empirical research to focus primarily on those modes that are public and formal. Thus negotiation, confrontation, and the interventions of third parties, whether insiders or outsiders, are the types of conflict management we hear most about (Thomas 1976; Walton 1987; Walton and McKersie 1965). Collective bargaining, interdepartmental relations, decision making over resources, and grievance and complaint procedures are the dominant examples we have of how people behave during episodes of conflict in organizations (Pondy 1967; Lawrence and Lorsch 1967; Pettigrew 1973; Pfeffer and Salancik 1978; Kuhn 1961). Relative to what happens backstage and off-line, these public, formal, and deliberate forms are probably rare in comparison with the ongoing skirmishes, the gossiping, the lumping, and the small vengeances that take place as part of normal daily activity.

The chapters in this book focus on different aspects of conflict in organizations. They view conflict as part of the social fabric of the organizations studied and so investigate its occurrences as part of the routines of work. In this respect, these works are an antidote to those that emphasize the public, formal, and deliberate aspects of dispute processing. Using field methods and narrative styles that differ significantly from most other studies of conflict in organizations, these chapters describe processes that are more likely to be private, informal, and nonrational but that exist in tenuous relationship to their opposites. They enlighten us about conflict as it is enacted in the crevices and crannies of organizations.[6]

What emerges from these studies is a picture of how disputes are handled in the context of ongoing operations in organizations. All of the studies attend to the private, informal, and nonrational forms of conflict and the interactions between these and their opposite forms. Different chapters, however, emphasize a particular dimension as a point of departure. Several focus on the private spheres of conflict, what kinds of activities occur there, and then how these connect with the more public aspects of disputing.

In Chapter 2, "Drinking Our Troubles Away: Managing Conflict in a British Police Agency," John Van Maanen considers "time-outs" from work where members of different divisions in a police agency get together to relax and share a drink. The pub tours and office and raiding parties are the ritualized occasions where, with alcohol-induced loosening of tongues, disputes over work and responsibility issues that are otherwise avoided, are privately raised and discussed. Van Maanen describes these occasions in detail as to place, participation, and the language in which differences are phrased. An explicit connection is made between conflict handling during time-outs and the formal requirements of the jobs in the different divisions.

Deborah M. Kolb considers issues of gender and mediation in the private management of conflict. In Chapter 3, "Women's Work: Peacemaking in Organizations," Kolb describes how three women come to be involved as peacemakers in conflicts within their organizations, the kinds of assistance they provide, their feelings about what they do, and the implications for their positions in their respective organizations. Working behind the scenes in a high-tech company, a small service firm, and a university, these "peacemakers" move between different interested individuals and groups, listening to what they have to say and advising them on actions to take. In so doing, these peacemakers provide a bridge between the private expression of difference and its public face.

The structure of a professional organization sets the context for Chapter 4, "The Private Ordering of Professional Relations." In it, Calvin Morrill uses observational and interview data in several offices of a large public accounting firm to describe and categorize the variety of forms that grievance handling takes among the partners. Given the structure of accounting practice, there are continued occasions for partners to find fault with each other around practice. Morrill identifies three ways in which the relationships among the partners are ordered: by tolerating behavior, by negotiating differences, and by invoking formal position. Morrill relates these patterns of private conflict management to various structural and professional characteristics of the firm and the likelihood that these professional orders will change.

Two of the chapters take as their starting points the dichotomous relationship between formal and informal structures. Jean M. Bartunek and Robin R. Reid, in Chapter 5, "The Role of Conflict in a Second Order Change Attempt," draw on interview and observational data collected at a private school to study a structural change. They trace the implementation of a new administrative "academic director" role at the school. The purpose of the position, one new to the school, was to increase the coordination of curriculum in a school whose culture had a strong "autonomy" ethos. Bartunek and Reid focus on the relationship between the school's patterns of conflict handling and this organization change, in which they show how the formal structural issues were handled informally among a small group of people. They conclude that strategies for avoiding conflict over the issue of role had historical roots and reinforced the school's autonomy ethos in ways that severely undercut the coordination mandate of the new academic director.

Collective bargaining is a formal and institutionalized mode of conflict resolution in many industries. In Chapter 6, "The Culture of Mediation: Private Understandings in the Context of Public Conflict," Raymond A. Friedman uses data about the collective bargaining relationship between International Harvester and the United Auto Workers to show how an informal subculture of shared meaning and understanding developed between negotiators for the company and the union. As boundary spanners of their organizations, these representatives were able, over time, to develop a trusting private understanding while maintaining a public conflictual stance in formal bargaining. This subculture of mediation was disrupted by a change of leadership and policy on the part of management, and this disruption contributed to a six-month strike in 1979.

Those who study conflict tend to emphasize the deliberate and rational aspects of it. In two of the chapters, the affective underside of disputes is developed in the analyses. Joanne Martin considers the indirect ways conflict is expressed and suppressed in Chapter 7, "The Suppression of Gender Conflict in Organizations." Observing that most studies of conflict focus on groups who have relatively equal status, Martin considers some of the subtle ways conflict between disempowered groups and those in authority is suppressed. Given that suppressed conflict cannot be directly observed, Martin uses the method of deconstruction to analyze a speech by a senior manager that is ostensibly about how the organization assists its women employees. From this analysis, she is able to show the dominance of public spheres of endeavor over the private, masculine perspectives over the feminine, and subtle expressions of sexuality that demean women managers in the workplace. These arguments begin to explain why the elimination of gender conflict and discrimination in the workplace has been so elusive.

In ongoing interactions, there are tensions in relationships that give rise to disputes. Whether or not these disputes are aired, or even resolved, the tensions remain and can cause deep feelings. In Chapter 8, "Culture and Conflict: The Cultural Roots of Discord," Frank A. Dubinskas describes such a relationship between the research scientists and the financial executives in a biotechnology start-up company. Basic conflicts over product and project planning frequently surface. Dubinskas depicts several examples of these disputes, many of which are quite acrimonious, and traces them to a clash of science and business cultures in which "time" and "human maturation" are understood differently by the two groups. Cultural notions of temporal reality affect not only the immediate projects but also deeply held beliefs about careers and the self. While immediate disputes are sometimes settled, these cultural differences lead to persistent and intense patterns of discord that mark interaction in the absence of a new shared model that incorporates different cultural understandings.

Finally, the concluding chapter, "Bringing Conflict Out From Behind the Scenes: Private, Informal, and Nonrational Dimensions of Conflict in Organizations," by Jean M. Bartunek, Deborah M. Kolb, and Roy J. Lewicki, develops the themes introduced in the empirical chapters. The characteristics of formal, private, and nonrational conflict handling are developed and their relationship to their opposites analyzed with reference to other studies of conflict in organizations. Some of the practical implications for diagnosing conflict in organizations and for intervening are developed. In the end, we come to appreciate some of the strengths and drawbacks of natural mechanisms of conflict handling that give rise to the picture of the peaceful organization with its turbulence kept out of sight.

Notes

1. There are other parallels as well. Legal scholars have argued that the existing study of law that examined law on the books and law in action replicated existing political biases and so looked to disputes as a way to describe legal action dynamically and within social contexts (Silbey and Sarat 1988). Likewise, within organization theory, a focus on the management or resolution of conflict serves to underscore the technical imperatives of existing authority.

2. This focus on negotiation has eclipsed the many other ways that conflicts are dealt with in highly political organizations. The study of negotiation is currently a major growth industry. In major academic enclaves across the country, various schools have grown up that suggest the variety of ways the negotiation process is conceived. The theoretical approaches include behavioral decision theory (Lax and Sebenius 1986; Raiffa 1982; Walton and McKersie 1965), psychological decision theory (Bazerman and Neale 1983; Neale and Northcraft 1989), the study of individual differences (Rubin and Brown 1976; Gilkey and Greenhalgh 1986), the structural approach (Pruitt 1981), and communications (Putnam 1990). Its suitability to mathematical formulation and to structured simulation in the laboratory may explain some of this popularity.

3. Conflict in organization theory, particularly its management wing, is described as being managed structurally, procedurally, and situationally. Formal structures of organization, its hierarchy, division of labor, and differentiation by task and function are means to regulate conflict (Weber 1968; Cyert and March 1963; Thompson 1967; Lawrence and Lorsch 1967). Conflict is contained not only through structure but also by way of organizational rules and procedures (Weber 1968; Edwards 1979). In the employment

relationship, conflict between employees and employers is managed within a context or a "web of rules" that prescribe the ways workers and managers are to deal with each other (Dunlop 1958). Grievance or complaint procedures are meant to handle those disputes that arise in daily working relationships (Scott, Nystrom, and Starbuck 1981). These procedures serve to channel conflict into certain legitimate forms and so minimize strikes and other forms of industrial action (Kochan 1980).

Situational models of conflict management shift the locus of conflict management from the systems level down to the particular occasions when disputes break out between organization members. These models are intended to assist would-be conflict managers to diagnose the conflict situation and adopt the mode of conflict management most likely to achieve these goals (Deutsch 1973; Thomas 1976; Rahim and Bonoma 1979). At times, this may mean encouraging or intensifying conflict to enhance the performance of a social system (Robbins 1974; Brown 1982).

4. *Avoidance* has a particular meaning in studies of community disputing; it is usually defined as the withdrawal or curtailment of a relationship (Nader and Todd 1978). This is not usually a viable option in organizations in which roles and tasks are generally given: Exit is extreme. When avoidance is set forth as a conflict management option, it is interpreted in the context of a particular conflict and not in terms of the overall relationship. Thus avoidance means simply the decision not to pursue a conflict, not to address an issue (Thomas 1976).

5. In legal disputes, the law obviously influences the forms of dispute processing. When legal scholars consider negotiation and other alternative dispute resolution procedures, they do so with reference to "the shadow of the law" (Mnookin and Kornhauser 1979). The point is that the channels of dispute processing—that is, what preceded negotiation or mediation and what is likely to follow—influence the structure and form of these procedures (Harrington 1985; Silbey and Merry 1987). In the context of grievance mediation, Kolb (1989b) describes how the previous steps of a grievance procedure and the possibility that arbitration will follow influence the ways problems are framed and the forms of argument used in the mediation process. Conflict in the shadow of authority is meant to suggest that the ways conflicts are managed in organizations are likewise influenced by the structure and context in which they occur.

6. These crevices are akin to what Turner (1969) labels "liminal spaces," the occasions when formal structure does not hold. While liminality is often used to account for rituals and ceremony (see Kunda 1986, 128), conflict as it is handled in the crevices of organizations displays qualities associated with conflict handling in liminal spaces—community, emotion, and spontaneity. It is in these liminal spaces, Turner argues, that low-level people acquire power and express it both to challenge and to reaffirm existing structures.

References

Abel, R. 1982. *The politics of informal justice.* New York: Academic Press.
Bacharach, S. B., and E. J. Lawler. 1980. *Power and politics in organization.* San Francisco: Jossey-Bass.
Bachrach, P., and M. S. Baratz. 1962. The two faces of power. *American Political Science Review* 56:947-52.
Barnard, C. 1938. *The function of the executive.* Cambridge, Mass.: Harvard University Press.

Baumgartner, M. P. 1988. Social control in suburbia. In *Toward a general theory of social control,* Vol. 2, ed. D. Black. New York: Academic Press.

Bazerman, M., and M. Neale. 1983. Heuristics in negotiation. In *Negotiating in organization,* ed. M. Bazerman and R. Lewicki. Newbury Park, Cal.: Sage.

Black, D. 1990. The elementary forms of conflict management. In *New directions in the study of justice, law and social control,* ed. Arizona School of Justice Studies, Arizona State University, 43-69. New York: Plenum.

Black, D., and M. P. Baumgartner. 1983. Toward a theory of the third party. In *Empirical theories of courts,* ed. W. O. Boyum and L. Mather. New York: Longman.

Blau, P. M. 1955. *The dynamics of bureaucracy.* Chicago: University of Chicago Press.

Braverman, H. 1974. *Labor and monopoly capital.* New York: Monthly Review.

Brown, D. 1982. *Managing conflict at organizational interfaces.* Reading, Mass.: Addison-Wesley.

Burrell, G., and G. Morgan. 1979. *Sociological paradigms and organizational analysis.* Portsmouth, N.H.: Heineman Educational.

Burroway, M. 1979. *Manufacturing consent.* Chicago: University of Chicago Press.

Cain, M., and K. Kulscar. 1982. Thinking disputes: An essay on the origins of the dispute industry. *Law and Society Review* 16:375.

Clegg, S. 1981. Organization and control. *Administrative Science Quarterly* 26:545-62.

Collins, R. 1975. *Conflict sociology.* New York: Academic Press.

Coser, L. 1956. *The functions of social conflict.* New York: Free Press.

Crozier, M. 1964. *The bureaucratic phenomenon.* Chicago: University of Chicago Press.

Cyert, R. M. and J. G. March. 1963. *A behavioral theory of the firm.* Englewood Cliffs, N.J.: Prentice-Hall.

Dalton, M. 1959. *Men who manage.* New York: John Wiley.

Deutsch, M. 1973. *The resolution of conflict.* New Haven, Conn.: Yale University Press.

Drucker, P. 1988. New organizational forms. *Harvard Business Review,* January-February.

Dunlop, J. 1958. *Industrial relations systems.* New York: Holt, Rinehart & Winston.

Edelman, L. 1990. Legal environments and organizational governance. *American Journal of Sociology* 95:1401-41.

Edwards, R. 1979. *Contested terrain.* New York: Basic Books.

Engel, D. 1980. Legal pluralism in an American community. *American Bar Foundation Research Journal* 980:325.

Ewing, D. 1977. What business thinks about employee rights? *Harvard Business Review,* September/October, 81.

Felstiner, W. 1974. Influences of social organizations on dispute processing. *Law and Society Review* 9:63-94.

Felstiner, W., R. Abel, and A. Sarat. 1981. The emergence and transformation of disputes: Naming, blaming and claiming. *Law and Society Review* 15:631-54.

Foulkes, F. 1982. *Personnel policies in large non-union firms.* Englewood Cliffs, N.J.: Prentice-Hall.

Galanter, M. 1974. Why the 'haves' come out ahead: Speculations on the limits of legal change. *Law and Society Review* 9, Rev. 95.

Galbraith, J. K. 1977. *Organization design.* Reading, Mass.: Addison-Wesley.

—1986. Behind the wall. *The New York Review of Books,* 10 April, 11-13.

Gilkey, R. W., and L. Greenhalgh. 1986. The role of personality in successful negotiations. *Negotiation Journal* 2:245-256.

Gluckman, M. 1955. *Custom and conflict in Africa.* Oxford: Basil Blackwell.

Goldberg, S., E. Green, and F. Sander. 1985. *Dispute resolution.* Boston: Little, Brown.

Goldman, P., and D. Van Houten. 1977. Managerial strategies and the worker: A Marxist analysis of bureaucracy. *Sociological Quarterly* 18:108-25.

Gouldner, A. 1954. *Patterns of industrial bureaucracy.* New York: Free Press.

—1965. *Wildcat strike.* New York: Harper & Row.

Greenhouse, C. 1986. *Praying for justice: Faith, order and community in an American town.* Ithaca, N.Y.: Cornell University Press.

Gulliver, P. H. 1979. *Disputes and negotiation: A cross-cultural perspective.* New York: Academic Press.

Harrington, C. 1985. *Shadow justice: The ideology and institutionalization of alternatives to court.* Westport, Conn.: Greenwood.

Hearn, J., D. L. Sheppard, P. Tancred-Sheppard, and G. Burrell, eds. 1989. *The sexuality of organization.* Newbury Park, Cal.: Sage.

Hill, S. 1981. *Competition and control at work.* Cambridge, Mass.: MIT Press.

Hirschman, A. 1970. *Exit, voice, loyalty.* Cambridge, Mass.: Harvard University Press.

Hyman, R. 1978. Pluralism procedural consensus and collective bargaining. *British Journal of Industrial Relations* 16:16-40.

Kanter, R. M. 1977. *Men and women of the corporation.* New York: Colophon.

Karambayya, R., and J. Brett. 1989. Managers handling disputes: Third party roles and perceptions of fairness. *Academy of Management Journal* 32:687-705.

Kerr, C. 1955. Industrial peace and the collective bargaining environment. In *Industrial peace under collective bargaining,* ed. C. S. Golden and V. D. Parker. New York: Harper & Row.

Kidder, R. 1980-81. The end of the road: Problems in the analysis of disputes. *Law and Society Review* 15:673.

Kochan, T. 1980. *Collective bargaining and industrial relations.* Homewood, Ill.: Irwin.

Kolb, D. 1983. *The mediators.* Cambridge, Mass.: MIT Press.

—1985. To be a mediator: Expressive tactics in mediation. *Journal of Social Issues* 41:11-27.

—1986. Who are organization third parties and what do they do? In *Research on negotiation in organizations,* Vol. 1, ed. M. Bazerman, R. Lewicki, and B. Sheppard, 207-227. Greenwich, Conn.: JAI.

—1987. Corporate ombudsman and organization conflict resolution. *Journal of Conflict Resolution* 31:673-91.

—1989a. Roles mediators play in different organizational settings. In *The mediation of social conflict,* ed. K. Kressel and D. Pruitt, 91-114. San Francisco: Jossey-Bass.

—1989b. How existing procedures shape alternatives: The case of grievance mediation. *Journal of Dispute Resolution,* 59-87.

Kriesberg, L. 1973. *The sociology of social conflict.* Englewood Cliffs, N.J.: Prentice-Hall.

Kuhn, J. 1961. *Bargaining and grievance settlement.* New York: Columbia University Press.

Kunda, G. 1986. Engineering culture: Culture and control in a high-tech organization. Ph.D. diss., Sloan School of Management (in press, Temple University Press).

Kunda, G., and S. Barley. 1988. Designing devotion. Paper presented at the annual meeting of the American Sociological Association.

Lawrence, P. R., and J. W. Lorsch. 1967. *Organization and environment.* Homewood, Ill.: Irwin.

Lax, D., and J. Sebenius. 1986. *The manager as negotiator.* New York: Free Press.

Lewicki, R., and B. Sheppard. 1985. Choosing how to intervene: Factors influencing the use of process and outcome control in third party dispute resolution. *Journal of Occupational Behavior* 6:49-64.

Lewin, D. 1987. Dispute resolution in the non-union firm: A theoretical and empirical analysis. *Journal of Conflict Resolution* 31:465.

Lukes, S. 1974. *Power: A radical view.* London: Macmillan.

March, J. G., and J. P. Olson. 1976. *Ambiguity and choice in organizations.* Bergen, Norway: Universitetsforlaget.

March, J. G., and H. Simon. 1958. *Organizations.* New York: John Wiley.

Marshall, J. 1984. *Women managers: Travelling in a male world.* Chichester, England: John Wiley.

Mather, L., and B. Yngvesson. 1980-81. Language, audience and the transformation of disputes. *Law and Society Review* 755-82.

Mechanic. D. 1962. Sources of power of lower participants in complex organizations. *Administrative Science Quarterly* 7:349-64.

Merry, S. E. 1987. Disputing without culture (a review of Goldberg, Green, and Sander: *Dispute resolution*). *Harvard Law Review* 100:2057.

Merry, S. E., and M. Rochleau. 1985. *Mediation in families: A study of the children's hearings project.* Cambridge, Mass.: Cambridge Children and Family Services.

Merry, S. E., and S. S. Silbey. 1984. What do plaintiffs want: Re-examining the concept of dispute. *Justice System Journal* 9:151.

Miles, R. 1980. *Macro organizational behavior.* Santa Monica, Cal.: Goodyear.

Miller, R., and A. Sarat. 1980-81. Grievances, claims and disputes: Assessing the adversary culture. *Law and Society Review* 15:525-66.

Mintzberg, H. 1979. *The structuring of organizations.* Englewood Cliffs, N.J.: Prentice-Hall.

—1985. The organization as political arena. *Journal of Management Studies* 22:133-54.

Mitroff, I. I., and R. O. Mason. 1981. *Creating a dialectical social science.* Dordrecht, Holland: D. Reidel.

Mnookin, R., and L. Kornhauser. 1979. Bargaining in the shadow of law. *Yale Law Journal* 88:950.

Morgan, G. 1981. The schismatic metaphor and its implications for organizational analysis. *Organization Studies* 2:23-44.

Morrill, C. 1991. Conflict management, honor, and organizational change. *American Journal of Sociology.* 97:585-622.

Mouzelis, N. P. 1967. *Organization and bureaucracy.* Chicago: Aldine.

Nader, L. 1965. The anthropological study of law. *American Anthropologist* 2:67.

Nader, L., and H. F. Todd, Jr., ed. 1978. *The disputing process: Law in ten societies.* New York: Columbia University Press.

Neale, M., and G. Northcraft. 1989. Experience, expertise, and decision bias in negotiation: The role of conceptualization. In *Research on negotiation in organizations,* Vol. 2, ed. B. Sheppard, M. Bazerman, and R. Lewicki, 55-75. Greenwich, Conn.: JAI.

Perrow, C. 1979. *Complex organizations.* Glenview, Ill.: Scott, Foresman.

Peters, T. J., and R. H. Waterman. 1982. *In search of excellence.* New York: Harper & Row.

Pettigrew, A. 1973. *The politics of organizational decision-making.* London: Tavistock.

Pfeffer, J., and G. Salancik. 1978. *The external control of organizations.* New York: Harper & Row.

Pondy, L. 1967. Organizational conflict: Concepts and models. *Administrative Science Quarterly* 17:296-320.

—1989. Reflections on organizational conflict. *Journal of Organizational, Change Management* 2:94-98.

Pruitt, D. 1981. *Negotiating behavior.* New York: Academic Press.

Pruitt, D., and J. Z. Rubin. 1986. *Social conflict: Escalation, stalemate and settlement.* New York: Random House.

Putnam, L. L. 1990. Reframing integrative and distributive bargaining: A process perspective. In *Research on negotiation in organizations*, ed. B. Sheppard, M. Bazerman, and R. Lewicki. Greenwich, Conn.: JAI.

Rahim, A., and T. V. Bonoma. 1979. Managing organization conflict: A model for diagnosis and intervention. *Psychological Reports* 44:1324-44.

Raiffa, H. 1982. *Art and science of negotiation.* Cambridge, Mass.: Harvard University Press.

Rawlins, W. R. 1989. A dialectical analysis of the tensions, functions, and strategic challenges of communication in young adult friendships. In *Communication Yearbook.* Vol. 12, 157-89. Newbury Park, Cal.: Sage.

Robbins, S. P. 1974. *Managing organizational conflict: A nontraditional approach.* Englewood Cliffs, N.J.: Prentice-Hall.

Rowe, M. 1987. The corporate ombudsman. *Negotiation Journal* 3:127-140.

Rubin, J., and B. Brown. 1976. *The social psychology of bargaining and negotiation.* New York: Academic Press.

Rubin, J. Z. 1983. Negotiation. *American Behavioral Scientist* 27:135-47.

Salipante, P. F., and B. Fortado. 1988. Reciprocity, equity, and responses to unresolved conflict. Case Western Reserve University. Unpublished paper.

Sarat, A. 1987. The new formalism in disputing and dispute processing. *Law and Society* 21:695-717.

Schein, E. 1985. *Organizational culture and leadership.* San Francisco: Jossey-Bass.

Scott, J. C. 1985. *Weapons of the weak.* New Haven, Conn.: Yale University Press.

Scott, W., P. Nystrom, and W. Starbuck, eds. 1981. *Handbook of organization design.* London: Oxford University Press.

Selznick, P. 1949. *TVA and the grass roots.* Berkeley: University of California Press.

—1970. *Law, society and individual justice.* New York: Russell Sage.

Sheppard, B. 1983. Third party conflict intervention: A procedural framework. In *Research in organizational behavior.* Vol. 6, ed. B. M. Staw and L. L. Cummings. Greenwich, Conn.: JAI.

Sheppard, B., K. Blumenfeld-Jones, J. Minton, and E. Hyden. 1990. Informal conflict intervention: Advise and descent. Unpublished manuscript.

Silbey, S., and S. Merry. 1987. The problems shape the process: Interpreting disputes in mediation and court. Paper prepared for the Law and Society meeting, June.

Silbey, S., and A. Sarat. 1988. Dispute processing in law and legal scholarship: From institutional critique to the reconstitution of the judicial subject. University of Wisconsin Law School, Institute for Legal Studies. Working paper.

Smith, K. K. 1989. The movement of conflict in organizations: The joint dynamics of splitting and triangulation. *Administration Science Quarterly* 34:1-21.

Starr, J., and B. Yngvesson. 1975. Scarcity and disputing: Zeroing-in on compromise decisions. *American Ethnologist* 2:553-66.

Thomas, K. 1976. Conflict and conflict management. In *Handbook of industrial and organizational psychology,* ed. M. D. Dunnette, 889-935. New York: Rand McNally.

Thompson, J. 1967. *Organizations in action.* New York: McGraw-Hill.

Tichy, N. 1981. Networks in organizations. In *Handbooks of organization design,* ed. P. Nystrom and W. Starbuck. London: Oxford University Press.

Trice, H. M. 1984. Rites and ceremonials in organizational culture. In *Perspectives on organizational sociology.* Vol. 4., ed. S. B. Bacharach and S. M. Mitchell. Greenwich, Conn.: JAI.

Trice, H. M., and J. M. Beyer. 1984. Studying organizational cultures through rites and ceremonials. *Academy of Management Review* 9:653.

Trubek, D. 1980-81. The construction and deconstruction of a disputes-focused approach: An afterword. *Law and Society Review* 81:727.

Turner, V. 1957. *Schism and continuity in an African society.* Manchester, England: Manchester University Press.

—1969. *The ritual process: Structure and anti-structure.* Ithaca, N.Y.: Cornell University Press.

Ury, W., J. Brett, and S. Goldberg. 1988. *Getting disputes resolved.* San Francisco: Jossey-Bass.

Walton, R. E. 1987. *Managing conflict.* Reading, Mass.: Addison-Wesley.

Walton, R. E., and J. M. Dutton. 1969. The management of interdepartmental conflict: A model and review. *Administrative Science Quarterly* 14:73-84.

Walton, R. E., and R. B. McKersie. 1965. *A behavioral theory of labor negotiations.* New York: McGraw-Hill.

Weber, M. 1968. *Economy and society: An outline of interpretive sociology.* New York: Bedminster.

Weick, K. 1979. *The social psychology of organizing.* Reading, Mass.: Addison-Wesley.

Westin, A. F., and A. G. Feliu. 1988. *Resolving employment disputes without litigation.* Washington, D.C.: BNA.

Wrong, D. 1979. *Power: Its forms, bases and uses.* New York: Harper & Row.

Yngvesson, B. B. 1978. The Atlantic fisherman. In *The disputing process: Law in ten societies,* ed. L. Nader and H. F. Todd. New York: McGraw-Hill.

Yngvesson, B., and L. Mather. 1983. Courts, moots and the disputing process. In *Empirical theories of courts,* ed. W. O. Boyum and L. Mather. New York: Longman.

Ziegenfuss, J. T. 1988. *Organizational troubleshooters: Resolving problems with customers and employees.* San Francisco: Jossey-Bass.

2

Drinking Our Troubles Away

Managing Conflict in a
British Police Agency

JOHN VAN MAANEN

Conflict often arises in unlikely places. Couples dining out in plush surroundings may seize on the occasion to express their mutual discontent between bites and before the bill arrives. Siblings may select the family outing to Disneyland as an ideal time to pursue festering grudges with one another. Neighbors may discover that the backyard barbecues of long summer evenings are perfect times to grumble about the unkempt lawns, barking dogs, or unruly teenagers of some of the residents on the block. And colleagues at work may decide that the company's Christmas party provides a convenient place in organizational time and space to insult or belt the boss free from the constraints of office decorum. Few situations, it seems, are inherently so happy, so peaceful, or so calm as to always drive out discord.

This chapter is about a class of recurrent social situations that mute or amplify conflict in work organizations.[1] Similar to the occurrences

AUTHOR'S NOTE: A number of readers have lent aid and comfort during preparation of this chapter. Among them are Steve Barley, Jean M. Bartunek, Gideon Kunda, and Peter Manning. I am particularly grateful to the coeditor of this volume, Deborah M. Kolb, for detailed comments and suggestions on an earlier draft as well as for introducing me to a literature of first-rate scholarship and, as might be expected, heated controversy.

mentioned above, the ones of interest here are considered by those who participate in them to be extracurricular activities, engaged in largely for the pleasures of the moment and therefore free from most of the troubles that mark the working day. They represent occasions designed on the surface for relaxing, promoting goodwill, encouraging fellowship, or simply celebrating the common pursuits of those gathered together. But more is accomplished in such situations than native accounts allow.

In particular, conflict between and among various individuals and work groups in the organization is routinely managed. Certain situations generate the unilateral expression and mutual fine-tuning of workaday grievances; others serve to more or less suppress and avoid such expressions; and still others provide ample opportunities for disputing parties to have a go at one another before a most interested and keen audience. In each case, there is something of an acknowledged normative order that guides interaction among the participants. Moreover, the rules that constitute such an order are sufficiently fixed and adhered to that participants rarely step out of line to press on matters seen as ill-suited for the occasion. What is most notable about these conflict management episodes is, however, the representation of them by participants as spontaneous, unstructured, and unpredictable. As I will argue, these claims are denied by the way the occasions are initiated, who takes part in them, the particular forms they assume, and the regularity with which they appear.

Conflict is, of course, a heavily studied domain. Accounts of it surface in all social science disciplines and figure prominently in cross-disciplinary fields as well. My treatment of conflict in this chapter lines up roughly alongside the studies conducted by sociologists and anthropologists interested in the disputing process.[2] Among other things, these studies suggest that disputes are handled in a variety of ways and that the choice of method and range of potential outcomes are culturally (and locally) governed. Individuals or groups can pursue grievances against one another formally or informally, privately or publicly, with or without third parties present, and in dramatic or mundane ways. Power, along with the material and symbolic resources to press claims, shapes the disputing process everywhere. Those with little of it find they must frequently tolerate their grievances and avoid conflict if they are not to be crushed ("lump it or duck it").

In work organizations, private and informal means of conflict resolution are, no doubt, more common than public and formal mechanisms; and, even when institutionalized dispute settlement processes—such as

mediation, negotiation, adjudication, or various grieving procedures—
are used, a good deal of what occurs takes place backstage and is
governed by a set of implicit rules of thumb often having little to do
with the specific conflict in question (e.g., Sudnow 1965; Emerson and
Messinger 1977; Kolb 1983; Friedman 1989). There is, in short, a good
deal known about the structure of conflict in organizations (who fights
and why) as well as the likely outcomes of such conflicts (who wins
and loses). I have neither the space nor the interest to go deeply into
such matters, and good reviews are available.[3] The management of conflict is indeed a substantive and theoretical field that has come of age
in organizational studies.

My contribution here to this broad field is a modest one. Most studies
of conflict at work concern themselves either with the origins and shape
of organizational rifts or with their consequences as observed in social
situations and practices designed explicitly to settle matters (e.g., strikes,
disciplinary procedures, bargaining sessions, conciliation processes). But
organizational members interact in a great variety of social situations,
and many, if not most, of these situations are more or less open as to
precisely what will unfold in the interaction itself (Silverman 1970;
Strauss 1978; Goffman 1955). Weekly staff meetings can turn into bitch
sessions or love-ins; coffee breaks can turn sour when participants turn
to ritual insults or shouting matches; and, of more than passing interest
here, office parties can get out of hand when aggrieved members of an
organization take advantage of a special occasion to make known in no
uncertain voice that they are most unhappy with some of those present.
By and large, lip service has been given to such occasions as venues for
conflict management but not much sustained study of them has been
offered.[4]

The particular occasion or social practice I am interested in here is
drinking at and away from work by members of an organization. More
specifically, it concerns the drinking behavior of police officers in the
Met (London's Metropolitan Police Department). The goals of this rep-
resentational and interpretive account are several. First, I want to
display how social drinking is patterned in this context and, by implication, suggest that drinking is likely to be patterned in all occupational
and organizational contexts (for example, by age, task, gender, rank,
shift, location, and so on). Drinking is, after all, one of the more
popular pastimes in American and British life and it would indeed
be surprising if we were to suddenly learn that such a frequent and

pleasurable activity is governed merely by personal whim or uncontrollable urge.

Second, I want to tie together the observed patterns of social drinking and the distribution and management of conflict within the organization. In part, I want to demonstrate that conflict is omnipresent in organizational settings and penetrates deeply into all the dealings members have with one another in the organization (dealings that may be guarded or spontaneous, work or leisure oriented, formal or informal, sacred or profane). Some interesting ideas emerge concerning the expression and suppression of conflict when one examines those sometimes frivolous and lightly regarded drinking episodes in organizational life that are thought by participants to be occasions of good cheer, devoid of instrumental purpose, ceremonial, or reverential, and (perhaps most misleading of all) without structure. "Having a few with the boys (or girls) in the office" is a normal, ordinary activity, but it is one that reflects far more than individual or group fancies.

Setting and Method

The Metropolitan Police Department in London employs roughly 25,000 sworn officers; 75% of these officers are deployed across 75 divisions with each division carrying (ordinarily) between 200 and 300 officers of assorted rank and function. A given division is headed by a chief superintendent, who, along with his immediate subordinates (usually one superintendent, two chief inspectors, and a detective chief inspector) constitute the "senior officers" of a division. They are known to the officers ranking below them as the "guv'nors." Each division operates within broad mandates, rules, and policy guidelines set by both law and higher police officials housed either in District Stations (24 in number) or at New Scotland Yard ("the Yard"), headquarters for the Met. Depending on how one counts, there are at least five administrative levels separating the commissioner of the Metropolitan Police (the highest office in the organization) and the respective divisional chief superintendents.

Most pertinent to this study, there are also five levels between the chief superintendent of a division and the lowest ranking officer on the force, the police constable or PC. Officers posted to the divisions regard themselves as "on the ground." The principal distinctions to be made within a division concern rank and function. Rank, running up the chain of command, goes from PC, to sergeant, to inspector, to chief inspector, to superintendent, to chief superintendent. Functions include a wide variety of specialist assignments as well as the traditional "reliefs" responsible for the routine foot and motor patrol of the division, responding to emergency calls for assistance from the public, communications at the police station, and running the front office of the station (affectionately known to all as "the nick"). In practice, officers posted to the nick sort themselves into one of two categories: uniform or CID. The term *uniform officer* can be misleading, however. Essentially, it means "not in the CID" even though the particular officer to whom it applies may not wear a uniform, work a relief, or be any longer designated a PC.

This uniform and CID distinction is crucial. On paper, one way of depicting a CID officer is simply as a police specialist, on par with other specialists like, say, dog handlers, traffic officers, or "homebeats." And, like other specialists, an officer joins the CID only after a period of service as an ordinary PC, after passing through a selection screen, and after completing a departmental training course. But to consider the CID equal to other functional groupings in this police agency would be a grave mistake. Important historical and structural differences exist.

First, the CID is the largest special function performed by the Met. Its membership represents 14% of the total officers on the force and, in the divisions, it is about 10% of the manpower (only about 3% of CID officers are women). This specialty operates in the shadow of its exclusive "crime focus" mandate, which all organization members take to be the core of the police mission (Manning 1977; Fielding 1988). Finding lost children (or cats), transporting prisoners and the intoxicated, chatting-up antagonists in a family dispute, or, more generally, "order maintenance" activities lie outside the CID domain, which is defined by its case-centered criminal apprehension objectives. The detective's job consists of "nicking people, not helping them."

Second, despite repeated attempts to "break up the CID," there remains a separate and parallel rank structure within the organization wherein the prefix *detective* is reserved only for those of the CID. Officially, the highest-ranking CID officer on a division (the detective chief inspector or DCI) reports directly to the chief superintendent of the division. In point of fact, the DCI usually reports (at least first) to the district detective superintendent, who looks toward the area detective commander, who reports to the chief CID officer located under the commissioner at the Yard. There is (and has always been) a good deal of ambiguity and conflict surrounding the CID chain of command and its supposed subordination to the uniform side of the organization (Newman 1984). For my purposes, it is merely worth noting that officers who enter the CID rarely wish to leave. Few do, and a rather splendid career can be carved out within the specialty. To transfer back to the uniform side of the house without a promotion in hand or without being forced back as a result of disciplinary proceedings (or threat of them) seldom occurs in the Met.

Third, as implied, the CID cultivates a separate and exclusive identity. These detectives of Scotland Yard not only have popular fiction and numerous London legends to assist them in the process, they have a number of organizational conventions as well. CID officers do not wear uniforms. At the division level, they typically work very closely together out of cramped quarters housed in the nick. The tasks of the CID officer are highly discretionary, investigating "major crimes" in a fashion that an officer's own style, mood, interests, and skill dictate. Supervision is relaxed. It is, for example, quite difficult for a naive observer to visibly separate the officers from their charges. Ranking CID officers (DIs and DCIs) are distinguished primarily on the basis of the administrative tasks they perform (e.g., reading diaries, approving overtime slips, organizing occasional raids) and the more serious crimes they themselves investigate (e.g., rape, murder, spectacular arson). Detective sergeants do not supervise but perform the same tasks as the DCs, who, in theory, report to them. Put simply, a position in the CID carries with it not only considerable prestige but a very loose and flexible task organization as well.

In sum, there is much truth to the CID officer's favorite description of the function, "a firm inside a firm." Separateness, exclusivity, status, and the relative freedom to pursue one's work without direct supervision characterize assignments in the CID. As one might surmise, it is a characterization that provokes more than a little hostility and envy from many uniform officers. And, as we shall see, it serves also to produce a regular string of lively disputes between the two groups.

My work with the Met took place between September 1983 and June 1984. During this eight-month period, I worked as a participant-observer in two divisions: one, an outer station, south of the river and far from the city; the other, an inner station located near to central

London in a more congested area. The outer division, closer to my home in England, received more attention from me than the inner division. In the South Downs (a pseudonym), I spent five months on a three- to four-day-a-week schedule performing the usual range of fieldwork tasks: formal and informal interviewing, touring with officers of the division, attending meetings, observing police work in various locales such as the charge and interrogation rooms, collecting official and unofficial documents, going to court with officers, schmoozing with officers after (and during) a tour of duty, and so forth. Much of this work differed very little from previous work of mine and is described in detail elsewhere (Van Maanen 1978, 1981, 1988).

Organizational Time-Outs

Midway through the afternoon of my second day of fieldwork in the South Downs, a quiet Saturday, the senior officer on the watch with whom I was talking about the business of the station reached down to his bottom desk drawer, withdrew a bottle of aged malt whiskey, and asked if I'd care to join him in a bit of a nip. My past experience within U.S. police agencies suggested that such a gesture of friendliness was uncommon but not entirely unknown. We proceeded to go through a good part of the bottle before we parted, me to go home and he to make his dutiful tour of subdivisional stations and inspect the books. I have, of course, no way of knowing just how often he engaged in office drinking of this type. If subtle disclaimers are to be believed, it was relatively rare. "Nice to have someone visit us from across the lake," he said. "We don't get to exchange views very often, and god knows the sort of talk we've been having is good for the soul if not the constitution."

Making my way unsteadily home, I spilled the day's observations and conversations into my trusty tape recorder and labeled most of the research day a waste—partly because I couldn't remember very much of it and partly because I was convinced that my talk with the senior officer, while cordial, did not get very far. Our talk, it seemed, rambled on in a boozy sort of way, touching here and there on matters of mutual concern but more often than not generating stories that were now only half remembered and of questionable value. We both seemed to take more delight in the moment by providing personal anecdotes embedded in those mannerly ways that polished both our characters. Only later did I come to label this interlude as an "organizational time-out" and only later did I come to recognize just how much there is to learn about things organizational during such time-outs.

For my purposes, an organizational time-out represents a gathering of organizational members during which some of the ordinary rules and norms of the workplace are situationally lifted. Broadly conceived, time-outs allow for discourse on nonwork topics, allow behavior patterns on the part of those present to deviate from those that obtain when they are working, and allow for the expression of sentiments typically unheard (or hushed) during the pursuit of organizational purposes. In most ways, time-outs denote autonomy for the participants (at least of a collective and claimed sort) and a general sense of freedom from organizational constraint. Time-outs are familiar to us all. In academic settings, the professor in the beer bar surrounded by students is a standard example. The sales meeting that finds its way to the golf course or tennis court is another. And, of course, my pleasant afternoon with the senior officer is still another.

Organizational time-outs are occasions launched by some sort of sign. Typically, there are strong symbols involved. Time of day and location are certainly obvious illustrations.[5] The symbol of interest to me in this chapter is, in Goffmanesque terms, the drinking of alcohol by two or more copresent persons. The raising of the first glass, bottle, aluminum can, or paper cup is a sign that participants may take to mean a relaxation of ordinary work rules. Precisely what rules are lost and, crucially, what different rules come into play are empirical questions. No easy answers are forthcoming, but some progress can be made toward uncovering them by considering, first, what common drinking situations exist for members of the studied organization, and, second, what sorts of conversations and activities occur in these time-out situations.[6]

Time-Out for a Drink

Going over my field notes on the many drinking occasions I encountered in the Met, a distinction can first be made between those times where alcohol use is strictly incidental to the activities that surround the time-out and those times where alcohol is the central, focal activity itself (and consumption will persist until the participants disband). The former category of events is certainly the most common and, for the most part, interesting in terms of conflict management only because so little conflict emerges. The second category of occasions involves those where alcohol serves to bring forth claims of drunkenness on the part of participants, a likely chain of events, and a particular focus of conversation and activity. When alcohol is incidental, its presence is usually fleeting and seldom missed when it is gone. When it is central to the occasion, its presence is keenly felt and sorely missed when it runs out (thus calling for its frequent replacement). I shall dispense with the first category quickly.

The specific occasion for incidental drinking might be a pub lunch attended by six or seven officers in the CID before undertaking a raid on local villains. From my field notes:

> We went to the Boy and the Donkey for refreshments. Most of the men ordered a pint along with the Ploughman's Special and a few put down two or three pints before we piled in the cars to hit Peter Olson's place. The DI drove the car. I jumped in and the men talked over his plans for the raid as we drove toward the council flats.

Or, CID officers may be shopping for information from those "in the business" while on duty in their favorite pub.[7] As one detective put it:

> You've got to be a bit of a trader to be a detective. You can't just go out there driving around and expect to nick some bloody thief. I make the rounds of my pubs every couple of days, have a pint or two with the boys and try to find out who's got something useful and what they want for it. The other day some yobo says he wants some help with his trespass case and wants to know what going equipped might be worth to me. So I tells him, "Look Jocko, going equipped's not worth all that much so you can come back to me when you've got something to deal." He will, mind you, it's all business. You just have got to let them know where they can find you, chat them up, and have a little something to offer and you'll get all the clear-ups you need.

Or, the occasion might be a ceremonial dinner in the officer's canteen on a division station. Again, from field notes:

> Several bottles of French wine were on the table. After dinner, brandies were served alongside the tarts and silver service coffee setting. The chief superintendent made a short speech, the district commander another, and the traditional "to the Queen" toasts were uttered. Even the CID officers, despite jokes to the contrary, were well behaved and somewhat out of character. From cocktails before dinner—beer,

sherry, or wine—to the gradual filing out from the elaborately decked out canteen, the entire do lasted about three hours. Everything was well planned, polite, stiff, yet rather charming and altogether pleasant. Somewhere between one-quarter and one-half of the dinner guests still had a tour of duty to complete before the workday would be over for them.

Or, the incidental drinking occasion may be quite unintended, as is the case recorded below when I accompanied a sergeant on his regular rounds of checking on those in his borough who apply for a gun license to allow them to keep a weapon in the home.

Sergeant Weatherwax and I went next to the posh house of an ex-chief superintendent. We were warmly welcomed even though Steve told me he had never met this man before. The elderly applicant asked his wife to bring us three brandies ("never did like Port, always went up my nose") and we went to the sitting room. Steve and I gratefully sipped our drinks while the ex-guv told long, involved tales concerning a variety of police misadventures in the good old days ("not like that nowadays, eh lads?"). Eventually, Steve got around to examining the documents associated with the various weapons as well as looking over the suitability of the storage plans the applicant had for the guns. With station sergeant crispness, Steve proclaimed, "All correct, Sir" and we took leave shortly thereafter.

As a final example, consider another incident structurally close to my initial encounter with the senior officer in the South Downs. This episode is interesting for the perfect symmetry of power relations (fully in keeping with the disciplinary image maintained on the uniform side of the organization) as well as for the uneasy response of the sergeant involved.

While I'm sitting in the chief inspector's office talking with him about the problems of staffing the special Christmas patrols, Sergeant Lindsey knocks on the door to report that one of the divisional vans is now back in service. The chief inspector and I each have a glass of scotch in our hand and, when Lindsey enters, he is asked to pour himself a glass and join us for a minute. Lindsey does but keeps glancing somewhat nervously toward the still-open door and soon says in half jest: "This will get around the office fast. Me sitting in the Ops-Inspector's office having a drink, very hotty-totty like. How can I tell me lads not to drink when I'm having one with the guv?" We all laugh and the chief inspector tells Lindsey that he's sure he'll find a way. Much later in the day, I run into Lindsey in the canteen and he tells me he's never had a drink in the office with a senior officer before today unless he counts the hello-goodbye parties (exit parties where an officer leaving a nick—on transfer or retirement—puts on a bottle for his left-behind mates) or the annual Christmas bash.

These examples could be multiplied many times over. The specific event seems to be either a round of drinks in the midst of the flow of everyday activities that are later picked up again or a round of drinks offered as part of a formal, planned, and highly structured affair of some sort. No one gets drunk. No one loses control. No one seems affected in any way by the alcohol consumed—although, at times, this amount can be substantial. Any signs of drunkenness arising during these events are likely to be ignored, treated as a joke, or, as happened on a few occasions, attended to quickly (and discreetly) by someone taking the offending officer for a short walk and a long "cuppa" (usually coffee). Conventionally defined roles and duties are respected, demeanor is strictly "sober," and whatever responsibilities the participants carry into the occasion will be carried out by them as well.

In these instances, it is apparent that situational demands rule how the alcohol is used by organizational members. When the drinking is over and time-in more or less declared, no one complains or suggests that more alcohol be brought on. The amount consumed is usually rather modest by Met standards, and all signs of drunkenness sternly discouraged. In the case illustrations, no one wants a drunk along on a police raid, taking part in an exchange with a "snout," spoiling a formal dinner put on with some care and expense, acting rowdy in the sitting room of a solid citizen, or lurching and leering at midday in the tidy office of a chief inspector.

More to the point, these episodes are not the sort that have given the police in Britain a rather well-deserved (if perhaps overblown) reputation for heavy, raucous drinking (Smith and Gray 1983). Nor do these sorts of episodic and casual drinking correspond to the kinds of evaluations Holdaway (1983) makes about the centrality of "hedonism" and its constituent elements, "hard drinking and brawling," as key aspects of the police culture. Nor do these occasions say much about the handling of organizational conflict in police agencies because so little of it is apparent in these events. Remaining at issue then: In what situations do conflicting and drinking appear together?

Time-Out for a Drunk

I will provide examples of three different types of drinking situations where the use of alcohol seems highly related to the character of social interaction observed. Drunkenness is very likely to be displayed across these situations, and the resulting interaction among the participants takes on quite different forms than those that mark the incidental drinking occurrences. My list of social drinking situations is not exhaustive, but it does contain all of the episodes in which I took part during the study. Whatever hidden, private, individual drinking patterns exist are, of course, unknown.

The settings I examine below differ with respect to the participants they typically attract, the allegiance maintained by various participants toward each other and others not present, the patterns of inclusion and exclusion in the setting itself, and the talk and turn of events developed during the course of the occasion. For reasons I will briefly speculate on in closing this chapter, the men of the CID figure far more prominently in all three types of situations than the men of the uniform branch, who, when they imbibe seriously, seem to do so in rather quiet, segmented, and less brittle ways.[8]

I must note too that, while each of these drinking situations is presented as a self-contained and relatively closed occurrence, situational peculiarities, like a chance meeting with others not recruited for the original escapade, can change one type over into another. Equally true, some drinking situations begin as purely incidental affairs but roll over into any one of the three situations discussed below (such as when CID officers ring up an informant to arrange a meeting in a local pub and the informant never appears—or, as once was the case, the informant appears well after a transformation from an incidental to a serious time-out had occurred, thus leaving the informant with stories only he could tell).

Pub Tours

Coming back to the CID office after a series of inquiries about the whereabouts of a suspected ("sus'd") villain, Thomas and Colin invite me to come along with them to a neighborhood Rugby Club for a couple of pints. I'm told the rest of the office will be there and it should turn out to be fun. When we arrive, all are CID men, all DCs except for DS Rourke and a couple of odd characters who turned out to be regular patrons of this semiprivate club frequented by detectives. I'm told by Duncan that this is a CID pub: "Just us and the local villains." Most of the crowd seems a bit drunk when we arrive. Thomas and Colin are not long in coming around to the general demeanor of the long table at which we sit. A good deal of conversation focuses on the various, obviously uncountable, stupidities of uniform officers: "A bunch of scarecrows standing around in uniform hoping to frighten off some slag."

The frankness of the discussion is surprising as I learn just what last month's skipper (the uniform station sergeant) was "done for" (put on report). I learn too of the various theories held by the men as to why Probationary Constable Peter Nash never made it to PC Nash. Tales were told of verbals gone sour, of successfully sus'd out leaks within the nick, and, prospectively, just who was going "to take the mickey out of whom." Personal revelations were far less common than revelations about others, but, still, the candor was unusual as the men covered office politics from their own perspective.

> I was sitting in the office working on my fishing flies when that wooden-top Inspector Dorkley comes marching up the back stairs to tell me they've got some yob downstairs just nicked for breaking off car aerials over behind the Rose and Crown. "Would I care to come down and interview him," he says. I didn't want to go down and chat him up, mind you; but, here was this inspector waiting for an answer all proper like. It was down to me so I jump outta the chair [demonstrating some swift moves to others in the pub], throw the ties on my desk, rub my hands together, and say, "Right guv, let's go push this little yobo around and maybe he'll shop us an axe murderer. I hope he's a fucking nignog too 'cause I hate them fucking coloureds." You should'a seen the look on his face. Left him standing in his own piss thinking he'd just released a nut case on some poor, unfortunate lad.

The participants in this little social drama of the pub all became self-proclaimed drunk as the night wore on. There were the typical loud voices, some falling down and staggering when going to the toilet, and, as suggested, some rather blunt talk concerning the CID version of the wonderful world of police work. Yet, all in all, the conversation was most able, sometimes witty, and altogether coherent. Tales were told that had recognizable beginnings, middles, and ends; and, by closing time, all of us left to go home agreeing that a good time had been had by all.

Several days later, I had a chance to ask the detective who held forth on disturbing the inspector's peace of mind about the eventual outcome of the story told in the pub. After pushing him a little and reminding him when and where he had told me of the incident with the inspector, he scratched his head and muttered, "Did I tell that story again? Shit. I must be getting old 'cause I can't remember telling you about it. Fact is, I don't remember all that much about Dorkley either. He's been gone sometime now, over at King's Gate I think. Must 'ave been the booze talking."

My field notes contain a number of structurally similar episodes that could have been provided in place of the one above. A few of them involve uniform officers from the reliefs or "Beatcrimes" and one involves a gathering at one of the Met's private sports clubs. Most involve the CID. There are several points of interest associated with pub tours that deserve summary mention. First, the participants are usually all of the same rank, shift, and function. The only time I saw CID men across ranks drink together outside the office on more than an incidental basis was during the petering-out phase of what had begun as an office party. Uniform officers occasionally drink with their sergeants but never did I witness pub tours that included an inspector or above.

Second, the topics of pub-tour conversation, while not tightly defined, center on establishing the distinctiveness of the little group gathered together and serve perhaps to further trust among them and ratify distrust among them toward other groups in the organization. Moreover, sentiments of hostility are focused on traditional out-groups. For the CID, this list is long. A partial list would include (in no particular order): senior officers in the division, except for the DCI; the uniform branches; court officials; women in the Met (often referred to as "plonks, PCs with cunts"); rotten villains (as opposed to "good villains" who go in for theft, burglary, robbery, and "throw their hands up when you nick them fair and square since they know that their turn has come"); most of the personnel posted to the Yard; most of those who study the police ("why don't they go out and study the slag"); and so on. By directing "aggra" (aggravation) toward these individuals and groups, the men affirm, by contrast, their loyalty to their mates.

Third, these events seem unplanned but nonetheless regular. Often they begin when two officers announce they are going to such-and-such pub (on one occasion, to an officer's flat in the city) and anyone in the office who cares to join them is welcome. By reputation, this is a two to three times per week occurrence in the CID offices in which I worked. These tours often include a series of pubs, and, in the process, the tour would pick up and lose participants. There appears to be a regular core of officers who always go. They appear to represent the insiders of the division CID office and have the longest tenure and most status among their colleagues. Officers who have not been pub crawling for a few weeks are noticeable by their absence and often made sport of (as aloof "Hooray Henry" types) to their face by regulars. I never met a nondrinker in the CID (although I met a number of modest and "smart" drinkers) and suspect, if they exist at all in the divisions, they must have very thick skins.

Fourth, because drunkenness is the state participants claim to achieve, they are not held responsible for their talk and action in the same way they are otherwise held in check by office norms. Pub-tour conversations are defined as "drunken talk" and therefore too unreliable to feed directly back into workaday matters. What pub tours offer participants is, however, an opportunity to question whether their thoughts and actions are in line with those of the other men present. They are times of reality testing and, through interaction, those present can correct idiosyncratic opinions and behavior. It gives each officer a chance to reassess and rethink his position on past or current events in the office in light of the criticism (or appreciation) of others.

Finally, those who take part in pub tours have a duty to participate— to get drunk and hold forth. If an officer doesn't join in the "drunken talk" and express his opinions, he is in danger of losing his right to participate at all. If his views are not shared by others, he is expected to modify them, not withhold them. Such a shift should not occur too swiftly. There is something of a proper form to observe. Capitulation is not the norm but small compromises and gradual concessions are. In the end, the function of pub tours is served when personal views are brought into line with those of the group.

Office Parties

The party for Andrew's transfer to the Yard began fairly early Wednesday afternoon at about three o'clock. It came about somewhat by chance because no one knew for sure whether or not the DI had other plans for the afternoon. Everyone agreed that no party could take place without his presence. Andrew had already brought in a bottle of good whiskey and a couple of cheaper bottles. Barry had stockpiled his normal supply of beer and all knew the guv'nor, in this case, the DCI, would come with his own port and brandy to mix, a habit he claims he picked up years ago while on the Flying Squad at the Yard. Collections for more drink will be catch-as-catch-can because the office party "kitty" is currently empty—a result of the busy Christmas calendar during which this party occurs. The affair is launched when the DI finally responds to a DC's gentle reminder that Andrew's last day in the office is to be this Friday. "Right," says the DI, "let's go see what's in the closet." Everyone knows what's in the closet, of course, but the signal has now been given to let the party begin.

Aside from the regulars in the office, other officers on the division are invited up for a drink. The party begins with only 6 or 7 people present but soon the office is crammed with perhaps 25 to 30 people and is spilling into the halls and offices surrounding CID quarters. The CID office on this division—as is true for most Met divisions—is located upstairs, above the charging room, and is relatively distant from the small public areas of the station. But anyone past the front desk of the division would have very little difficulty knowing that there was a party going on and just where it was taking place. Noise drifts astray, and several times the skipper appears to plead for a little restraint ("We've got some juveniles and their parents downstairs"). In his final appearance, he is hooted at for interrupting the flow of the party, plied with a drink, mollified to a degree, and sent on his increasingly merry way to keep the nick running.

There are many ranks represented at the party. The DCI appears and proceeds to start drinking his strange brew. The superintendent puts in a brief appearance (bringing with him an honorary bottle of wine for Andrew bearing the label, "Chateaux CID, 99% Rotten"). The district detective chief superintendent shows up and stays for several hours. Eventually, all the DCs and DSs of the division arrive and stay for the duration. Some of their friends from other divisions come too with glasses in hand. A friendly barrister drops in as do several Met solicitors (lawyers) who are apparently good friends with the DI.

As people arrive and mingle, others leave. Recruitment to this party (as contrasted with a pub tour) is ongoing, haphazard, and seemingly democratic. It is clear, however, that the party group is made up of friends. Persons unlikely to get along with the hosts of this affair do not appear or, if they do, are made to feel uncomfortable through the choice of conversational topics. Statements such as "lemme tell you just how thick the Homebeats really are" (or uniform officers, or chief inspectors, or traffic officers, and so on) drive the unwanted from the room.

On the whole, there is an open door to these parties but a good number of guests arrive and depart with dispatch.

These parties are marked by an obvious emphasis on being drunk. The CID men swagger, swear, stumble, and put on an ostentatious but convincing display of drunkenness. People are obnoxious, aggressive, and physical and seem to have lost any pretension of courtesy. The few women present are sometimes fondled in meant-to-be-seen ways but they are mostly ignored unless subjected to bawdy commentary or outright scorn. Moreover, the usual deference CID officers provide one another during ordinary working hours (or even during pub tours) slips from view. Interaction among the officers is marked by uncharacteristic rudeness and personal attack. Between the ranks, there is an interactive separateness in the room as the more senior officers cluster at one end and their inferiors in rank at the other. Verbal swipes are taken at one another within each of these groups but such swipes are most remarkable when they take place between the ranked groups. When they occur, the attention of all in the room is riveted on the exchange, slowing down the party and sometimes bringing forth lengthy collective arguments concerning a particular grievance(s). Consider the mutual "bollocking" (verbal critiques) that took place between the DI and a DC:

> You've got to stop fucking around with this nowhere Lawrence case, Guv. We've got to show results sometime. I'm sick and tired of chasing down the numbers on all the videos that have been done in Greater London for the past month.

> You're winding me up, sunshine. I'm doing my job and if you were just doing yours like it's supposed to be done, you wouldn't be coming on to me now.

> Sod off, David. You know everything we've got so far is dodgy. This isn't going anywhere.

> You're the wrong bugger to be talking, Barry. Look at the overtime slips I've signed for you on this one. You better knock off or I'll have you back where you belong—downstairs pushing a broom.

> You're a bloody fool, David, to worry about Lawrence and his punters. What's with you on this one, anyway? Is he putting it to your Mum?

> You're a fucking cunt, Barry. Shut your lips before you and me take a little walk outside.

It seems that the question of how officers and men of the CID are to relate to one another during (and, presumably, after) the party is of some significance. It is also a complex matter in light of the overlapping duties, sometimes interdependent tasks, independence, and high visibility of their work relative to other police functions.

CID officers form something of a clan wherein expressions of distrust or dissatisfaction with the work behavior of one another within and across the ranks are normally avoided. Those in the clan tolerate a good deal of activity (or lack thereof) on the part of others of whom they privately do not approve. Moreover, there is, at least in this unit, a good deal of frustration with what are perceived to be low detection rates, uncaught villains, unsympathetic courts, inadequate resources to do the job, manpower shortages, careless deployment strategies, inadequate dedication of certain officers to their jobs, tight constraints on overtime, lack of skill and loyalty within the fold, the current apprenticeship program, and with what is generally seen as the Yard's desire to "put the CID in its place."

In short, the conditions surrounding CID work make for relatively fragile interrank and sometimes between-rank relations. Each expects more of the others than the others seem willing or able to provide. To talk about some of these matters openly during the course of the normal workday would be very difficult for the parties involved. Communications across the ranks are typically restricted to practical matters of immediate interest. A serious discussion about some of these believed personal and organizational shortcomings might trigger heated debate, arguments during which those involved might say and do things they would later come to regret.

Given this hothouse microenvironment, the office party allows for some often blunt discourse across the CID ranks. With alcohol obvious and everyone drunk, an officer is not responsible for what he says and does. Higher officials can criticize lower ones and, more important, lower ones can "come on about their complaints" with the higher ranks (occasionally with remarkably higher ranks). It is also possible, because of the public venue of the office party, to discuss what might otherwise be viewed as individual "personality conflicts" as if they were collective problems.

In some instances, these "discussions" seem to produce tension-relieving procedural changes. The Lawrence case mentioned above was, for example, dropped several days later by the DI on the face-saving grounds that the manpower was more urgently required to catch up on some homicide inquiries. Sometimes, much desired personnel transfers result. In any case, participants will almost always claim they were thoroughly "out of their minds" at the party and rarely will they admit to remembering much at all other than what horrible hangovers they had the following day. The office party seems then to have the consequence of allowing officers with some differing and often strong views on their work to communicate with each other and to do so in a way that the consequences of such communication need not be directly faced.

Like pub tours, my field notes contain descriptions of a number of structurally similar CID parties. They are, in fact, rather frequent affairs, and few weeks went by without at least one party taking place. Exits and entrances to the unit provide typical excuses for "putting on the bottle," as do post-raid debriefings, monthly management meetings, certain holidays and local events of traditional significance, birthdays and births, and, if nothing else was available, a party could be justified by the same principles as American college students who invent pseudoholidays such as TGIFs (thank god it's Friday). I never witnessed a party on the uniform side of the organization (in or out of the nick) that came anywhere close to duplicating the group dynamics of CID parties.

Raiding Parties

In late January, I went on a pub tour with Barry, Thomas, Colin, and Clive, all CID officers of undistinguished rank. We began by putting down pints in a familiar pub close to the nick. All the assembled are disturbed by the way the new burglary screening program is working. In the past, CID officers were assigned all burglary cases to do whatever follow-up they alone deemed necessary (within general inquiry and reporting guidelines). Since the first of the year in the South Downs, Beatcrimes, a uniform specialty, has taken a good deal of the burglary load away from the CID. The purpose of the program is, on the surface, benign: To free up CID time for more serious matters. Massive amounts of time (and, of course, overtime) can be spent on burglary inquiries that are, strictly speaking, entirely routine and symbolic functions. A point system has been put into effect such that, if the program works as its designers wish, only a few burglaries will flow to the CID office (presumably only those with a high probability of yielding a suspect and charge). The men sitting with me in the pub are not, however, happy with the program. They smell changes afoot that they do not like.

> Those buggers will keep all the good stuff for themselves. They've always given us shit in the past and it's not going to change now. What winds me up the most is watching those silly blokes go out together on cases and then spend hours putting out a trivial report. They've got a list of enquiries as long as my arm just sitting on Owen's desk downstairs. The Boy Detective [a term CID officers often used to denote the chief superintendent] will be squirming if this keeps up. To top it all off, Owen's got the bottle [courage] to put that note in the Parade Book about the rape case Hughie fucked up. God damn Herberts. It's all going downhill I tell you. Pretty soon there won't be any CID and won't the villains be pleased. Thank god I'll be gone by then.

The pints keep coming and the talk turns increasingly bitter. As the evening wears on, the tired lament of the CID officer is heard again and again (as, no doubt, it has been heard for many years). Eventually, the men, led by Barry, decide to move on to another pub. I bid everyone a drunken goodnight and drive home thinking vaguely that I've just been on another pub tour. I found out later, however, that the men piled into Colin's car feeling rather "stroppy" and proceeded to descend on the Three Virgins, a club thought to be frequented by Beatcrime officers. Apparently, no one from Beatcrimes was present but the men ordered multiple rounds anyway and, according to Colin, stood about the bar talking loudly with each other about the kind of silly people from the department that go to the Three Virgins. They claimed to have left no doubt in any of the customers' or publicans' minds that they were from the CID and they were mad about being insulted by people who exhibit oddly shaped heads (a pointed reference to the bobby helmets some-times worn by uniform officers). One of the patrons was said to have made a move for the door during an allegedly moving monologue by Barry, and the other CID men jammed the customer back on the bar stool with the remark, "You should stay put when DC Cobb is enlight-ening you." The atmosphere, according to the tale, was electric and, to a listener, whatever order remained in the club was clearly not the doing of the CID, who claimed they were entitled to a brawl.

Eventually, things cooled down as the clock moved toward closing time and it became apparent that no one else would be arriving for a drink that evening. No Beatcrime officers appeared. Final rounds were put down without incident and the men again piled into Colin's car for the ride back to the station parking lot.

This incident differs in several important ways from what I have called pub tours and office parties. First, the specifics of the evening's adventure are readily recalled. The episode became known as "Stalking the Downstairs' Wally" (referring to a particularly disliked Beatcrime officer) and was told and retold by the CID men with relish. Because the raid was ultimately thwarted by the Beatcrime officers' failure to appear, it does not possess all the character of the truly legendary stories that circulate throughout the CID, but, for the moment, to those in the local office, the story would do. It tells of an attempt to restore CID honor—believed to be degraded by Beatcrime officers—undertaken unilaterally with vengeance in mind. The intent was to settle a dispute by evening the score and putting Beatcrime men in their proper place.

Second, recruitment to this event was far from random. Had I remained with the drinking party, I suspect a normal pub tour would have been the result. Each of the men in the raiding party claimed to have run into recent difficulties with Beatcrimes and had personalized tales to tell regarding the slights and injustices visited them when dealing with men of the other office. Moreover, each was of low rank, and would have, if the plan had been realized, bumped into uniform officers of equally low rank. The sides were more or less balanced. There could be no parties of high rank or outsider status along on such a raid because both are more or less "above" insult or injury directed toward them by those of lesser or irrelevant rank. Moreover, given their station, both are believed to have other, more proper, means at their disposal to pursue whatever grievances they may have directed to the lower order—disciplinary procedures for one and the written word for the other.

Third, the four CID men who stayed the course were all very good friends. Their talk throughout the evening apparently produced something akin to a flash-point agreement that things were so bad for them that they might rightly try to remedy the situation. Nothing could really be done about the situation, of course, because it was the result of organizational forces located well beyond the divisional boundaries. But some redress was possible and "Stalking the Downstairs' Wally" was the form that it took. In essence, the raid was an identity display on the part of the participants. It was a demonstration that CID officers are

CID officers and uniform blokes are uniform blokes. What one is, the other surely is not.

No one in the CID would claim that these men were so drunk that they did not know what they were doing. Indeed, in many ways, the group behaved in the most stereotyped and unflattering ways to outsiders for whom the image of a reeling and pushy CID man is well established. Yet it seems that what the detective constables of the South Downs were up to was more than merely to enliven an evening with an uncontested, familiar performance of the drunk and nasty CID man acting true to form and out for a little fun. They were out to do a little conflict management too in a fashion that had tradition and just cause on its side.

There are more stories I could recount here of structurally similar episodes—none of which I witnessed, however. All are told with pride, and some flow from the uniform side of the department as well. All involve groups going up against other groups and all involve raiding parties made up of status equals descending on like foes. A variation on this theme is found in the "Boxing Day" stories told by CID officers. These are tales about the annual, departmentwide CID bash held each year that is said to conclude when divisional groups are unleashed to visit their most detested and villainous pubs, there to bust up the place and anyone who gets in their way. Sometimes the enemy is inside the organization, sometimes outside.

Comment

Allow me now to come back to a few of the themes with which I began this chapter. In particular, let me say some things about these little drinking episodes that I think touch on matters beyond the Met or the South Downs. I will be mercifully brief. Four comments, with some additional elaboration on the last two, are relevant.

First, much of the literature on conflict and its many forms, uses, and settlement patterns (if any) strikes me as exceedingly empty of those concrete nitty-gritty details about the everyday situations within which conflict is publicly put up for display. My chapter is, in large measure, a reaction (perhaps an overreaction) to the vacuous prescriptive literatures favored by those who worry about it in organizations (e.g., "getting to yes," "team building," "win-win negotiation") as well as those imposing but abstract theoretical explanations for conflict favored by those who want to model it in organizations (e.g., the causal structure of organizational conflict as told by a log-linear regression with n + 1 variables). That the descriptive literature on conflict in organizations remains thin may only suggest that we prefer reading about what could or should be done rather than what is done. It may also suggest that a good deal of conflict is avoided or otherwise lumped or tolerated during the routine workaday encounters of organizational members and groups. A look into the cracks of organizations may be of some use in this regard. As a move in this direction, I propose the serious study of time-outs as one (of many) ways to develop more accurate, interesting, and sensitive studies of conflict. We might start by looking at some of the functions of the legendary "businessman's lunch," complete with its now customary bottle of white wine replacing the gone but not forgotten multiple martini.

Second, conflict might usefully be viewed as a dramatic rendering, a symbolic display, or a performance to which various audiences attach certain meanings under certain circumstances. Such a view might suggest that conflict itself is often a rather permanent state among certain parties rather than a temporary midpoint stage in an ongoing dispute process with clear beginnings and endings. Such a view might also suggest that, because conflict varies by setting, various associated conceptual attributes like grievances, gripes, and grudges also vary by setting. I am not arguing that there is no substance behind such concepts, but I am arguing that researchers often give far too much credit to those folk theories informing us as to the facticity of an issue in dispute. In this regard, we again need close case studies of conflict—studies that probe conventional definitions, look behind appearances, and do not divorce the study of conflict from the various situations in which it appears (or disappears).

Third, if context is to be given its due, some ways must be found to harness elements of it that are describable. I have tried here to suggest that social relations are always relevant to contextually sensitive descriptions. The small group may even have to be rediscovered because it seems that it is here that a good deal of meaning, especially of the organizational sort, is constructed and affirmed (Schein 1985; Van Maanen and Barley 1985). Meaning is so critical because there is absolutely nothing inherent in the notion of conflict that is strictly independent of human observation and the making of meaning. To understand what one can and cannot get away with inside (or outside) an organization requires a rather elaborate theory of conflict and its consequences—folk or academic. Such a theory, if it is any good, must allow a good deal of context sensitivity (e.g., as to timing, place, local history, relationships, and risk). Consider, in this regard, some of the conflict theory leads provided by certain patterns of social relations that stand behind the wobbly time-outs I observed among the police.

In many respects, senior officers on the uniform side have more power over their subordinates than their counterparts and rank equals in the CID.[9] They seem to use it as well. During my time at the South Downs, 14 officers from the uniform side were put "on report" (initiating disciplinary procedures) while no CID officers suffered a similar fate. Police constables, by and large, do their jobs within broad outlines set by the senior officers of the division. They may not like these officers or their guidelines but they do their bidding. They virtually never talk back and, despite grumbling for what are seen as the foibles of senior officers, they perform most of their required tasks in civil and competent ways (at least most of the time). CID officers are, however, another story. They are, perhaps by vocational socialization and experience, a distrustful lot. They bicker among themselves and constantly thwart, with some success, the aims of their superiors. What might explain such a pattern?

Keeping in mind that this glossy discussion is a highly relative one, we can approach the above pattern by noting first that managerial performance standards on the uniform side are far less ambiguous than on the CID side. Uniform supervisors have access to many yardsticks to measure the performance (or lack thereof) of their officers. While some critics (such as myself) may find these standards woefully inadequate, police supervisors do not. The arrest book, the PAS (person-at-station) book, and the traffic book are examples in this regard. By listening in on the radio communication of officers in a district and examining the work they log on other books, a reasonably aware sergeant or inspector will soon come to some judgments about who is working and who is not. There is little overlap or sharing across jobs (except in the generic sense of "patrol"), and visible uniforms and insignia support the command structure that is intended to keep everyone in his or her proper place.

The officers and men who constitute the uniform reliefs rarely confront one another with complaints and, when they do, invariably do so timidly, casting their complaints in terms of requests or favors needed from the other. Avoidance and the curtailment of interaction among squabbling parties is the norm. The fluidity of the division is partly responsible because troublesome supervisors or workmates can usually be slipped by requesting a new assignment, switching shifts, or, more drastically, moving to another nick. Moreover, police communities embody something of a mock or soft bureaucracy within which higher officials maintain good relations with lower ranks by virtue of leaving them alone (Van Maanen 1974; Jermier and Berkes 1979; Holdaway 1983). When grievances do bubble up and become public, they are almost always put forth by superior officers and handled therefore as matters of discipline. For those of low rank who find avoidance difficult and the toleration of a grievance impossible, their only recourse is revolt. Revolts are rare, of course, but not entirely unheard of (e.g., blue flu, ticket campaign, strike).

Moving upstairs to the CID office, a very different pattern of conflict is observed. While there is little formality among the officers and relationships appear settled and warm, there is not much sharing of information. Access to information is personalized and often kept very private. Officers working particular cases are reluctant to discuss much about them during the ordinary workday—for fear of leaks, poaching; appearing unduly confident, incompetent, lazy, dishonest; or being drawn away from the case in hand. CID officers are even more suspicious of written documents than are their uniform brethren. Supervisors lose power accordingly because there is very little opportunity to see what it is their officers do all day, and, informationally, there is little they can learn about what they do unless the officers choose to tell them. Commands in the CID, at least at the local level, take the form of requests, subject to amendment by those to whom they apply.

It is very tempting to conclude that the relatively high alcohol consumption rate in the CID is something of a functional equivalent to some of the more predictable informational and disciplinary channels operating on the uniform side. Under some pressure to produce, CID officers work in a low-information context, under strained interdependencies, and face, for all practical purposes, detection goals that are more often than not impossible to achieve. Moreover, they work in and out of crowded offices under conditions of relative rank equality and make use of an all-purpose, well-established entrepreneurial language and set of case-making practices that are shared (and continually worked on) by the membership. In Black's (1990) terminology, the CID represents a "tangled network" of social relations where conflict is neither entirely avoided nor unilaterally crushed. As the office party suggests, they do something in between; they talk (loudly) to one another and try to negotiate settlements. Sometimes these settlements require a little help from their friends, sometimes not.

Further, there is the matter of the tense social relations between the CID and the uniform branches. Most of the time, the two appear to lump their grievances and carry on. When a charging sergeant calls for the CID to come down and interview a nicked villain, he will leave the room (perhaps reluctantly) and return only when the CID has completed their inquiries. When an investigating detective takes over a case based on the material put in the file by a relief officer, he may "bitch" about the quality of the report but rarely will he seek out the uniform officer for further information or to make known to him his displeasure (a practice not overlooked by uniform officers). Sometimes, however, such muted conflict explodes when the two groups rub up against each other and find they can no longer simply tolerate one another's presence. Raids, fights, reciprocal insults, and not-to-be-missed disdainful glances are forthcoming. There is a feudal-like code of honor at work behind these gestures, yet neither group seems willing to press things too far. A fight now and then with a story to tell seems to be the norm. When uniform officers feel they are pushed about too roughly by their CID counterparts, they push back (and vice versa). Those up in the hierarchy overlook a good deal of this mutual give-and-take and are perhaps more often amused by it than offended. There are limits, of course, to which such a toleration policy can be put, and the raiders of both camps seem to respect them.

Fourth and finally, drinking occasions in the Met can also be viewed as ritual.[10] The incidental drinking episodes represent rather frozen but entertaining rituals wherein conflict is masked and largely ignored. Both high ranks and low ranks talk and behave on these occasions as if there were no troubles between them and all were members of a common community within which each has an appropriate location. The rules suggest, however, that the ritual is strictly a reaffirming one insofar as category differences are concerned, for it is virtually always the higher rank who initiates and closes the time-out. Provided one does not upset the interlude by behaving as if the time-out were for serious drinking, the incidental drink honors the collective pursuits and interests of distinctly unequal organizational members.

When drinking becomes central to a gathering, ritual becomes more specialized. Pub tours for little groups of CID officers provide occasions whereby they can distance themselves from and contrast themselves to others in the organization. Through gossip, tale telling, and the rigors of joint drinking, trust and rank loyalties are at stake and typically confirmed while a group perspective is hammered out and celebrated. Office parties offer opportunities for rituals of resistance as official taboos are momentarily set aside and negotiations entered into between status unequals. Evil talk is legitimized and challenges to the everyday divisional routines and power relations allowed. The framework and temporal boundaries surrounding these challenges are more or less fixed and apparent to all participants; but the mere frequency with which these festivities appear on the ritual calendar of the office and the intensity of feelings generated on such occasions suggest that these parties provide welcome opportunities for persons and groups to dramatize their contrasting interests and problems. And raids across organizational boundaries symbolize in some very concrete ways the common aims and values of subgroup membership. The honor of the group is at stake. Stories and myths are created that provide the group with memorable events; these stories and myths aid in demonstrating and therefore institutionalizing the character, strength, and style of the group to which the raiders belong.

All this is to say that conflict has both structural and ritual dimensions. An instructive place to observe these dimensions is in the time-outs created by organizational members. There is irony here too because time-outs are often thought by those who take part in them to be among the least rule-governed and least conflictual occasions associated with organizational life; but, as I have argued, they may be among the most. Essentially, by examining time-outs, we can peek behind the onstage performance of organizational drama and learn of the backstage work that keeps the production together. Conflicts as managed in one region or the other are not any more or less real or necessarily any more or less important, but they will surely appear in different forms. To know more about how we are sometimes able to drink our troubles away might just prove instructive (and fun).

Notes

1. In this chapter, I follow the conceptual framework developed by Nader and Todd (1978) and later elaborated on by a number of writers including Mather and Yngvesson (1980-81), Miller and Sarat (1980-81), Cain and Kulscar (1981-82), Kolb (1986), and, critically, Black (1990). This framework organizes the disputing process into rough stages: grievance, conflict, and dispute settlement. Conflict emerges when a party or parties make public their grievance against another party or parties and is the focus of this analysis. Modes of conflict management range from self-help varieties, to intervention on the part of third parties, to doing nothing and ducking, or tolerating the particular grievance altogether. An exemplary treatment of how disputes come to the surface and are shaped by the situations within which they are expressed is that of Felstiner, Abel, and Sarat (1981).

2. I have in mind a long list of studies and conceptual writings on disputing that are illustrated in anthropology by Gluckman (1985), Bohannon (1967), Nader (1965), Moore (1977), Gulliver (1979), Merry (1979), and Merry and Silbey (1984) and in sociology by Becker (1963), Sudnow (1965), Bittner (1967), Black (1976, 1980), Strauss (1978), and Gusfield (1981). This is but a small drop in a large bucket.

3. Pondy's (1967) paper is the classic. Other review pieces include Pfeffer (1981), Kolb (1986), Sheppard (1983), and Thomas (1976).

4. As always, there are exceptions. Among them are Rosen (1985), Kunda (in press), Sheppard, Blumenfeld-Jones, and Roth (1989), and Friedman (1989). It is interesting that some of the descriptions of the role drinking groups play in the day to day affairs of Japanese managers appear structurally similar to the role drinking groups play in the Met as examined here. See, for example, Rohlen (1974).

5. Donald Roy (1960) has written most tellingly on time-outs—although he didn't call them that. His were nonalcoholic ones, of relatively short duration, and geared into a tightly run, production-conscious work context. Banana time, coke time, shut-the-window time were all routine and ritualized activities breaking up the workday for the otherwise highly scheduled human cogs attending to stamping machines on a small shop floor. But, as Roy rightly argued, such episodes allowed workers to attach certain meanings to the workplace and to the social relations that obtained there, provided occasions of mutual sport, support, and entertainment, and, generally, allowed for a more fulfilling experience at work than might otherwise have been the case. At about the same time, Melville Dalton (1959), writing about middle managers in a large corporate environment, also suggested just how frequent time-outs were for those men he studied. Dalton's careful work noted that many executive offices were empty for goodly portions of the day while the managers took time-outs for long, liquid lunches; and, toward the end of the day, those same offices often hummed to the tune of social interaction made more melodic by alcohol. Both writers argue for the importance of time-outs in the business of business.

6. Two studies provide something of a structural model for the representation and analysis of my police drinking materials. One is a sharp look by Lithman (1979) at an Indian community in Canada with a provincewide reputation for "hard and incessant drinking." Lithman rejects psychological explanations for the so-called functions of alcohol (e.g., "to allow the venting of pent-up frustrations," "to get happy," "to get feelings out in the open") in favor of a distinctly sociological explanation resting on the social relations that characterize the community and the cultural norms of conduct that go with heavy drinking. The other study is provided by Todd (1978), who examined disputing as it took place around the *gastaimmer* (drinking table) in a public house located in a rural

Bavarian village. Both studies suggest that what appear to be spontaneous, freewheeling drinking occasions carry with them quite firm rules about who drinks, how they are to carry on while drinking, and what topics are to be raised and dealt with while drinking. Both writers develop comparative taxonomies of the social situations they observed and do so with respect to the kinds of conflict likely to emerge in each situation. Both pay attention to the differing participants in each situation as well as the tone, manner, and direction in which participants spill or swallow their grievances along with their drinks. And both interpret the behavior they witnessed in terms of existing social relations that linked (or blocked) members of each community to (or from) one another.

7. Interpreting CID accounts of this sort is tricky because such talk is largely rhetorical, designed to put forth an idealized representation of their trade. CID officers do indeed spend a good deal of on-duty time in pubs (one study estimated 17%; Smith and Gray 1983). But it is far from clear that the information they obtain in such locales is all that helpful to them. Part of the CID officer's attraction to pubs, beyond whatever crime-relevant information he may gather, is that in them he is typically welcomed by the publican and occupies a prestigious social position in the hierarchy of patrons (as something of a local celebrity). On the CID craft, see Hobbs (1988).

8. This is as good a time as any to note that whatever indication I provide about the frequency of drinking in particular domains is, at best, a nervous guess. There is no control on my groups or observations and I have only field notes on which to base my rough counts. I trust my data more than I would a survey on such matters but I recognize their limitations as well. In terms of the textual comment that prompts this disclaimer, I am simply reporting that drinking in the office was an uncommon activity in the uniform areas of the station.

9. This statement should not be taken very far. I am merely making a relative comparison here, not an absolute one. Even on the uniform side, one would be hard-pressed to demonstrate that the guv'nors very often exercise their power. By and large, much of police control inside the organization is ceremonial, staged, and highly ritualized (e.g., the parades before each relief, the stream of memos and orders that appear in the nick from senior officers, the traditional visitations to the substations where an inspector may occasionally place his hand on the engine bonnet of a Panda or R/T car to check whether they have been driven recently, or a nocturnal tour of the canteen to see who's playing cards, pool, or sleeping, and so on). Such ceremony is not entirely empty because the work of the division does get done and usually done rather well (here the comparison is with the patrol divisions in the United States).

10. To decide on a working definition for *ritual* from the disputes of social anthropologists is no easy matter. Leach (1968, 526) writes: "Even among [ritual specialists] there is the widest possible disagreement as to how the word 'ritual' should be used." I bypass this debate and adopt Lukes's (1975, 290) definition of ritual: "Rule-governed activity of a symbolic character which draws the attention of its participants to objects of thought and feeling which they hold to be of special significance." This is useful for my purposes because organizational time-outs gracefully slide in under its cover. Moreover, as Lukes suggests, this definition allows ritual to be seen as a mode of exercising power (including the handling of disputes).

References

Becker, H. S. 1963. *Outsiders*. New York: Free Press.

Bittner, E. 1967. The police on skid row: A study in peace-keeping. *American Sociological Review* 32:699-715.

Black, D. 1976. *The behavior of law*. New York: Academic Press.

—1980. *The manners and customs of police*. New York: Academic Press.

—1990. The elementary forms of conflict management. In *New directions in the study of justice, law and social control*, ed. School of Justice Studies, Arizona State University, 43-69. New York: Plenum, 1990.

Bohannan, P. 1967. *Law and warfare: Studies in the anthropology of conflict*. Austin: University of Texas Press.

Cain, M., and K. Kulscar. 1981-82. Thinking disputes: An essay on the origins of the dispute industry. *Law and Society Review* 16:375-402.

Dalton, M. 1959. *Men who manage*. New York: John Wiley.

Emerson, R. M., and S. L. Messinger. 1977. The micropolitics of trouble. *Social Problems* 25:121-34.

Felstiner, N., R. Abel, and A. Sarat. 1981. The emergence and transformation of disputes: Naming, blaming and claiming. *Law and Society Review* 15:631-57.

Fielding, N. G. 1988. *Joining forces*. London: Routledge.

Friedman, R. A. 1989. Interaction norms as carriers of organizational culture. *Journal of Contemporary Ethnography* 18:3-29.

Gluckman, M. 1985. *Custom and conflict in Africa*. Oxford, England: Basil Blackwell.

Goffman, E. 1955. On face-work. *Psychiatry* 3:213-31.

Gulliver, P. H. 1979. *Disputes and negotiations: A cross-cultural perspective*. New York: Academic Press.

Gusfield, J. R. 1981. *The culture of public problems*. Chicago: University of Chicago Press.

Hobbs, D. 1988. *Doing the business: Entrepreneurship, the working class, and detectives in the east end of London*. Oxford, England: Clarendon.

Holdaway, S. 1983. *Inside the British police*. Oxford, England: Basil Blackwell.

Jermier, J., and L. J. Berkes. 1979. Leader behavior in a police command bureaucracy. *Administrative Science Quarterly* 23:1-23.

Kolb, D. 1983. *The mediators*. Cambridge, Mass.: MIT Press.

—1986. Who are organization third parties and what do they do? In *Research on negotiations in organizations*, ed. M. Bazerman, R. Lewicki, and B. Sheppard. Greenwich, Conn.: JAI.

Kunda, G. In press. *Engineering culture*. Philadelphia: Temple University Press.

Leach, E. 1968. Ritual. In *International encyclopedia of social science*. Vol. 13, ed. O. L. Sills. New York: Free Press.

Lithman, Y. G. 1979. Feeling good and getting smashed: On the symbols of alcohol and drunkenness among Canadian Indians. *Ethnos* 44:119-53.

Lukes, S. 1975. Political ritual and social integration. *Sociology* 9:289-308.

Manning, R. 1977. *Police work*. Cambridge, Mass.: MIT Press.

Mather, L. M., and B. Yngvesson. 1980-81. Language, audience and the transformation of disputes. *Law and Society Review* 15:755-816.

Merry, S. B. 1979. Going to court: Strategies of dispute settlement in an American urban neighborhood. *Law and Society Review* 13:891-925.

Merry, S. E., and S. Silbey. 1984. What do plaintiffs want? Reexamining the concept of dispute. *The Justice System Journal* 9:151-78.

Miller, R., and A. Sarat. 1980-81. Grievances, claims and disputes: Assessing the adversary culture. *Law and Society Review* 15:525-66.

Moore, S. F. 1977. Individual interests and organizational structures: Some aspects of strict liability, self-help and collective responsibility. In *Social anthropology and law*, ed. I. Hamnett, 159-89. London: Academic Press.

Nader, L. 1965. The anthropological study of law. *American Anthropologist* 67 (2): 3-32.

Nader, L., and H. F. Todd, eds. 1978. *The disputing process: Law in ten societies*. New York: Columbia University Press.

Newman, G. F. 1984. *Law and order.* London: Panther.

Pfeffer, J. 1981. *Power in organizations.* Marshfield, Mass.: Ritman.

Pondy, L. R. 1967. Organizational conflict: Concepts and models. *Administrative Science Quarterly* 17:296-320.

Rohlen, T. 1974. *For harmony and strength.* Berkeley: University of California Press.

Rosen, M. 1985. Breakfast at Spiro's: Dramaturgy and dominance. *Journal of Management* 11:31-48.

Roy, D. 1960. Bananatime. *Human Organization* 18:158-68.

Schein, E. H. 1985. *Organizational culture and leadership.* San Francisco: Jossey-Bass.

Sheppard, B. H. 1983. Third party conflict intervention: A procedural framework. In *Research in organizational behavior.* Vol. 6, ed. B. M. Staw and L. L. Cummings. Greenwich, Conn:. JAI.

Sheppard, B. H., K. Blumenfeld-Jones, and J. Roth. 1989. Informal thirdpartyship: A program of research on everyday conflict intervention. In *Mediation of social conflict*, ed. K. Kressel and D. Pruitt. San Francisco: Jossey-Bass.

Silverman, D. 1970. *The theory of organizations.* London: Heinemann.

Smith, D. J., and J. Gray. 1983. *Police and people in London.* Vol. 4, *The police in action.* London: Policy Studies Institute.

Strauss, A. 1978. *Negotiations.* San Francisco: Jossey-Bass.

Sudnow, R. 1965. Normal crimes. *Social Problems* 12:255-76.

Thomas, K. 1976. Conflict and conflict management. In *Handbook of industrial and organizational psychology*, ed. M. D. Dunnette, 889-935. New York: Rand McNally.

Todd, H. F. 1978. Litigious marginals: Character and disputing in a Bavarian village. In *The disputing process: Law in ten societies*, ed. L. Nader and H. F. Todd, 86-121. New York: Columbia University Press.

Van Maanen, J. 1974. Working the street. In *The potential for reform of criminal justice*, ed. M. Jacob. Newbury Park, Cal.: Sage.

—1978. Watching the watchers. In *Policing: A view from the streets*, ed. P. K. Manning and J. Van Maanen, 309-349. New York: Random House.

—1981. Notes on the production of ethnographic data in an American police agency. In *Law and social enquiry*, ed. R. Luckmann. Uppsala, Sweden: Scandinavian Institute for African Studies.

—1988. *Tales of the field.* Chicago: University of Chicago Press.

Van Maanen, J., and S. Barley. 1985. Occupational communities. In *Research in organizational behavior,* Vol. 6, ed. B. Staw and L. L. Cummings. Greenwich, Conn.: JAI.

3

Women's Work

Peacemaking in Organizations

DEBORAH M. KOLB

I often find myself drawn into conflicts at work. Colleagues come in, close the door, and then confide in me about some problem they have with a mutual associate or boss. I listen and, probably more often than is wise, agree to take the matter up with the other person(s). Sometimes I succeed in altering the situation and at other times I report back what I have learned. I often wonder why I get involved. Is it because I am accessible—my door is usually open—or because I relish good gossip or because people know of my interest in mediation or because they think I will make a difference? Whatever the reasons for my own involvement, I have recently become aware of how pervasive this kind of informal peacemaking is.

It is often said that conflict (and its management) is a major growth industry. One of the major areas of expansion in the dispute resolution

AUTHOR'S NOTE: I presented a preliminary version of this chapter as part of a symposium titled "Women's Ways of Developing Organizations," chaired by Joanne Martin at the annual meeting of the Academy of Management, San Francisco, August 1990. As I revised the draft, several people helped me think about the intersection of gender and informal peacemaking. I thank Dafna Izraeli, Lotte Bailyn, Linda L. Putnam, Bill Breslin, Jean M. Bartunek, Eileen Babbitt, and Joanne Martin for their contributions. I enjoyed the interaction with the three women profiled in this study. I hoped they learned from it as well.

field generally, and one that has had considerable impact on organizations, is the use of mediation to resolve conflicts in wide-ranging domains of social life. Within organizations, it is seen as an alternative to traditional grievance and complaint procedures (Kolb 1987; Rowe 1987), to grievance arbitration (Kolb 1989b; Ury, Brett, and Goldberg 1988), and to authoritarian managerial decision making (Karambayya and Brett 1989; Sheppard 1983). Despite positive claims made regarding its efficiency and user satisfaction, formal channels of dispute processing are relatively underutilized, and mediation is rarely the choice of managers when faced with conflict among their subordinates (Kolb 1987; Sheppard, Blumenfeld-Jones, and Roth 1989).

Members of organizations may shun these official processes because they have other, less formal and public avenues open to them. There is evidence that a considerable amount of conflict management is handled privately and informally by people who have no mediation function or credentials but have become involved because they feel compelled for some reason(s) to aid in the resolution of disputes between their associates (Kolb 1989a). Indeed, it is likely that informal peacemaking is one of the most common forms of conflict management within organizations. At some point, many managers, supervisors, secretaries, colleagues, and friends will find themselves involved as behind-the-scenes intervenors in some disagreement or conflict.

Despite the prevalence of these informal activities, they are rarely the subject of systematic study. In part, the lack of scholarship is related to how difficult it is to document these phenomena (see Dalton 1959). But the dearth of work may also be related to the characteristics of those who take on the function as well as the importance, from the organization's perspective, of these activities. Given the structure of contemporary organizations and the support roles in which women are represented in large numbers, they are likely to be major practitioners of behind-the-scenes peacemaking. To the degree therefore that behind-the-scenes peacemaking remains largely invisible as a topic of inquiry, it means that the women who are likely to get involved in and enjoy this type of activity remain invisible as well.

The research reported here is an effort to redress this situation. It explicitly focuses on three women who do informal peacemaking in their organizations. The telling of their stories highlights the practice of informal conflict management in organizations and suggests how these activities contribute to the integration of effort and the possibilities for change. It also explores the intersection of informal peacemaking and gender. Clearly, this activity is not the sole province of women but represents an option open to members of organizations who lack more direct forms of influence (Johnson 1976). By exploring how these women construct and give meaning to their experiences, it is possible to untangle some of the ways in which gender may influence dispute processing and how these modes of conflict management contribute to gendered definitions of organization activity.

Studying Conflict in Organizations

Conflict is part of the routine of everyday life in organizations. Given the social structure within which we operate and the open-endedness of most social interactions, the possibilities for conflict at work are seemingly infinite (Collins 1975; Goffman 1967; Kriesberg 1973). Most research on conflict in organizations highlights either formal structures by which conflict is contained, overt negotiation and bargaining processes over rationed resources, and/or institutionalized procedures that channel complaints and disputes toward what are deemed organizationally productive ends (Cyert and March 1963; Lawrence and Lorsch 1967; Pfeffer and Salancik 1978; Pondy 1967). Likewise, normative models of practice rely on expert interventionists who enter a defined dispute to assist in its resolution (Blake, Shepard, and Mouton 1964; Blake and Mouton 1985; Brown 1982; Walton 1987).

These approaches to conflict intervention share some significant features that distinguish them from the kinds of peacemaking activities reported here. First, people who intervene, whether consultants or mediators, are typically outsiders, not only to a given dispute but also to the organization(s) in which the conflict is located. They are brought in as experts, often paid, to assist in conflict resolution. Their expertise lies in their conflict management skills, in their ability to invent agreements, and in their detached professional, objective stance (Brown 1982; Walton 1987). In contrast, peacemakers are insiders who generally have far greater knowledge of their colleagues than an outsider could possibly have. Their expertise comes from their insider status, the fact that they understand the psychology of the situation, and the political realities of the systems within which they work.

Second, the involvement of outside intervenors is prompted by identified problems, whether patterns of dysfunctional behavior, impasse in the resolution of disputes, and/or in the face of significant disruptions, such as strikes and walkouts. In contexts where harmony and collaboration are prized, public expressions of conflict can be seen as antisocial and as detrimental to getting on with the work (Boulding 1964; Greenhouse 1986; McCauley 1963). What happens is that disputes go underground and become the topic of "off-line" meetings and other time-outs (Kunda 1986; Van Maanen, this volume). Internal peacemakers are often privy to these situations, such that there is a timeliness and immediacy to their involvement because they are accessible and available.

Finally, the process of formal conflict intervention is frequently a discrete event that is separated from the daily activities of those involved. Such an activity might be a laboratory-type intervention of the sort advocated by Blake and his colleagues (1964, 1985), a dialogue over dinner (Walton 1987), training in conflict skills (Brown 1982), or a formal mediation where bargaining representatives come to a table to negotiate (Susskind and Cruikshank 1987). Internal peacemaking is an informal activity that is part of the daily workings of the organization. Indeed, the efforts of behind-the-scenes peacemakers often precede and lead to the formal conflict resolution interventions conducted by outsiders.

While these modes of formal conflict intervention are no doubt important in dealing with significant conflicts in organizations, they represent only the public face of conflict management. What has been missing from most of this body of research and accounts of practice is a consideration of the informal and private ways for dealing with differences and how these activities support and make possible the approaches we are more likely to notice (Barley 1991; Kolb and Putnam, this volume). If we want to develop a fuller appreciation of the dynamics of conflict management in organizations, it seems critical to study both the public, overt, and formal channels that have been considered in the past and—perhaps more important—to peek behind the scenes to learn more about the peacemaking that goes on there.

An interesting question, then, is why these overt and public forms of conflict management have been the primary focus of scholarly inquiry. These reasons appear to be political, methodological, and theoretical. From the perspective of those who lead organizations, *conflict* is a dirty word. It signals contention, dissatisfaction, and potential disruption. A focus on structures for containing conflict (i.e., integrative roles, teams, and task forces), processes for resolving differences (i.e., negotiation and problem solving), and dispute resolution procedures (i.e., grievance arbitration and mediation) contributes to the belief that conflict can be settled and dealt with in ways that promote mutual interests or at least reconcile conflicting interests between organizations and their employees. Advocating that managers mediate, for example, is a stance based on an ideal about humanity and concern on the part of those who lead. To focus on less public forums of disputing is to acknowledge the pervasiveness and ubiquitous character of conflict in contemporary organizations and the frequent taboos against its public expression (Martin 1991).

There are also methodological reasons why overt forms of disputing provide the data for most research. Certain forms of dispute resolution are isolated from the social encounters in which they occur and become the province of professionals—mediators, arbitrators, and organization development consultants. These practitioners can be studied in the compartmentalized case world in which they occur (Kolb 1989b). Similarly, labor negotiations, formal complaint handling (e.g., grievance procedures, ombudsman roles), and disputing procedures are bracketed as events separated in time and space from routine interaction and so can be isolated for empirical study (Barley 1991; Brett and Goldberg 1983; Ewing 1989; Kolb 1987). Other forms of conflict processing are not as easy to separate from ongoing interaction and so require the researcher's presence in the setting (Dalton 1959; Izraeli 1975; Van Maanen, this volume).

Finally, there are differences in the academy as to what constitutes significant phenomena for study.[1] Feminist critics take the position that much of what is considered problematic in social life (and therefore subjects worthy of inquiry) are themes drawn from the experience of men, especially those who are white and of the middle class and, in the case of organization theory, those who manage corporations (Harding 1986). Millman and Kanter (1987, 32) observe some of the ways that sociological inquiry privileges certain theoretical concerns and closes out others:

Sociology has focused on public, official, visible, and/or dramatic role players and definitions of the situation; yet non-official, supportive, less dramatic, private, and invisible spheres of social life and organization may be equally important. . . . In consequence, not only do we underexamine and distort women's activities in social science, but we also fail to understand how social systems actually function because we do not take into account one of their most basic processes: the interplay between informal, interpersonal networks and the formal, official social structures.

It is not that private peacemaking has been neglected by scholars because women are involved, nor does the focus of this chapter imply that this kind of activity is unimportant to men. Rather, because behind-the-scenes conflict management is ignored in both scholarship and assessment of practice, despite its importance to organizations, women remain invisible in this sphere of activity that may be a major one for them.

The research reported here is an effort to complement existing study of conflict management in organizations by considering informal and invisible peacemaking activities of three women who work for different organizations. Their activities offer a way to peek behind the public facade of conflict handling and begin to understand more about how it is that certain people get involved in this process, what they actually do, and how they complement the more public and visible domains of conflict management. It is also a way to begin to consider some of the ways that gender and peacemaking may become intertwined. Peacemaking is not exclusively a woman's activity. In the manner in which they carry out their activities and the meaning they attribute to them, however, the women profiled here seem to contribute to a gendered construction of their activities as unimportant and, ironically, to the reproduction of a gender-based system of relationships in organizations.

Background and Methods

I became involved in this project through two different routes. One developed directly from ethnographic research that I was doing on informal conflict management (Kolb 1989a). In one of these organizations, Baker Systems,[2] a large computer manufacturer, the person I studied was a woman named Olivia Lane. At the time, Lane was a manager of executive training and development and was married to one of the firm's senior executives. During a nine-month period, I closely observed the workings of the training and activities of a major task force in which she was a member. During that time, she kept a diary of her activities, especially as they concerned the work of another project on strategic planning. This diary and my observations formed the basis of our periodic debriefing and interview sessions.

At about the same time, a former student came to consult with me about a role she found herself playing more and more in her organization. Patricia Loomis was working at Infotrend, a consulting and training firm in the information technology field. She began in the sales and training area. Her background in social work, however, led the president of the company to seek her out for advice on "how to deal with people." Observing this relationship, others in the firm would come to see her about problems they were having with colleagues, the president, and the vice-president. Uncomfortable and unsure about what she was doing, she began to keep a diary and, during a six-month period, we would meet periodically to discuss her activities.

During the same period, I also met occasionally with a third colleague, Betty Armstrong, a professor at a local university. When we discussed my work, she noted that she too found herself engaged in giving advice primarily to women graduate students and junior faculty who sought her out for help on a variety of professional and personal matters. During the past two years, when one of these situations arose, Armstrong kept notes about what occurred and I would interview her about it.

I describe the opportunistic nature of these case studies for several reasons. One is that the sample is, at this point, exclusively women. Each was interested in working with me because of our past relationships and because they knew of my interest in conflict management. It is also likely that they consulted me because I am a woman who they suspected would empathize with them (and perhaps help them think through what they were doing) based on my own experience. Indeed, I functioned behind the scenes with them in ways that parallel their work with members of their organizations.

As a result of my entry into these situations, I have only limited knowledge of the degree to which what I report is generalizable to other women and whether there are male variants of the same activity. I do know that, when I mention this work to others, they frequently tell me about a woman in their office I should interview.

Finally, this work is ongoing. While my interest began with dispute resolution, it has shifted during the past several years and the intersection of gender and conflict management is now paramount. All this is to say that these cases and the work they represent are just the beginnings of an ongoing project.

The Cases[3]

Behind-the-scenes peacemaking is a common activity that can take many forms within organizations. The three women described here occupy different formal positions in their respective organizations. Further, there are differences in how they became involved in peacemaking activities, what constitutes their efforts, and how they see their contributions to their respective organizations. My purpose is to describe these women and tease out some of the common themes that mark this informal peacemaking activity.

Olivia Lane

Olivia Lane had been associated with Baker Systems, a computer software developer and manufacturer, for 15 years in the marketing organization. Five years ago, while she was on educational leave from the firm, she dated and then married Ed Sims, one of the senior executives. When she returned after completing her degree, she moved from marketing into the human resource area. As manager of executive training and development, she was charged with developing programs for the vice-presidential level of the company at a time when it was in serious financial shape for the first time in its history.

As an outgrowth of the vice-presidential training project, she organized a series of task forces to deal with specific organizational issues. Lane was a frequent and, by her choice, silent attendee at these task force meetings. After the formal meetings, it was not unusual to find several members staying behind to chat about what had occurred. Lane was usually part of these groups. Also, because of her direct and indirect access to senior management, some of the vice-presidents (VPs) began to see her as a link to their superiors. Sometimes they asked her to bring up a concern about the performance of another department with the relevant senior vice-president. Several came to her office on a regular basis to complain about specific and general problems in the organization. She became, as she described it, a "welcome pest" to a core group of VPs who came to view her, or so it appeared, as their advocate with senior management around a range of conflictual issues. In this way, she emerged as a kind of go-between who passed on information, reactions, and interpretations among the VPs and between one level of the organization and another.

Lane was often consulted on personnel matters, especially as they concerned women at Baker:

> Alice came to see me. She's not happy about what's been going on in the research area. She came to let me know that she plans to resign. She says she's in a rut and feels alienated from her team. There's a lot of storytelling going on. Alice is an important asset for us, but maybe she needs some time doing something else. I think her boss is threatened by her but I want to keep her. She's been here for eight years and knows the history. I think it will look bad for us if she leaves. It's also part of my commitment to the women here. I want to help her. So yesterday we talked strategy. I spoke to Jim [VP of human resources] and told him we needed to do something. I also spoke to Dave, one of our consultants on the networking project, and told him Alice might be available if they needed more staff. I spoke to Alice about it; she was enthusiastic. So what we did is arrange for her to work on one of our projects while she is employed by the consultant. It's great for both of us. She really knows the product, but it also gets her out of Baker for a while. It was all my initiative.

One of her interventions that Lane views as most successful concerned a problem regarding strategic planning at Baker Systems. Four VPs had been at work on a strategic planning task force, one of those Lane organized and then attended as a silent observer. The VPs were discouraged and pessimistic about their ability to implement any of the changes they were discussing. "They were really angry at what was going on here. Nobody was willing to take responsibility for planning and then driving it down. They would say we all know that, here at Baker, we are strategy rich and implementation poor," reported Lane.

> What they want from me is some sense of where Charles Ray [senior VP of administration] is on this. They feel, and I agree, that without him driving it and some commitment and resources for a consultant the project will die. I know Ray well; I could talk to him and because I'm Ed Sims's wife, he'll listen.

Lane met with the VP of administration and tried to arrange for a presentation by a consultant, but Ray rejected any involvement in strategic planning that was not of his own design.

I went back to the task force and told them what Ray had said. It was hard to see them so discouraged. I decided to get Adam Black [senior VP for marketing] involved. I know Adam well and I knew that he felt we had to do something to put a stake in the ground for ourselves. He also has clout with Ray; Charles listens to him.

Based on her discussion with Black, Lane arranged a series of meetings with Black, the task force, and the potential consultants where everyone got excited about the possibilities. But the question remained, according to Lane, "How to get Charles Ray on board? As a last resort, I knew that I could get Ed involved. But I didn't think the time was right."

The group asked her to meet with Ray again. "I went to see Ray. I knew I had to handle him with kid gloves. He's pretty sensitive and this is a sensitive issue. So I went in and asked him for his advice." At Ray's suggestion, Lane arranged a meeting where he would present his plan for implementing a strategic plan.

At the meeting, Ray and the others present seemed to go along, confining their questions only to clarifying how he planned to roll out the program in the short run. I was surprised. I had gotten this together and at least I thought Adam would speak up. I knew that even though they weren't challenging Ray that this was more of the same. Before I knew what I was doing I said, "Does this mean that I should cancel the consultants and end the task force?" They were shocked; maybe because this was the first time I had opened my mouth. Anyway, it opened it up and it was the first time they really discussed the pros and cons. When I look back, I think that the reason I did it was that it bothered me that these two activities (Ray's and the task force's) were happening and everybody was ignoring it and not talking.

Based on this discussion, a formal planning process was initiated in which both the task force and other people from senior management along with the consultants developed and implemented a strategic plan, the first one in this entrepreneurial company's history. Lane was appointed liaison for the process, making her role more or less official. She continued in this capacity for several months until she went on maternity leave.

Patricia Loomis

Pat Loomis was a psychiatric social worker before she returned to graduate school to get an MBA. After graduation, she went to work for Infotrend, a small but growing educational and consulting firm in the technology industry. The company had 10 employees when she joined and grew to 35 by the time she left full-time employment with the firm four years later. She was hired to do training on some of Infotrend's programs and to help with sales as well. Her role as a peacemaker evolved over time.

> My role at Infotrend changed when I began to spend more time with Jack Bates, the president. Because of my interest in Third World countries, I started to travel with Jack down to Washington to market to the World Bank. He began to talk to me about a lot of business as well as people issues inside and outside the company. Now he consults me about most of the major people decisions in the company. When I asked him once why he seems to listen to me, he said that he sees me as being able to do things that he cannot—that I understand psychology. It became clear to others in the company that I had a good relationship with Jack. Liz March, the senior vice-president, suddenly started paying attention to me but I knew she was always testing me to see whether I was swayed by Jack or not. She once said to me that as soon as she saw me disagree with Jack on an issue and take a stand, then she would trust me. That was hard, because I often agreed with Jack.

Loomis found herself increasingly drawn into disputes between management and others in the company:

> I'm involved in a situation where one of the administrators is not working out. The administrator thinks people are out to get her. She works for Liz. Liz has a strong personality and wants everything done her way so the administrator doesn't get to do much on her own. But when things go wrong, she gets blamed. The administrator has gotten very defensive; the organization has really done a number on her self-esteem. I met with Liz for three hours. She only sees the world through her eyes. I never met anybody who did it more. I try to calm her down and get her to see the reactions she generates in people.

Loomis's role changed after she took a short leave to participate in a summer institute at one of the nation's prestigious graduate schools of management. When she returned, she agreed to set up a human resource function in the company. In addition to her systems design responsibilities, she began to work with the members of the Management Committee (MC).

> At this time my role has been defined by the MC as someone who each can talk to. When I am talking to one of the MC members about their conflict with another, I try to present the other's side in a way that either explains the other person's perspective, helps them understand some of the psychology involved—why they may have said what they did given who they are—or I try to point out how in fact

they have similar goals or even how the other person really has this person's best interest in mind but they can't communicate it well.

A major part of Loomis's efforts were devoted to the relationship between Jack and Liz. Liz, given her bottom-line performance (she generates 60% of the revenues), wanted to become the operating officer for the company. Jack was concerned that she was too controlling and, if he promoted her, people might leave. Loomis described a session with Liz:

Most of the conversation focused on her upcoming discussion with Jack. She is the #1 contributor to the company and feels that her compensation and title should reflect this. She wants to be the operating officer with Jack as CEO. After she laid out her concerns, I spent time trying to clarify with her what exactly it is that she wants because so much of the trouble between her and Jack stems from assumptions between the two. . . . I talked to her about some of Jack's hot buttons. I suggested that she might give on some of his ideas, preferably early in the conversation so that he would feel she was listening and be more likely to give back later. She said she tries never to concede to Jack because then she gets it thrown back in her face later on. We talked about how problematic that was because of course Jack was going to think she was inflexible. I recommended that if she couldn't concede anything, then she needed to put that right on the table with Jack and have a conversation about what gets in the way of her being able to talk to him. She asked me to talk to Jack before their meeting to help him be more open to understanding their different assumptions.

I wrote an MCI note to Jack and mentioned my conversation with Liz. I suggested that he be clear about definitions and that he watch for falling into automatic assumptions. He sent an angry note back—"How can I know about my automatic reactions if they are automatic?" I heard from Liz that the meeting went well, that she thought they had listened to each other. They agreed to set up a biweekly meeting to plan a process for succession.

This relationship between the president and chief producer around the issue of succession is ongoing. Loomis thinks that those involved value her contribution. But she is not always sure: "I worry sometimes that I am keeping a bad system alive. I am preventing them from hitting bottom. On the good side, I get them to see things from a broader perspective; I am teaching them about psychology."

Loomis is now a consultant with Infotrend and works part-time on contract work with some of their major clients.

Betty Armstrong

Betty Armstrong is one of very few tenured women professors at a Midwestern university. She teaches a full load of courses and pursues an active research agenda. As one of the few senior women at the university, she has had more than her share of appointments on committees that touch on women's issues such as parental leave policy, child care, and faulty recruitment and retention. She is frequently asked by school administrators to assist with the problems of the clerical and other support staff, a group primarily composed of women. Against the background of these more or less visible activities are many that occur behind the scenes.

Over the years, female graduate students and junior faculty have asked Armstrong for help on a variety of professional and personal matters. Some come for help because they feel unfairly treated and want help in dealing with both the person and the problem at hand. For example, a junior faculty member, Connie Marks, learned that an administrator had canceled her assignment to teach part of a summer executive program. The cancellation was unexpected. Marks had prepared a letter to the faculty member (Bob Smith) who was coordinating the program to protest the move. Before she sent it, she went to see Armstrong:

> Connie sees me a lot. She uses me as an adviser. It's not known; I'm in the background. I do the same thing with others, but mostly with women. So she came to me with the draft of her letter to Bob Smith. That's how I got into it. She was very upset. This was going to be good visibility for her, and besides, she had counted on the money. I felt badly for her. This happens a lot around here. I told her that the letter she wrote seemed wrong. She was assuming that Bob Smith was behind the cancellation. I suggested that she go to Bob Smith, not to change his mind but to get information, to ask him what was going on. Connie was not happy. She thought Bob Smith was stubborn and hard to talk to. I told her to think of it as an information visit. Ask him what went on. So she did it and decided not to send the letter. She told me later that Bob Smith knew nothing about the change. With Connie in his office, he called the administrator and asked him why he had made a curriculum decision without consulting him, Smith. He said he understood why Connie was so angry. Now we don't really know what happened, but at least she got to teach in the seminar.

While Armstrong described this situation as a "little one," she has also been involved in situations where graduate students or members of the faculty have problems in which sexual harassment, conflicts of interest, and other forms of possible exploitation are the major issues. In these situations, Armstrong says she helps people think clearly about the problem and come up with solutions. There are other situations in which Armstrong works behind the scenes to bring conflict that is underground out into the open. One case concerned a controversial tenure case:

> With Sarah Chase's appointment, I have taken a more active role. We have a number of cases coming up and they all have difficulties. I am trying to facilitate in Sarah's case. The real constraint is Phil Grand [the chair of area]. He says, "Sarah is great and it is too bad that we can't keep her. Her work is high quality, but not enough of it is out. She takes too long to get it out." The problem was that these things get said and there's nobody to challenge them. It builds a negative perception of Sarah.

> The first thing I did was to have an informal talk with Sarah about strategy and what I wanted to do. Then I went to Jim [senior member of the department] to get him to support the strategy. My plan was to get people together, to get Phil Grand in the same room with the people who support Sarah. I picked the group—Jim, Sam Adams, me, and Bob Jones and then Phil and Frank Short, both of whom thought Sarah was not a strong case. I told them that the purpose of the meeting was to discuss area appointments. I told Jim that I was counting on him to intervene to change Phil Grand's mind. I got all of Sarah's work together; all the working papers, the background on all of them. My secretary set it up, but I called everybody. I had it prepared.

> Before the meeting, I went to see the dean and asked him if he would be willing to push Sarah based on quality and not quantity. He said he would if the group was firmly behind her. I had the meeting. Phil and Frank talked about their concern regarding her output. Jim didn't talk at first but I had briefed him before the meeting. Then in his ponderous way he said, "I am interested that we are so interested in quantity." At the meeting, I forced each one there to give their views on this and their advice for Sarah to strengthen her case. I started with the most positive first. At the end of the meeting, Phil was a little less against her. They all agreed that each would talk to her. Then I met with Sarah to talk strategy. I told her that we had done what we could. She had to help by getting some more work out.

Armstrong said that she felt Sarah's case was being compromised by the negative comments people made in one-on-one meetings. She wanted them to make their stands in public. "Getting to have the meeting was most important. I wanted to orchestrate it. I was pretty invisible. I don't think, except for Sarah and Jim, the people realize the hand I had in it," Armstrong said.

There have been several other occasions when Armstrong has seen the consequences of back-room gossip for young faculty members, especially women. She tries to orchestrate situations in such a way that people are forced to air their concerns so that others can respond. Sometimes these efforts have become public, and there have been negative consequences for her personally in undertaking these efforts.

Themes in Behind-the-Scenes Peacemaking

The three women described here are engaged in behind-the-scenes maneuvering in the context of conflictual situations. Each gets involved in a variety of activities that include giving advice and support to people, trying to get them to see situations in different ways, acting as go-between, and working behind the scenes to arrange meetings where disputes can be publicly aired. They all act out of concern for others and take risks on their behalf. At the same time, there are contrasts in how these women think about and give meaning to the activities in which they are engaged. Each works from an agenda of change but sees that agenda differently and so evaluates her contributions accordingly.

Getting Involved

Informal peacemaking is not a part of Lane's, Loomis's, or Armstrong's job descriptions. They become involved in conflicts because of a number of situational and personal reasons. First, they are located in positions where they can learn about emerging problems and conflicts. Thus Lane's involvement with the various task forces put her in touch with a network of vice-presidents through which she was privy to issues that concerned them. Loomis's position, first informally and then via the human resource function, meant that people came to her with their problems and difficulties with others at Infotrend. Armstrong's involvement with various women's groups at the university makes her visible to the community of women faculty who call on her for help.

Second, the three women provide a sympathetic ear to those who seek them out. They allude to the fact that they are nonthreatening, easy to talk to, and sensitive to "people" issues. Each thinks that her gender is related to this stance. Lane claims, for example, that people come to her because she has these skills:

> This is a typical thing a woman is good at. I'm not threatening; I'm sympathetic and I'm comfortable to speak to. They know that I will let them come in and talk and that I will listen.

Likewise, Loomis alludes to her psychological skills:

> From the start, people were aware of my psychology background, joked a little nervously about it, and slowly began to use it, coming to me for advice on how to deal with this person or that issue.

Armstrong takes a more matter-of-fact stand on why people come to see her: "I think they think that I will help them solve their problems." In response to my query about whether she is seen as a maternal figure, however, and whether this is relevant, she said, "I guess that's part of it as well."

Hochschild (1983, 172) observes that frequently women are expected to take on these kinds of functions within their organizations because these functions are seen as congruent with other gendered societal roles:

> Because they are seen as members of the category from which mothers come, women in general are asked to look out for psychological needs more than men are. The world turns to women for mothering, and this fact silently attaches itself to many a job description.

Those in lateral or lower positions turn to these women not only because they are sympathetic and good listeners but also because they believe that the women can help. One of the reasons they can help is that they have access to important people. Lane is the wife of a senior executive. This position was critical, she argued, in explaining her successful intervention:

> If it hadn't been me pushing for this, it would have died. It's because I was Ed's wife. I can't imagine that anybody else doing what I do. One of the VPs said that he listened to me 99% because I was Ed's wife.

Similarly, Loomis had a special relationship with the president, based on their mutual interest in psychology. The access these women have to important people make them attractive to others who have problems because it signals the possibility that they can do something about a problem. The access they have, however, is based on personal relationships and is generally unrelated to their formal roles or functions. Because their access is personal and because they work on behalf of others, it is unlikely that these women are seen as competitive or out for their own personal advancement. Thus, from the perspective of those at the top, they probably do not appear threatening. At the same time, their actions (and whatever results they might achieve) are likely to be attributed to personal relationships (perhaps sexual) that are not quite legitimate in the organizational context (see Martin this volume).

Armstrong has access too, but of a different sort. She is one of the very senior women at the university, a position that singles her out and influences the actions she takes on behalf of other women (Kanter 1977). She, like the other women, however, does not use her influence directly or seek recognition or other rewards but prefers to work behind the scenes, where her contributions remain invisible.

Complementing the interest others have in their peacemaking role, the women also have their own reasons for getting involved in these activities. First, they have a loyalty to their organizations and care about the ways it treats its members. Thus, when they get involved, they have in mind specific outcomes for a better workplace. Loomis described her agenda in the following manner:

> Increasingly I began to take on causes, things I wanted changed at Infotrend. A lot of their treatment of people, especially the women, was very poor. It fascinated me because I liked the top people, especially Jack, and I felt that they genuinely wanted to have a company that was better than others as far as human resources was concerned and yet they kept screwing up.

Similarly, Armstrong and Lane both believed that their efforts would enhance the position of women in their organizations.

Second, the three women seem to be genuinely motivated by the helping role. They enjoy taking responsibility for others. The cases are replete with examples of situations in which the women take on the causes of others—both male and female. Sometimes these causes involve some risk to their own positions, especially when the situations are public. Armstrong's advocacy on behalf of Sarah Chase's tenure case exemplifies this willingness to take risks on behalf of others. The meeting that she organized amounted to an open confrontation with the area chair. Likewise, Lane, during the meeting she organized with Ray and the members of the task force, challenged them to go public with their disagreements.

Finally, their attitudes about conflict also drive their participation. Loomis puts it well:

> Sometimes I think this is a woman's thing. For myself, I am terrible at dealing with conflict. I want to make people get along. I don't like it when they disagree. I keep hoping that they'll see the good side of each other.

Because they dislike conflict, they want to avoid its potential disruptive tendencies. Ironically, their dislike of conflict seems to engage them in it. But the engagement is not a public one that might merit notice or benefit; it is enacted through a variety of peacemaking activities that are largely invisible.

Peacemaking Activities

However they become involved in conflicts within their organizations, their interventions are made up of a set of specific activities. It is these activities that come to define the type of peacemaking roles that each of these women play (Kolb 1983). Four major types of activities are observed in the reported interventions. They are (a) providing *support* by giving people the opportunity to tell their story, (b) *reframing* people's understandings of a situation by providing alternative explanations and choices, (c) *translating* people's perceptions of each other either directly through message carrying or indirectly through responding, and (d) *orchestrating* occasions for private conflicts to be made public.

Each of the women provided opportunities for people to voice their grievances, tell their stories, and do so in emotional ways if they preferred. Loomis thought that sometimes that was all people really wanted. Armstrong saw this as necessary in certain situations. She described a case involving a doctoral student who was having serious difficulties with dissertation advisers:

> She came and said, "May I close the door?" She looked very upset. And then she said, "I'm sorry to bother you—I'm sure you get bothered a lot of times about

things like this, but I really don't know what to do." She told me her story and I listened. We sat there and talked about it for a long time. She was very upset. I just let her talk and then I made the following suggestion. . . .

Being available to help people vent their feelings often gives rise to a form of mediation that has been labeled "therapeutic" (Silbey and Merry 1986). Although each of the women is sensitive to the psychology of organizational relationships, their efforts involved more than a sympathetic ear.

In each of the cases, the women tried to help people reframe the problem. This was accomplished in several ways. Loomis tried to help Liz March appreciate how her own role contributed to the administrator's performance problems. Likewise, Lane helped Alice see that it was possible to continue an affiliation with Baker as a consultant and yet not be an employee. And Armstrong, in several cases, made suggestions that helped people see that they had other choices than the ones they initially perceived. Loomis relates her efforts to alter people's perceptions to her dislike of conflict:

> Personally I hate conflict and try to avoid [it more than I should] so I emphasize all the areas they agree on that they think they disagree on. I try to come up with ways to get them to see how if they do something differently (such as not taking it personally when someone makes a certain type of remark, but see it as that person's problem) then they will in fact get what they want.

This search for common ground by helping people explore other options is a contribution traditional third parties make (Susskind and Cruikshank 1987).

Probably the activity that is most associated with a peacemaking or mediation role is that of go-between or message carrier. This type of activity places the peacemakers in the middle between different individuals and groups. From that position, the go-between can assist people to understand the others, act as advocate for one or the other, and use the information as a basis for suggesting possible resolutions to problems (Kolb 1983). These activities were a prominent part of Loomis's and Lane's activities in particular. In the strategic planning case, Lane spent a considerable portion of her time meeting with different players, reporting on what others thought, and bringing that information back to the central planning group. On a whole range of smaller issues as well, she met with people to report on others. Similarly, Loomis used back-and-forth diplomacy between Liz and Jack to help them deal with the issue of succession:

> Liz says that she feels my go-between role is useful because there are some issues that she and Jack just can't talk about openly because of past history. She believes that he will hear things from me that he won't from her. I believe she sees me as a messenger and on some level an advocate for her in her struggles with Jack. Jack sees me as someone who might be able to get Liz to see what she is doing wrong.

The go-between function can also serve as a preliminary step in the orchestration of public occasions for the airing of conflicts.

Orchestrating public expressions of conflict is a dimension of peacemaking that has not been much documented in studies of dispute processing. Each of the women, on some occasions, uses her peacemaking activities to arrange a meeting at which differences that had only been confided privately could be confronted in a more public setting. Lane, for example, orchestrated a meeting between the two groups who were fighting over the control of strategic planning and brought the conflict to a head by challenging their silence. She described the efforts as ones of "orchestrating the agenda." Likewise, Armstrong facilitated the arrangements for the faculty meeting to make public the behind-the-scenes gossip regarding Sarah Chase's chances for promotion. She commented: "From my standpoint, getting the meeting organized was most important. That's why I spent so much time orchestrating it." Similarly, Loomis organized a retreat among the senior people at Infotrend to bring out into the open conflicts about who was going to run the company and what directions it would take:

> It seemed to me that the top people were really having trouble working together. Things had become so political that nobody was talking to anybody else. I organized a retreat in an attempt to bring the company together. People were leery at first but the day was a success. People said that they felt more connected to the company as a result.

There are several observations to be made about this aspect of the peacemaker's activities. First, arranging these meetings involved a significant amount of behind-the-scenes maneuvering. But such practices are one of the means that these peacemakers use to achieve the outcomes they seek. Indeed, public occasions of conflict intervention (even when outsiders are involved) will always require this kind of backstage organizing.

Second, just as their orchestration of these meetings is invisible to many, so too they continue to remain behind the scenes during the actual event; that is, they reject a public role for themselves at the public session. Thus Lane remained silent until the very end; Armstrong asked Jim to take the lead in bringing up the issue of quality versus quantity in judging faculty output; and Loomis arranged for an outside consultant to facilitate the retreat. In this way, their roles in orchestrating the public expression of difference continue to remain invisible to most of those present.

Orchestrating is one approach to mediation (Kolb 1983). In implementing this approach, professional mediators defer to influential leaders for guidance on how to manage the substantive issues in dispute. The preference for this approach is based on the mediators' assessment of relative expertise and knowledge and the belief that, in situations of conflict, it is easy to make mistakes that could jeopardize the mediator and the chances for possible settlement. There are analogies to the peacemakers here. They too prefer to let others handle the process. In part, they may realize the risks associated with public conflict management. Armstrong, for example, has had experiences where the orchestration of an event backfired. Rather than addressing the problem at hand, a public incident of sexual harassment, she became the focal point and those present tried to appease her rather than seriously explore ways to solve an institutional problem. Or they may prefer a more invisible role because it is one that is more comfortable and less stressful for them.

Whatever their reasons for undertaking the role, it is clear that orchestration of public conflict is a significant contribution that peacemakers make. Numerous studies of conflict in organizations, as well as in other settings, suggest that conflict is rarely articulated. For whatever the reasons, people generally prefer to avoid or "lump" their differences (Bumiller 1987; Greenhouse 1986; Morrill, this volume).

The consequences of avoidance are serious. Not only does an organization miss possible opportunities for innovation and change, but suppressed conflict can generate resistance to goals. Thus, by facilitating the public expression of conflict, these peacemakers may make more of a contribution than those who actually resolve differences (Miller and Sarat 1980-81). Because of the high risks sometimes involved, the strengths of the orchestrating role may also paradoxically be its weaknesses. Consider, for example, what could have happened to

Sarah Chase's tenure hopes if Betty Armstrong had failed to make all the contacts she did prior to the faculty meeting.

Evaluating the Peacemakers' Contributions

It is never easy to evaluate a conflict management intervention. Actual agreements are inadequate because they ignore quality and compliance with outcomes (McEwen and Maiman 1984). Mediators themselves do not hold up agreement as a necessary end; rather, they emphasize the learning and understanding that will result (Sarat 1990). Further, most peacemaking activities occur in the context of other concurrent modes of dispute management, making it difficult to separate the impact of one approach from that of another (Buckle and Thomas-Buckle 1986). In the contexts in which these women operate, it is even more difficult. While some of the conflicts are resolved, others continue. Indeed, one of their major contributions may be to channel conflict into arenas where it can be made public and perhaps resolved if not better understood (Miller and Sarat 1980-81). What is interesting is how the women themselves evaluate what they do. They express concern about the isolation and precariousness of their situation yet do little to legitimate or institutionalize it.

Each of them alludes to problematic aspects of the role. Loomis describes her worries concerning position, problems about confidentiality and honesty, and the politics of her relationships:

> This position is not official. It ebbs and flows and I'm always a little nervous about it. I sometimes feel deceptive and that I am double-dealing. I'm very honest with Jack but I'm not nearly as direct with Liz as I have less of a bond with her. She sees me as her advocate. I will help her; I've told her that, but I don't do as much as I could. And then I'm always worried about my relationship with Jack.

Lane echoes these feelings that the position is not legitimate, a perception that limited her participation in one of the meetings:

> Nobody told me to keep my mouth shut. I just felt I should. Even though I put this together I don't feel I have earned a place. I'm even embarrassed to sit at the table. I'd like to open my mouth. At other times I think I have earned a place, but hardly anybody knows what I have done.

Armstrong also reflects on the isolation of the role:

> At one point I felt that I had really solved this problem and yet I'm not getting any of the credit. Nobody's even telling me what's going on.

This sense that what they do is not valued and not important is supported by some of the language they use to describe themselves. Lane is the most emphatic:

> This is baby-sitting. I feel like I'm dealing with multiple children who fight with each other. When people ask me what I do, I say I do social work. I ask myself what good does this do?

Loomis says that she tired of "playing an unacknowledged role—the woman behind the scenes." Armstrong resents that she is continually drawn into situations in which the topic is "women's problems."

They are often critical of their contributions, a judgment that balances organizational concerns with their sense of taking responsibility for others. Loomis wonders whether "I'm keeping a bad system alive." Lane is concerned that the efforts make no difference: "I keep going over and over the same issues with the same people." And Armstrong feels that she sometimes jeopardizes her and others' interests. In a situation where she confronted a male colleague on behalf of a junior faculty member, she found herself snubbed and excluded and wondered whether in the end it would help the junior faculty member.

At the same time, the women seem to act in ways that perpetuate some of the problems they identify. It is clear that they find their roles intrinsically rewarding. It is a comfortable position for them. As a result, they make few demands on the organization. Despite some of the benefits they claim for what they do, the peacemakers don't translate their accomplishments into something that might require reward. They don't use their position, their skills, and their contributions as the basis to negotiate for benefits or advancement for themselves. By keeping their activities behind the scenes, they make recognition of their accomplishments less likely.

The picture that emerges from these assessments is a mixed one. On the whole, the women think that they make a difference, that they help individuals in specific situations and contribute to the improvement of their organizations. They are not clear, however, about the value of the role to themselves and to the organization. In organizations, where status is officially related to one's track record and accomplishments, activities like peacemaking that occur behind the scenes and out of sight may not be highly valued.

Comment

There are several insights about conflict management in organizations that come from an investigation of these three women's peacemaking activities. One concerns the position of the peacemaker relative to the people she helps and how these activities aid organizational function and process. The other concerns the women themselves and how this peacemaking aspect of their work can be understood in a broader context of gender and organization.

From the organization's standpoint, peacemaking behind the scenes is essential to its work. By keeping many disputes out of sight and by fostering the resolution of some, peacemaking serves an important integrating function that has been overlooked in much organization theory. Peacemakers are also important in linking informal mechanisms for conflict management and those that are formally designated. Through their activities, some conflicts are channeled into official systems and others become focused such that outside intervenors can join the process. The personal interest that motivates their participation, however, can result in a smoothing and depoliticizing of conflict that leaves basic relationships intact.

Peacemakers may also act in ways that extend authority within their organizations. Loomis and Lane, for example, make the claim that they try to be neutral and be fair to all parties. Their stories are told within a particular structure of authority, however. Consider Loomis's situation. She strives, for pragmatic reasons, to maintain neutrality—"I always have to act neutral between Liz and Jack. The minute she perceives that I am with him too much, she closes me out." Yet it is clear that her allegiance is with Jack and the advice she gives Liz is often of the accommodating sort. Thus, in the ways she carries out her activities, she seems to become more of an aid to Jack than to Liz. In this way, her behind-the-scenes activities may have the effect of reinforcing, or even extending, the authority structure that exists at the firm (see Abel 1982). The same argument could be made for Lane, as her activities rarely challenge existing structures.

Armstrong's case seems somewhat different. She seems to see her role as advocate for women at the university on a host of issues. To the degree that her work is behind the scenes, however, it may not pose much of a threat to existing power structures. Indeed, in one of her cases, she learned of serious charges of sexual harassment, conflicts of interest, and exploitation of graduate students. In the interests of resolving more immediate issues—that is, those that were of most concern to the graduate student—these larger concerns were not as diligently pursued.

Peacemaking behind the scenes can result in social relations and norms of the workplace being subtly redefined. Clearly, certain individuals were helped by these women. To the degree that this peacemaking occurs behind the scenes, however, it serves to individualize conflicts that may be structural or systemic at their root and tends to support existing social and authoritative arrangements. By keeping conflicts out of sight and providing an outlet for individuals, peacemakers may dampen the impetus for significant change (Cain and Kulscar 1982). In this way, behind-the-scenes peacemakers become an instrument of social control in organizations.

It is worth considering what role gender plays in all of this. Some might argue that these women act in ways consistent with a "woman's voice." *Voice* is a metaphor that is meant to capture alternative ways of seeing the world, being with others, and caring about them that emphasize connection and caring, seeing oneself and others not in opposition but in terms of mutual aid and support. Thus the preference for behind-the-scenes activity and harmony and for finding ways around the system might be seen as examples of ways to accommodate differences that are associated with a woman's approach (Gilligan 1982; Keller 1985).

Such a perspective, however, ignores the importance of *place*, which is a metaphor for the social structures and cultures in which disputing or other activities are set (Kolb and Coolidge 1988). In most of the legal, political, and economic spheres in which conflict management and peacemaking occur, the status of women is not assured and the meanings attached to their activities are often perceived in terms of gender (MacKinnon 1982; Menkel-Meadow 1985). What has been labeled the voice of caring and relationship, some argue, is the voice of those who lack status and position (MacKinnon 1982; Weedon 1987). Further, experience in subordinate or marginal social positions means that women have had to learn how to be alert and observant in order to fit in (Miller 1976). Hence skills associated with women—listening, observation, and empathy—may be the general skills any subordinate group uses to make its place (Scott 1985).

In the organizations in which these women work, power is an important dimension in understanding position and status (Bacharach and Lawler 1980; Pfeffer and Salancik 1978). *Power,* as it is used in the organizational literature, concerns the degree to which outcomes can be attributed to individuals' actions (Mintzberg 1983). In this regard, politics is distinguished from the exercise of formal power. This view of power is one of domination over others (Ferguson 1984). Some suggest that women think about power differently than men and use it not to seek control over others but to empower them (Miller 1976).

The way power is understood by these women is somewhat different. It is not public power that they seek. When they talk of power, it is more of a personal sort. That is, they feel rewarded for what they do even if their efforts are not publicly known or acknowledged. In actually carrying out their activities, they rely on what Johnson (1976, 100) calls "indirect power," which she says "occur[s] when the influencer acts as if the person on the receiving end is not aware of the influence."

The exercise of indirect power tends to keep its users in subordinate positions (Johnson 1976). Indeed, the women tend to perceive their behind-the-scenes maneuvering as compensating for what they cannot do directly, that is, their inability to take their place. There is some evidence in these cases and elsewhere that, when legitimate power is conferred on women, peacemaking may cease to be as integral to their identity and work (see Kanter 1977).

There is a certain irony here. Because peacemaking benefits the organization, it may be a vehicle of upward mobility for women who take on the role. In the work they do privately and behind the scenes, however, their efforts often go unremarked and unnoticed. Therefore its importance is rarely acknowledged. Women peacemakers contribute to this perception. The women in these cases, who may be marginal to their organizations in the first place, may serve to reproduce their marginality by the private efforts they undertake and the value they claim for them. In this way, behind-the-scenes peacemaking can come to be seen as a devalued and gendered activity.

And now I know why I'm always doing it: It's woman's work.

Notes

1. In the organizational field, the critique might be extended to say that what has been considered problematic reflects the interests of those who manage corporations, a popu-

lation that is still predominantly male. Thus scholarship in the conflict area concerns itself primarily, despite claims about the beneficial effects of tension and disagreement (Coser 1956), with the means and mechanisms by which conflict can be controlled, resolved, and managed according to some general ideals of effectiveness, efficiency, and perhaps fairness (Lewicki, Weiss, and Lewin 1987).

2. The names of the organizations and the players within them are disguised.

3. My research assistant, Susan Staub, provided able assistance in pulling together the transcripts and other case materials.

References

Abel, R. 1982. *The politics of informal justice*. New York: Academic Press.

Bacharach, S. B., and E. J. Lawler. 1980. *Power and politics in organizations*. San Francisco: Jossey-Bass.

Barley, S. 1991. Contextualizing conflict: Notes on the anthropology of disputes and negotiations. In *Handbook of negotiation research*, ed. M. Bazerman, R. Lewicki, and B. Sheppard. Greenwich, Conn.: JAI.

Blake, R. R., H. A. Shepard, and J. S. Mouton. 1964. *Managing intergroup conflict in industry*. Houston: Gulf.

Blake, R. R., and J. S. Mouton. 1985 *Solving costly organizational conflicts*. San Francisco: Jossey-Bass.

Boulding, K. 1964. A pure theory of conflict applied to organizations. In *The frontiers of management*, ed. G. Fisk. New York: Harper & Row.

Brett, J., and S. B. Goldberg. 1983. Mediator-advisors: A new third party role. In *Negotiating in organizations*, ed. M. Bazerman and R. Lewicki. Beverly Hills, Cal.: Sage.

Brown, D. 1982. *Managing conflict at organizational interfaces*. Reading, Mass.: Addison-Wesley.

Buckle, L. G., and S. R. Thomas-Buckle. 1986. Placing environmental mediation in context: Lessons from "failed" mediations. *Environmental Impact Assessment Review* 6:55-72.

Bumiller, K. 1987. *The civil rights society*. Baltimore: Johns Hopkins Press.

Cain, M., and K. Kulscar. 1982. Thinking disputes: An essay on the origins of the dispute industry. *Law and Society Review* 16:375.

Collins, R. 1975. *Conflict sociology*. New York: Academic Press.

Coser, L. 1956. *The functions of social conflict*. New York: Free Press.

Cyert, R. M., and J. G. March. 1963. *A behavioral theory of the firm*. Englewood Cliffs, N.J.: Prentice-Hall.

Dalton, M. 1959. *Men who manage*. New York: John Wiley.

Ewing, D. W. 1989. *Justice on the job: Resolving grievances in the nonunion workplace*. Cambridge, Mass.: Harvard Business School Press.

Ferguson, K. E. 1984. *The feminist case against bureaucracy*. Philadelphia: Temple University Press.

Gilligan, C. 1982. *In a different voice*. Cambridge, Mass.: Harvard University Press.

Goffman, E. 1967. *Interaction ritual*. New York: Doubleday.

Greenhouse, C. 1986. *Praying for justice: Faith, order and community in an American town*. Ithaca, N.Y.: Cornell University Press.

Harding, S. 1986. *The science question in feminism.* Ithaca, N.Y.: Cornell University Press.

Hochschild, A. R. 1983. *The managed heart.* Berkeley: University of California Press.

Izraeli, D. 1975. The middle manager and the tactics of power expansion: A case study. *Sloan Management Review* 8:57-70.

Johnson, P. 1976. Women and power: Toward a theory of effectiveness. *Journal of Social Issues* 32:99-109.

Kanter, R. M. 1977. *Men and women of the corporation.* New York: Colophon.

Karambayya, R., and J. Brett. 1989. Managers handling disputes: Third party roles and perceptions of fairness. *Academy of Management Journal* 32:687-705.

Keller, E. F. 1985. *Reflections on gender and science.* New Haven, Conn.: Yale University Press.

Kolb, D. M. 1983. *The mediators.* Cambridge, Mass.: MIT Press.

—1987. Corporate ombudsmen and organizational conflict. *Journal of Conflict Resolution* 31:673-91.

—1989a. Labor mediators, managers, and ombudsmen: Roles mediators play in different contexts. In *Mediation research,* ed. K. Kressel and D. Pruitt. San Francisco: Jossey-Bass.

—1989b. How existing procedures shape alternatives: The case of grievance mediation. *Journal of Dispute Resolution* 1989:59-87.

Kolb, D. M., and G. Coolidge. 1988. Her place at the table. Harvard Law School, Program on Negotiation, Working paper.

Kriesberg, L. 1973. *The sociology of social conflict.* Englewood Cliffs, N.J.: Prentice-Hall.

Kunda, G., and S. Barley. 1988. Designing devotion. Paper presented at the American Sociological Association, August, San Francisco.

Lawrence, P. R., and J. W. Lorsch. 1967. *Organization and environment.* Homewood, Ill.: Irwin.

Lewicki, R., S. Weiss, and D. Lewin. 1987. *Models of conflict, negotiation, and conflict intervention: A review and synthesis.* Unpublished manuscript.

MacKinnon, C. 1982. Feminism, Marxism, method and the state: An agenda for theory. *Signs* 7:515-44.

Martin, J. 1991. Deconstructing organizational taboos: The suppression of gender conflict in organizations. *Organization Science.*

McCauley, S. 1963. Non-contractual relations in business. *American Sociological Review* 28:55.

McEwen, C. A., and R. J. Maiman. 1984. Mediation in small claims court: Achieving compliance through consent. *Law and Society Review* 18:11-50.

Menkel-Meadow, C. 1985. Portia in a different voice: Speculating on a women's lawyering process. *Berkeley Women's Law Journal* 1:39-63.

Miller, J. B. 1976. *Toward a new psychology of women.* Boston: Beacon.

Miller, R., and A. Sarat. 1980-81. Grievances, claims, and disputes: Assessing the adversary culture. *Law and Society Review* 15:525-66.

Millman, M., and R. M. Kanter. 1987. Introduction to another voice: Feminist perspective on social life and social science. In *Feminism and methodology,* ed. S. Harding. Bloomington: Indiana University Press.

Mintzberg, H. 1983. *Power in and around organizations.* Englewood Cliffs, N.J.: Prentice-Hall.

Pfeffer, J., and G. Salancik. 1978. *The external control of organizations.* New York: Harper & Row.

Pondy, L. 1967. Organizational conflict: Concepts and models. *Administrative Science Quarterly* 17:296-320.

Rowe, M. 1987. The corporate ombudsman. *Negotiation Journal* 3:127.

Sarat, A. 1990. *Professional pride, professional practice: Control, commitment and "minor miracles" in family and divorce mediation. A profile of Patrick Phear.* Paper prepared for the Project on Building Theory from Practice, Program on Negotiation.

Scott, J. C. 1985. *Weapons of the weak.* New Haven, Conn.: Yale University Press.

Sheppard, B. 1983. Third party conflict intervention: A procedural framework. In *Research in organizational behavior.* Vol. 6, ed. B. M. Staw and L. L. Cummings. Greenwich, Conn.: JAI.

Sheppard, B., K. Blumenfeld-Jones, and J. Roth. 1989. Informal thirdpartyship: A program of research on everyday conflict intervention. In *Mediation research,* ed. K. Kressel and D. Pruitt. San Francisco: Jossey-Bass.

Silbey, S. S., and S. E. Merry. 1986. Mediator settlement strategies. *Law and Policy* 8:7-32.

Susskind, L., and J. Cruikshank. 1987. *Breaking the impasse.* New York: Basic Books.

Ury, W. L., J. Brett, and S. Goldberg. 1988. *Getting disputes resolved.* San Francisco: Jossey-Bass.

Walton, R. E. 1987. *Managing conflict.* Reading, Mass.: Addison-Wesley.

Weedon, C. 1987. *Feminist practice and poststructuralist theory.* Oxford, England: Basil Blackwell.

4

The Private Ordering of
Professional Relations

CALVIN MORRILL

A central tension in organizational life is that between the search for certainty, the maintenance of routines—in short, the preservation of organizational order—on the one hand, and the necessity of organizational change on the other. This tension is most visible during public conflicts over such issues as succession to top leadership posts, corporate mergers and acquisitions, major technological innovations, and changes in state policies affecting organizations. Yet the tension between order and change also occurs less visibly and in informal ways, often prompted by what will here be termed *private grievances*.

Private grievances can be defined as interpersonal complaints that have low visibility to nonparticipants and are managed informally. They are analytically important for the study of organizations because (a) they can involve threats to organizational order, (b) they can involve attempts to preserve organizational order, and (c) they can lead to necessary incremental changes through the adoption of new routines.

AUTHOR'S NOTE: An earlier version of this chapter was presented at the International Communication Association meetings, Dublin, Ireland, 1990. Support for this work was provided by a Junior Fellowship at Harvard Law School and the Program in Law and Social Sciences of the National Science Foundation (Grant No. SES-8508349). Donald Black, Michael Burgoon, Roberto Fernandez, Deborah M. Kolb, Dirk Scheerhorn, and Harrison White made helpful comments on earlier drafts.

Strauss's (1978; Strauss et al. 1963) "negotiated order" approach provides a useful theoretical point of departure for the study of private grievances, order, and change. He emphasizes how organizational order and incremental change emerge from explicit and implicit negotiations and bargains among organizational members, often prompted by disagreements and interpersonal friction. This chapter examines these interpersonal processes among high-ranking partners in a large accounting firm using ethnographic data. After an overview of the negotiated order approach, the following pages examine the study site of the investigation and the methods used, present cases illustrative of private grievances and their management among partners in the firm, and discuss the relationships between social structure, private grievances, organizational orders, and change.

The Negotiated Order Approach to Organizations and the Disputing Process

Within the negotiated order approach, organizational stability rests on bureaucratic structures as well as explicit and implicit informal agreements among organizational members. Navigating organizational life inevitably leads to continual reappraisal of existing agreements among organizational members as they differentially pursue their interests within the same and different value systems through time. Such reappraisals can then result in the breach or modification of agreements. This approach thus focuses on the interplay between old and new agreements, and the emergence and change of the normative boundaries of behavior in organizations via negotiation.

Strauss and his associates' (1963; Strauss 1978) original formulations sought to capture the processual nature of negotiated order in a psychiatric hospital populated by doctors, nurses, lay people, and clients. They argued that the approach was appropriate for understanding organizations containing personnel (especially professionals) trained in different occupations with different occupational philosophies. Under such conditions, the possibility of interpersonal misunderstandings and troubles that are not easily resolved with formal procedures is more likely. This suggests, then, that private grievances may be an important triggering behavior for negotiations over order and change. Strauss and his associates also argued that different mixes of personnel might produce different levels of articulation for negotiated agreements or even different ordering processes. For example, doctors explicitly complain to nurses about how they act in certain treatment situations with patients and impose orders for future behavior. Among themselves, however, doctors' grievances might be largely unexpressed and their negotiated agreements more private and less explicit—a kind of "silent bargaining" (Strauss 1978, 224).

In the years following this work, many researchers have used the negotiated order approach to study a variety of phenomena within different organizational contexts, yet have been less rigorous in defining the processes of negotiated order or the relationship between negotiated orders and their social contexts (see the review in Fine 1984).

To address these shortcomings in the use of the negotiated order approach, private grievances were conceived as being at the base of what is generally called the "disputing process." Following Nader and Todd (1978) and Morrill (1989), the disputing process involves a tripartite distinction between grievance expressions, conflicts, and disputes. *Grievance expressions* occur when people define (perceptually or otherwise) and respond to deviance by their fellows. *Conflicts* arise when principals exchange grievance expressions privately or publicly. *Disputes* occur when third parties become involved (as supporters or settlement agents) and the conflict becomes the public knowledge of its social audience. It is not for the mere sake of classification that these distinctions are used. Whether or not a grievance evolves into a conflict or a dispute has important implications for how it relates to organizational order and change. It should also be noted that these behaviors need not slowly unfold from unilateral grievances, to dyadic conflicts, to triadic disputes. Indeed, many disputes snowball quickly from grievances for which parties can quickly mobilize supporters (Koch 1974).

Study Site

The evidence on which this chapter rests was gathered from a "Big Eight" public accounting firm, which for reasons of confidentiality was given the pseudonym Independent Accounting. As with many large accounting firms, the partnership level contains professionals from different backgrounds and with different specializations and so it seemed an especially appropriate context to investigate negotiated order. The specific site was chosen for its accessibility. The Big Eight (whittled down to the Big Five in 1989 due to mergers) audit more than 90% of the largest corporations in the United States (Stevens 1981). Working at Independent Accounting are more than 10,000 employees in several dozen branch offices who generated more than $1 billion in revenues during 1985. The firm is owned and managed by a few hundred partners organized into three specialties called "practices": tax, audit, and management consulting. Each branch office has a partner in charge of each practice and a managing partner who heads the office. The firm is also divided into several geographic regions headed by an executive committee composed of partners from each practice. A managing committee oversees the regional committees and is located at the firm's world headquarters. Similar to executives in other businesses, partners tend to be white, male, with college degrees, and between the ages of 35 and 65 (see Kanter 1977, 29-68). The nonpartner professional members of the firm—associates—tend to exhibit the same demographics and have the same division of labor. The specific site for this investigation was Independent's western regional office, containing 21 partners, more than 300 associates, and several hundred clerical workers collectively known as "staff."

Production at Independent is organized around one-on-one professional-client encounters, called "engagements." The audit of an engineering firm's assets prior to its purchase by an oil company, the preparation of taxes for a large commercial bank, or the design of an information management system for a manufacturer are all examples of engagements. Engagements vary in length from a few weeks to several months. They also vary from "one-shot deals," such as the design of an automated payroll system by management consulting partners, to multiyear "repeat" engagements exemplified by yearly tax preparation.

Method

To observe and learn of private grievances, ordering processes, and change at Independent Accounting, a "trouble-case method" was employed during fieldwork. This method originates in the anthropology of law and consists of searching for "instances of hitch, dispute, grievance, trouble; and inquiry into what the trouble was and what was done about it" (Llewelyn and Hoebel 1941, 21). Beyond this general notion, there is little agreement about the method or about what constitutes a "trouble case." Turner (1957), for example, defines trouble cases as behaviors that ritually act out discontinuities in the social structure of particular settings, thus emphasizing their *dramaturgical* aspects. Silberman (1985, 2) regards a trouble case as a "*disruption* in daily or other routines produced through violations of normative expectations [emphasis added by the author]." Baumgartner (1990) argues that trouble cases occur only when initial complaints by one party against another are met with overt resistance by the latter; trouble cases thus involve open *struggles*.

The current investigation adopted an operational definition of trouble case closest to that of Black (1976, 105), who argues that trouble cases begin with grievance expressions. The focus on grievance expressions as the raw materials of conflict and disputing thus allows for a wider sampling frame of trouble cases than the dramaturgical, disruption, or struggle approaches. It provides the opportunity for the researcher to study idiosyncratic or reactive grievance expressions of which offending parties and other members in the same social setting may be unaware. A trouble case may look like routine, nongrievance behaviors from a casual observer's or outsider's vantage point. By acknowledging that cases occur during ongoing interaction, this method also enables the researcher to view cases as an integral part of social structure, order, and change. The key in such a method, then, is the link between particular grievances and their pursuit by complainants.

Trouble cases among partners were collected via semistructured interviews and direct observation at Independent Accounting during a 12-month period in 1984 and 1985. In all, partners and associates were studied for a total of 236 hours on 54 different days; 19 of 21 partners were interviewed, as were 21 associates and several clerical staff members. Direct observations of partners were conducted at meetings, social gatherings, breakfasts, lunches, and dinners. Although it was initially difficult to "hang around" partners' offices, members of the firm soon became used to an observer as they become used to the many clients who constantly circulate through the regional branch.

Data collection methods similar to these have been fruitfully used in anthropological studies of conflict management in other cultures (see the discussions in Koch 1974, 1-25; Nader and Todd 1978, 5-8) and most recently in sociological investigations of urban disputing in the United States (Merry 1979). Despite their overall effectiveness for uncovering information about very delicate issues, other investigators have found that they tend to overestimate dramatic cases of conflict management while underestimating more subtle strategies (Koch 1974, 23-24). Such a shortcoming might be especially harmful to the current effort because of the interest in covert and overt ordering. In addition, the researcher's inability to "live" with members of the firm (as an anthropologist might while studying a traditional society) further constrained the collection of every trouble case that occurred at the firm during this fieldwork.

In this investigation, these problems were addressed via triangulation. The efficacy of triangulating data collected from informants and direct observation is well illustrated in classic organizational ethnographies by Blau (1955) and Dalton (1959). When grievances were not openly stated by participants in interaction (as they frequently were not), subsequent interviews with partners and associates focused on asking partners and associates what they were thinking and how they felt while engaged in the interaction observed. These conflict accounts thus became data for establishing the links between grievances and their expressions. Two informants who worked at the firm for nearly 30 years, who knew where "most of the bodies were buried," and who trusted the researcher aided considerably in this regard. Nearly every case collected independently by the researcher surfaced during these conversations and was obliquely cross-checked without revealing case sources to the deep informants who intuitively understood the consequences for the researcher and subjects should the confidentiality of case sources be compromised. It should also be noted that the findings presented here do not solely rest on observations and interviews with partners and associates but reflect broader inferences drawn from the considerable contact I had with clerical personnel and consultants working with Independent Accounting during fieldwork.

The current investigation yielded information on 77 grievance expressions embedded within 54 partner trouble cases. All cases were either observed at the firm or described to the investigator by participant, third parties, or uninvolved informants in the partnership. In addition, the observer also relied on clerical staff and clients for some of the information contained within trouble cases. Grievance expression categories were drawn both from informants and from sociological and anthropological literatures. This strategy allowed for coding that is analytically rigorous but also close to the way informants actually experience grievances, conflicts, and disputes.

The sections below first present a brief overview of the issues that prompt grievances among partners and associates, followed by trouble cases that illustrate the grievance expressions, conflicts, and disputes that round out the entire sample. The cases were selected to highlight how particular types of grievance expressions unfold, although many of the cases contain multiple types of grievance expressions centered on the same case themes.

Private Grievances Among Partners

Grievance Issues

On a day-to-day basis, partners find fault with each other in terms of client relations: for losing accounts to competitors, for proposing ineffective strategies to maintain or develop new accounts, or for "stealing" clients or associates working with fellow colleagues. A range of behaviors involving interpersonal etiquette may also be the basis for trouble: not sharing innovations, poor work performance, technical matters related to accounting procedures, being too flamboyant in one's personal effects or dress (such as not wearing a dark suit to work), being drunk or obnoxious at office parties, or wasting time in meetings with tangential or self-indulgent pronouncements. Interpartner trouble also turns on questions of selection for largely honorific posts (at the regional level) or the evaluation of associates. It is also interesting to note what rarely prompts private grievance expressions between partners: hiring practices (e.g., affirmative action), sexual discrimination or harassment, and ethical conduct (e.g., taking company resources for personal use, fabricating expense accounts). Agreements surrounding these issues are therefore rarely reappraised as a result of private grievances and, at the time of fieldwork, neither were these issues at the base of formal, public grievance proceedings.

Less Visible Grievance Expressions

Rarely do interpersonal grievances among partners escalate to conflicts and almost never to disputes. As will be seen in the case example that follows, many of the understandings that emerge between

Table 4.1 Private Grievance Expressions Among Partners at Independent Accounting

Behavior	Frequency	Percentage
Less visible expressions:		
temporary avoidance	24	31
toleration	16	21
strategic alienation	11	14
surveillance	(3)	—
exit	(3)[a]	—
	57	73
Open expressions:		
conciliatory negotiation	7	9
counseling	6	8
accusations	5	6
replacement	(2)	—
	20	27
Totals	77	100

a. Figures in parentheses are used whenever the total number of cases is too small to generate meaningful percentages. Percentages are provided to account for the total sample.

partners in the aftermath of grievances, conflicts, or disputes are punctuated by what was earlier referred to as silent bargaining: unarticulated agreements to simply not pursue the matter any further. In one sense, order is negotiated by what does not happen among the principals. The frequencies of the less visible and less open private grievance expressions used by partners among themselves appear in Table 4.1 and are discussed below.

One of the most common grievance expressions, toleration, illustrates silent bargaining among partners. It involves inaction by an aggrieved party but intrapersonal recognition that whatever is at the basis of a grievance or conflict still exists (Baumgartner 1984a, 83-84). Partners recalled specific situations or explained cases that I witnessed by using expressions such as "learning to live" with their colleagues' "eccentricities" or "problems," for example, or not letting "stupid things around the office" committed by other partners disturb their work. A case involving appropriate auditing techniques illustrates this grievance expression among partners:

Case 1. Depreciation Hell
Principals: Bailey and Hornish of Audit

Bailey and Hornish had both been audit partners at Independent for five years. They had worked together once as associates and had decided to work together again on an audit of a large utility firm about to be acquired by another firm. During Bailey's previous work with Hornish, he had remembered having doubts about the depreciation accounting procedures Hornish preferred. Whereas Hornish championed methods that computed depreciation using a traditional "age-life method" (based on the depreciation of an organizational asset over its "lifetime"), Bailey preferred a "unit of production" method, which takes into account the downtime of production facilities. Bailey especially believed that the unit of production method should be used in the current audit because a recent downturn in the local economy had led to many of the utility's facilities standing idle. He also suspected that Hornish had "cut some sort of deal" with the utility to use the age-life method to inflate their assets prior to the utility's acquisition by another utility. As he inspected the utility's records and facilities, Bailey firmly believed the age-life method to be inappropriate. But he allowed Hornish to frame the determination of depreciation at the utility using the age-life method. He did, however, hold two "seminars" during the course of the engagement for his associates on how one can "cheat" in an audit using the age-life method. He also made it policy that the method was not to be used by his associates unless he approved it.

Note Hornish's and Bailey's silent bargain in this case. Bailey allowed Hornish to continue with his method during the engagement without direct challenge in exchange for inoculating associates against its future use. As Hornish put it, "We did what we could to make a difference of accounting philosophy not become divisive on the engagement." Thus this silent bargain, prompted by Bailey's private grievance, contributed to order on the engagement by reducing disruption. The implications for change in this case are clear for associates who were forbidden to use the age-life method. For partners, the implications of this case for change related to their accounting procedures because of Bailey's inability to impose rules on them. Subsequent interviews with partners, however, revealed that some had been confronted with similar choices while working with Hornish and had taken similar courses of action with their associates.

When partners pursue their private grievances against colleagues, they most often do so via the temporary curtailment of social interaction with them or temporary avoidance (for general discussions of this concept, see Felstiner 1974; Baumgartner 1988). Temporary avoidance constitutes the largest single kind of grievance expression (31%) in the sample. Partners would refer to temporary avoidance as "keeping out of a peer's way until the dust settles" or "going underground for a while." The case below illustrates this strategy:

Case 2. Green's Misrepresentation
Principals: Green of Tax and Banks of Audit

Green had just been elected partner, specializing in financial service corporation tax preparation. He was eager to capitalize on his new status by aggressively going after several new accounts. Banks, the regional audit partner, while having lunch with an insurance firm executive whose company he had previously serviced, learned that Banks had been referred to the client by a financial services executive to prepare taxes for one of the client's subsidiaries. Green had told the client that he had extensive experience in financial service and insurance taxes but was hesitant to give the insurance executive any specific references. Banks was careful not to criticize Green when the client asked about the latter's knowledge of the insurance industry. Instead, he suggested the client use a tax partner whose work "he [Banks] knew better [and believed] would better serve the client." Banks expressed dismay to the observer that a partner would "misrepresent" himself to a client because of the potential liabilities for the firm. At no time did Banks confront Green with these issues or mention them to colleagues. Instead, he "carefully steered himself and his clients clear" of Green by not referring any of his audit clients to Green for tax work, although he always framed the issues for not recommending Green to them as technical matters. Two years after this incident, however, Green had successfully cultivated a small insurance clientele, and Banks met with him to discuss a "regular referral relationship." Banks believed that, as long as one kept Green "on a leash," he was a "good technician."

This case demonstrates temporary unilateral avoidance that lasts for several months before ending with a spontaneous rekindling of social relations. Other cases involving partners who have had some previous interpersonal tie demonstrate bilateral temporary avoidance that lasts for only a few days or even hours. Such was the situation in the aftermath of a particularly intense competition for a client during which two partners believed the other to be using questionable "sales tactics." In the week that followed, the two partners would avert eye contact with one another when in the same room or pretend to be on the phone when the other walked into his office. At the end of the week, the two partners were seen laughing about a lopsided loss that a local professional basketball team had suffered the previous night.

Case 2 also underscores the spontaneous resumption of social relations with offenders and, once again, the silent bargain not to escalate the matter further. The ease with which partners strike silent bargains in these types of cases is facilitated by cover stories (Jackall 1988) that draw attention away from grievance issues and facilitate the rekindling of relations with offenders. Cover stories during or in the aftermath of avoidance also constrain the "snowballing" of old cases into new ones with different themes or into open conflicts and public disputes directly involving partners other than the principals. This is consistent with what partners want for themselves and their colleagues: to be left alone to handle their trouble without interference, without visibility, and without open hostilities.

Partners also engage in other private grievance expressions when toleration or temporary avoidance of the offender is infeasible. Such cases often evolve into private conflicts in that they involve the exchange of grievance expressions by the principals themselves. Even then, such tactics are likely to "keep the peace" either because of a lack of visibility to other partners or because those who do become adept at "tracking" even the most subtle grievance expressions respond in equally oblique fashions. Consider the face-to-face expression of a private grievance in the case below:

Case 3. The Pipe Cleaner
Principals: Dales and Simpson of Management Consulting

Dales and Simpson are regular participants at the practice's monthly marketing meetings. These meetings can be valuable to partners for developing new clients and for "pitching" their services in line with the firm's overall advertising strategies (begun only one year prior to the fieldwork for this investigation). Dales and Simpson have been partners for seven and twelve years, respectively, but, like many partners, do not have much contact except during these meetings. For six straight meetings, every time Simpson began a long a oration on marketing strategy, Dales, who found Simpson a "bag of wind and a nuisance," began an elaborate process of cleaning and loading his pipe. Dales would continue this process for as long as 15 minutes or as long as Simpson spoke, until he would finally light his pipe. He would then stare out the window of the regional office's 43rd floor executive conference room engrossed in smoking his pipe as though no one else were in the room, often with his body nearly turned away (in a swivel chair) from Simpson. All the while, Simpson never outwardly reacted to Dales's lack of attention.

Subsequent interviews with Simpson revealed that he simply tolerates what he calls Dales's "rude" behavior; Simpson allows Dales to be rude in exchange for continuing to talk. In general, this kind of private grievance expression is similar to Goffman's (1967, 63) notion of alien-ation from interaction in which individuals "spontaneously become in-volved in unsociable solitary tasks" during interaction with others. This behavior is purposive, however, functioning to express some sort of griev-ance about another's behavior. It therefore might be labeled "strategic alienation." Its other manifestations in the sample include carefully stacking and restacking computer printouts or drawing intricate pat-terns on paper while colleagues are talking. For some partners, these behaviors are nervous habits. When such activities express a grievance toward a colleague, however, they become strategic alienation.

Yet another type of private grievance expression among partners is surveillance: the systematic gathering of information by aggrieved par-ties about each other. Partners refer to this practice as "watching" or "keeping tabs" on an offender. In such cases, surveillance may seem like toleration to offenders and uninvolved observers. Such was the case when a partner believed a colleague in the same practice was "underutilizing" a talented young associate and kept track of the engagements the associate worked on and the interaction she had with her supervisors over a pe-riod of months. The offender and aggrieved greeted each other and even occasionally lunched as though the grievance never existed. The case simply withered away as the complainant moved on to other activities.

In rare cases, private grievances take the form of exit from the firm. Partners generally remarked that this strategy is a method of last resort used only in response to persistent problems with colleagues. Moreover, partners were generally reluctant to talk about colleagues who had left the firm, referring to them as "burnouts." The three cases of exit, in fact, followed exactly the same pattern. Each complainant moved sev-eral times within the firm (temporary avoidance), partially rekindled relations with former colleagues, developed new problems with new colleagues, and eventually left Independent.

Open Grievance Expressions

Many of the basic themes across Cases 1 to 3 also appear in Case 4 below: The principals are restrained in their grievance pursuit even when confronting one another. Case 4 also illustrates the open and strategic negotiation of order and change at the interpersonal level found in Strauss (1978) and explicitly defined by Gulliver (1979, 3) as an "exchange [of] information and opinion . . . argument and discussion . . . [to] propose offers and counter offers relating to the issues" of trouble between two or more parties. The agreement reached at the conclusion of the negotiation in this case, it should be noted, is quite different than the earlier silent bargains. It is explicit in its relevance to the grievances at hand as well as in laying out rules for handling similar situations in the future:

Case 4. Scavenging
Principals: Dokes and Freidberg of Management Consulting

When a partner moves to a different branch, decides not to service a client any more, or retires, questions arise about who among the other partners will be allowed to seek out the newly freed clients for his or her own. Managing partners may be consulted by the disengaging partner but never become involved in "settling the issue." Instead, partners make direct claims to the disengaging partner based on their expertise with similar kinds of clients. Partners call this process "scavenging." Williams was retiring from Independent after more than 20 years as a management consultant partner. Two younger partners, Dokes and Freidberg, had previously worked together as associates and partners on large engagements. They continued to have a working relationship on two engagements, but they handled the majority of their engagements independently of one another. They both wanted Williams's two largest active clients. Both partners met several times with Williams during a two-month period, often taking the older partner to lunch and breakfast (breakfast meetings are common at Independent). Knowing Williams's fondness for sailing, Dokes also hosted Williams and his wife on a weekend sailing trip to some islands just off the coast. In kind, Freidberg treated Williams to a weekend at his resort condominium at a nearby golf course. Each of these outlays prompted grievances by the two younger partners against the other. In interviews, they both claimed the other had overstepped the boundaries of appropriate behavior and argued that their own behavior had been in response to the other's actual or anticipated behavior. For a few weeks after their weekend soirees with Williams, neither Dokes nor Freidberg spoke to the other, communicating about a joint client they serviced through their associates. They also visibly averted eye contact and did not speak to each other at a Halloween party for their children thrown by the wife of another partner. During this time, Williams confessed he felt "awkward" about the situation but simply avoided both men and was considering giving the clients to a third partner, Halsted, whom he had not yet contacted. Finally, nearly four months after the scavenging had begun, and with Williams still undecided about whom to give the clients to, Freidberg had one of his associates relay a message through Dokes's associates that he wanted to have lunch with his colleague to talk over some "important matters." They met the following week. Freidberg described the meeting as "cordial," while Dokes commented that two men "never really accused each other of anything, but talked over what had happened and how to get the most out of Williams's clients."

In the end, they agreed to approach Williams with a joint offer to handle the clients together. They did so and Williams agreed to give them the clients. They also agreed that in the future the most experienced partner in a particular specialty (demarcated by industry) should have the first "shot" at clients. By this time, however, Williams had talked to Halsted, who expected to receive the clients. Upon finding out that Williams had given Dokes and Freidberg the clients, Halsted became upset but neither confronted nor avoided [Williams]. He simply did nothing.

Much of the negotiation among partners occurs as addenda to other activities, which allows the principals to mask (to their colleagues and themselves) the fact that they have problems with each other. Quick negotiations often occur at the end of phone calls about other issues, at the conclusion of meetings in the hallways, or even at the few parties the firm has. With one exception, negotiated conflicts were only collected from among management consultant partners. The one exception involved two partners who had joined Independent from another firm in the audit practice. In all of the cases in which conciliatory negotiation occurred, the principals avoided or tolerated one another to some degree prior to engaging in conciliatory negotiation. It should also be noted that partners engaging in conciliatory negotiation typically use their associates to keep lines of communication open even when the principals are avoiding each other.

The two cases below demonstrate the limits to which partners go in mandating changes in the behavior of their colleagues. In each, a form of "counseling" occurs, either to alter the behavior of the partner in question (as in Case 5) or to remove a partner with "problems" from the firm (as in Case 6). In Case 5, the complainant, Vega, counsels Jimson about how to return his behavior to an "acceptable standard." His grievance expression focuses less on Jimson's boasting and more on the future changes he must make in his behavior. Consistent with their general sentiments about interference in another partner's affairs, partners expressed great reluctance to counsel their fellows even at another's request. Thus the order and change that emerge from this situation are not negotiated implicitly or explicitly. Rather, they are mandated, albeit in a restrained fashion, by Vega:

Case 5. The Boastful Partner
Principals: Jimson and Vega of Management Consulting

Jimson had recently made partner due in no small part to his mentoring by Vega, an older partner in a nearby office on the same floor. As they greeted one another each morning, Jimson repeatedly boasted about his latest engagements and laughingly added that "a new era had dawned" in which he (Jimson) would mentor Vega on how to deal with clients. Vega tired of these "pronouncements" and soon began hurrying into his office when he saw Jimson coming down the hall and closing the door muttering something about having to make a phone call. After two months of this behavior, Vega bid good day to Jimson in the hallway one morning and asked him to step into his office. Once inside, he congratulated Jimson on his "success" during recent months and commented that when he (Vega) had a "run of particularly good success," he sometimes felt "a certain intoxication." He then asked Jimson if he ever felt the same thing. Jimson replied with a chuckle that he had felt "very confident" and maybe a bit "cocky" with his recent accomplishments. Vega ended his five-minute conversation by telling Jimson that one of the distinguishing marks of an Independent partner is a "reserved and professional perspective." Too much confidence, Vega warned, "could lead one to arrogance and ruination." Vega then suggested that Jimson let his "accounts" speak for themselves "through client referrals and year-end [profit] shares." Jimson partially heeded the advice by curtailing his boasting when Vega was within earshot but continued it to some of his trusted junior associates.

Case 6 presents one of two such cases in the sample where other partners became directly involved in disciplinary action against another partner for lack of performance. Even here, the restrained and covert manipulative qualities of the ordering repertoire among partners is apparent. This case also illustrates highly strategic action on the part of the partners involved as well as a blurring of the boundaries between formal and informal grievance pursuits. Smith, the managing partner, is reluctant to suggest a leave for Samuels (the object of the grievance) or that Samuels give up some of his accounts, but he did "piggyback" on Samuels's suggestion of leave. In this way, Smith transforms the dispute from one focusing on the prerogatives of older partners to hold on to "dormant" clients to one in which Samuels himself was the problem. He also issues memos reinforcing the customary rules on client-partner liaisons and setting up procedures for leaves of absence from the partnership:

Case 6. The Partner Replacement
Principals: Samuels and Garcia in Tax and Smith the Managing Partner

Samuels seemed to drive away as many clients in the audit practice as he generated. He had joined the firm several years earlier than Smith, the managing partner of the regional office, and Garcia, the head of the tax practice, but had been "golfing friends" with both since he had made partner. While playing golf one day with Smith, Garcia, and Lindsey (a member of the audit practice), Samuels began talking about his recent woes with a large savings and loan that he had just lost to a rival Big Eight firm. Samuels spoke at length about the pressures of dealing with savings and loans in the aftermath of the deregulation of the industry in 1982 and how some of the older partners in the firm had a "stranglehold" on some of the more financially stable savings and loans despite not having serviced them as clients for some time. Partners were said to keep clients "dormant" until such time as they might service them. This practice, Samuels argued, left the weaker savings and loans to younger partners "who might have a harder time collecting fees and maintaining a relationship" with the client. Smith listened to his friend and asked Samuels several times what he "thought should be done" to ameliorate the situation. Samuels suggested some sort of policy to give every partner a chance at "good" clients. He also suggested to Smith that he might need a "leave of absence from the firm to sort out some things for himself." In the clubhouse after their game and after Samuels and Lindsey had left, Smith discussed Samuels's leave with Garcia, who recounted several instances he knew of (some from his associates who were "watching" Samuels) where Samuels had "mishandled accounts." They agreed that Samuels's proposal "made sense for the good of the firm and the partner." The next week, Samuels, Garcia, and Smith met and discussed Samuels's "situation." They agreed that Samuels had faced undue pressure in the newly changed savings and loan industry and that problems with his family (namely, the arrest of his son on narcotics possession) may have contributed to his troubles with clients. Smith urged Samuels to take a three-month leave effective during the summer of that same year (nearly two months later). Samuels also insisted that he draw up a plan about who would replace him on his accounts during his absence. Samuels, who was 53 at the time, took his leave but never returned to the firm. Instead, he opened a small consulting firm in another part of the country and slipped into semiretirement. This case prompted Smith to issue a memo in which he argued that the "spirit of the firm recognized that partners were bound to pursue whatever clients they wished within the boundaries for proper etiquette." He also drew up procedures for partnership leaves in similar situations.

Two more aspects of Cases 4 to 6 bear mentioning. First, all of them occurred in the management consulting practice, where partners tend to have ongoing or prior work ties with one another over and above simply being partners at Independent. In Case 4, Dokes and Freidberg shared several associates through joint engagements. In Case 5, Vega and Jimson had a longtime mentoring tie. Finally, in Case 6, Samuels, Garcia, and Smith were longtime friends but had never worked together.

Second, counseling appears to occur between partners of different ages as in Case 5, where Vega was much older than Jimson, and in Case 6, where Smith was not only managing partner but had been with the firm much longer than Samuels. In similar cases, younger partners tend to defer to the advice of older partners, sometimes even seeking it out.

Partners were not involved in, and I did not observe, however, any cases in which younger partners or partners of lower rank referred a conflict to or allowed a conflict to be settled by an older colleague or a partner in a management position. As with their beliefs about mobilizing colleagues as supporters, partners disdain the idea of a peer presiding in judgment in interpartner disputes.

Multiple Organizational Orders

Recall the vision of the negotiated order proposed by Strauss (1978): The social order of an organization is a living tapestry of interpersonal agreements and bargains woven together by explicit or implicit negotiation. Organizational change is a function of the breakdown or refashioning of agreements and bargains.

Now consider the vision of the partnership at Independent Accounting. It is a social setting in which few open negotiations occur but in which order inheres largely because of what does not happen between aggrieved parties. Partners in the tax and audit practices routinely fill their days with efforts to deny, avoid, and endure trouble among their fellows to minimize the possibility that grievances will be pursued in any but the most oblique and truncated fashions, resulting in silent bargains between the principals regarding normative behavior. Working in the tax and audit practices at the partnership levels does not require that partners have the interpersonal skills expected in an openly negotiated order where communication is paramount; instead, partners' skills consist of being independent of their fellows. Partners in management consulting display the same general propensities but also evidence a greater willingness to deal with their conflicts openly. Finally, trouble between partners of sizable age, experiential, reputational, or rank differences displays some tendency to be handled by unilateral action on the part of the senior partner.

The first of these patterns (illustrated by Cases 1-3) is best captured by what Baumgartner (1988) terms "moral minimalism" to underscore the nonconfrontational behaviors that are used under such conditions to maintain order. A second pattern (illustrated by Case 4) comes closest to capturing the sense of an openly negotiated order with explicit agreements and bargains. A third pattern (illustrated by Cases 5-6) resembles authoritative orders in most managerial hierarchies with their emphasis on the prerogative of status superiors (e.g., Chandler and Daems 1980; Morrill 1989). Thus three different organizational orders can be identified: a *minimalist,* an *openly negotiated,* and an *authoritative* order. The findings above also suggest that particular normative orders couple with social structure in systematic ways. Such an argument is consistent with cross-cultural typologies of social structure and conflict management contained in Koch and Sodegren (1978), Baumgartner (1984b), and Black (1990). The sections below first turn to the issue of the couplings of social structures and ordering processes and then briefly speculate on the relationship between different organizational orders and the origins and diffusion of incremental organizational change.

Social Status, Interdependence, and Ordering Processes

The structuring of work into independent engagements does indeed reflect general professional "freedom . . . to practice one's craft without interference, advice, or regulation by others" (Freidson 1970, 98) but not with direct efficacy. Continued adherence to such arrangements may more accurately reflect historical and rhetorical processes begun long ago as public accountants carved out space in the societal division of labor for themselves as a profession with particular jurisdictional boundaries (Abbot 1988). In one sense, then, the autonomy Independent accountants reserve for themselves is the perpetuation of a myth about how professional work is to be accomplished and regulated. Regardless of the mythical qualities of the way partners organize work, such arrangements have real consequences for their work lives because they create weak formal structure and weak interpersonal ties among partners and in so doing couple with their minimalist order along the lines argued by Baumgartner (1988), and is discussed below.

The formal hierarchy among partners only weakly stratifies the partnership and also appears to discourage the submission of disputes for the judgment of their parties who might diminish hostilities. Submitting a dispute to a third party for such functions generally entails a reduction of the disputant's autonomy—in effect, a relinquishing to the third party of some or all of the "ownership" of the conflict by its principals (Christie 1977). In social situations where the status of all the parties involved is roughly equivalent, where status is not clearly defined, or where an individual's formal position only slightly increases his or her ability to impose and enforce a decision, disputants are unwilling to forgo control of their conflicts. Partners who come into conflict also have little interdependence and can curtail their interaction without costs to themselves or their adversaries.

Also contributing to the weak interpersonal ties among partners is intrafirm mobility. Few partners remain in any of the firm's branch offices for their entire careers. Many transfer on their own initiative because of better opportunities in newer or bigger offices. Some are asked to fill particular needs in other regions. Others are voted by their colleagues to take local, regional, or national management positions that may require relocation. Even after several moves, only a few partners appear committed to spending the rest of their careers at the same branch office, although the vast majority of partners spend their careers in the firm. At the regional office, several partners even had secondary offices at other branches at which they spent considerable time. When hitches in interpersonal relations among partners arise, therefore, partners can often look forward to moving from the annoying situation or to having their opponents leave.

To the degree that work among all Independent partners is structured around autonomous engagements, all partners participate in the minimalist order by pursuing their grievances privately and informally and by striking silent bargains with their adversaries. Deviations from this social organization, however, create the possibility of different kinds of orders. Consider the management consulting practice. It is not surprising that management consulting partners are the partners most weakly tied to the accounting profession, and so the historical emphasis on independence in their work is less pronounced than among their brethren in other practices. They place greater emphasis on "team projects" and being "team players." The durability of their intercollegial relationships is therefore greater. Management consulting partners engage in an openly negotiated order, striking explicit agreements born of interdependence rather than independence. The situation of management consulting partners is thus very close to that described by Gluckman (1955) in his analysis of how the interdependence contained in crosscutting ties induces open negotiation of conflict.

The weak status differences among firm members along lines of age and experience also enable different ordering processes to occur. A weak authoritative order also seems to predominate when partners of

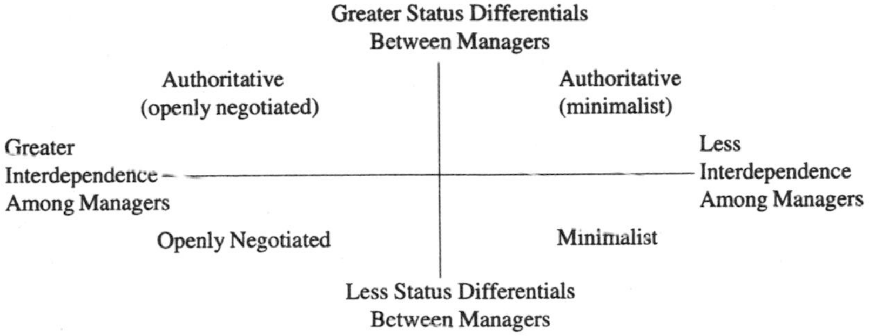

Greater Status Differentials
Between Managers

| Authoritative (openly negotiated) | Authoritative (minimalist) |

Greater
Interdependence ———————————————————————— Less
Among Managers   Interdependence
Among Managers

| Openly Negotiated | Minimalist |

Less Status Differentials
Between Managers

Figure 4.1. Social Structure and Organizational Orders

different ages and experience are involved in trouble. In such instances, older and more experienced partners are able to draw on their informal status to influence colleagues to settle or give up their conflicts. The overall minimalist character of the moral order in the management consulting practice and among partners of different ages, however, is still evident despite these variations.

Theoretically, this suggests that different levels of status differences and interdependence among managers are associated with different kinds of orders. Figure 4.1 portrays the coupling between these variables and micro orders.

Where managers are independent of one another (in terms of controlling the resources necessary to perform their duties) and weakly stratified (in terms of having very little differentiation of their formal status as defined by their authority relations or informal status in terms of their experience with the firm, age, and reputation), a minimalist order will predominate, held together by silent bargains. Where managers are more interdependent but only weakly stratified, an openly negotiated order will predominate, held together by explicit agreements. Where managers are strongly stratified and interdependent, an authoritative order held together by imposed prescriptions will predominate, peppered by explicitly negotiated agreements. This is the situation in organizations that have begun to introduce lateral coordinating structures (e.g., project teams in their traditional managerial hierarchies; Drucker 1988). By deduction, where actors are independent and stratified, a strong authoritative order will predominate, peppered by minimalism and silent bargaining. This is the situation in traditional managerial hierarchies without lateral coordinating structures (Morrill 1989).

Table 4.2 Origins and Diffusion of Incremental Change in Three Organizational Orders

	Minimalist	*Openly Negotiated*	*Authoritative*
Origin of change	Boundary invasion (independence threatened)	boundary closure (interdependence threatened)	Boundary blurring (challenge to status position)
Diffusion of change	structural equivalence (similar structural conditions)	cohesion (direct contact)	imposition (direct or via bureaucratic rules)

Organizational Orders and Organizational Change

Finally, it is to the issue of organizational change that the discussion now turns. Although the data presented in this chapter do not allow for a complete investigation of the implications particular organizational orders hold for incremental organizational change, Table 4.2 contains some speculation regarding the etiology and diffusion of change in organizational orders.

Minimalist orders would appear to be inimical to change. Yet it does occur, as suggested here, when actors encroach upon one anothers' spheres (boundaries) of influence (e.g., at Independent, engagement staffs). When threats to independence occur, partners barely interact with each other and then run to their own engagements to innovate (as illustrated in Cases 1-3). In this sense, the diffusion of change in a minimalist order may approximate that which occurs through "structural equivalence" (see Burt 1986). Widespread incremental change among partners emerges as they individually adapt to similar structural situations but without direct contact with one another. This may explain why large-scale collaborative change, such as the development of explicit merger and acquisition strategies, has been so difficult within Big Eight accounting firms (Maister 1983). The structure of work, and its attendant social relations and minimalist order, militates against it. Public accounting firms only began merging in the late 1980s—nearly 15 years after such intercorporate practices became a part of the standard repertoire of American business (Hirsch 1986). It may also explain why the partner levels of large public accounting firms still appear staid and stodgy: The impact on partners of such large-scale occurrences is so decentralized in such firms that it appears not to exist.

One could argue that openly negotiated orders exhibit very different etiologies and diffusion patterns of change. In such orders, change associated with private grievances arises from threats to *interdependence* (when the boundaries of one's resources are metaphorically "closed"). Change occurs via openly negotiated agreements and bargains, and such agreements diffuse through an organization via direct contact, or through what Burt (1986) refers to as "cohesion," between actors (as illustrated in Case 4).

Change in authoritative orders poses yet another contrast to change in minimalist or negotiated orders. In this kind of order, change originates from challenges to the prerogatives of superordinates. In this sense, the very normative boundaries that status hierarchies create are challenged by those that would overstep them and create new ones. Diffusion likewise has a different pattern, taking the form of direct imposition from above, as when a superior issues a direct order about how a subordinate should behave (as the more experienced partner did in Case 5). Change can also be diffused within such an order in an indirect way through the establishment of rules that specify new routines to be followed and attach negative sanctions to the performance of replaced, old routines (partly illustrated in Case 6).

Conclusion

Different social structural conditions within Independent Accounting lead to distinctly different organizational orders and change processes on any given day. Whether such orders and their attendant change processes can be identified in other organizational contexts awaits further study.

Also awaiting further study are numerous questions related to organizational orders and the central themes of this volume: the public-private, formal-informal, and rational-nonrational dimensions of conflict. This chapter, for example, has largely considered private and informal change that occurs *within* organizational orders. Under what conditions do organizational orders change? What are the relationships between more formal and less private grievances, and changes from one organizational order to another? At what point do organizational orders come into conflict with, or reinforce, one another? How do different organizational orders couple with different formal processes of grievance handling? Do different organizational orders contain different mixes of habituated versus conscious and premeditated grievance expressions? How do different organizational orders couple with different levels of efficiency and productivity (however defined)? Can the conceptual framework developed here to describe interpersonal processes apply to macroconflict and change, either within entire organizations or organizational populations? Each of these questions deserves investigations in its own right and may ultimately yield greater insight into the tension between order and change in organizational life.

References

Abbot, A. 1988. *The systems of professions.* Chicago: University of Chicago Press.
Baumgartner, M. P. 1984a. Social control in suburbia. In *Toward a general theory of social control.* Vol. 2, *Selected problems,* ed. D. Black. Orlando, Fla.: Academic Press.
—1984b. Social control from below. In *Toward a general theory of social control.* Vol. 1, *Fundamentals,* ed. D. Black. Orlando, Fla.: Academic Press.
—1988. *The moral order of a suburb.* New York: Oxford University Press.
—1990. War and peace in childhood. In *The Virginia Review of Sociology.* Vol. 1, *Law and conflict management,* ed. J. Tucker. Greenwich, Conn.: JAI.
Black, D. 1976. *The behavior of law.* New York: Academic Press.
—1990. The elementary forms of conflict management. In *New directions in the study of justice, law, and social control,* ed. Arizona School of Justice Studies, Arizona State University. New York: Plenum.
Blau, P. M. 1955. *The dynamics of bureaucracy.* Chicago: University of Chicago Press.
Burt, R. S. 1986. Social contagion and innovation: Cohesion versus structural equivalence. *American Journal of Sociology* 92:1287-1335.
Chandler, A. D., and H. Daems, eds. 1980. *Managerial hierarchies: Comparative perspectives on the rise of the modern industrial enterprise.* Cambridge, Mass.: Harvard University Press.
Christie, N. 1977. Conflicts as property. *The British Journal of Criminology* 17:1-15.
Dalton, M. 1959. *Men who manage.* New York: John Wiley.
Day, R. A., and J. V. Day. 1977. A review of the current state of negotiated order theory. *Sociological Quarterly* 18:126-42.
Drucker, P. F. 1988. The coming of the new organization. *Harvard Business Review,* January-February, 45-53.
Felstiner, W. L. F. 1974. Influences of social organization on dispute processing. *Law and Society Review* 9:63-94.
Fine, G. X. 1984. Negotiated orders and organizational cultures. *Annual Review of Sociology* 10:239-62.
Freidson, E. 1970. *Professional dominance.* New York: Atherton.

Gluckman, M. 1955. *The judicial process among the Barotse in Northern Rhodesia.* Manchester, England: University Press for the Rhodes-Livingstone Institute.

Goffman, E. 1967. *Interaction ritual.* New York: Anchor.

Gulliver, P. H. 1979. *Disputes and negotiations: A cross-cultural perspective.* New York: Academic Press.

Hirsch, P. M. 1986. From ambushes to golden parachutes: Corporate takeovers as an instance of cultural framing and institutional integration. *American Journal of Sociology* 91:800-837.

Jackall, R. 1988. *Moral mazes: The world of corporate managers.* New York: Oxford University Press.

Kanter, R. M. 1977. *Men and women of the corporation.* New York: Basic Books.

Koch, K. 1974. *War and peace in Jalemo: The management of conflict in Highland New Guinea.* Cambridge, Mass.: Harvard University Press.

Koch, K., and J. A. Sodegren. 1978. Political and psychological correlates of conflict management: A cross cultural study. *Law and Society Review* 10:443-66.

Llewelyn, K. N., and E. A. Hoebel. 1941. *The Cheyenne Way.* Norman: University of Oklahoma Press.

Maister, D. 1983. Beyond garbage-can-decision-making. *The American Lawyer*, December, 6-7.

Merry, S. E. 1979. Going to court: Strategies of dispute settlement in an American urban neighborhood. *Law and Society Review* 13:891-925.

Montagna, P. 1968. Professionalization and bureaucratization in large professional organizations. *American Journal of Sociology* 74:138-45.

—1971. The public accounting profession. *American Behavioral Scientist* 14:475-91.

Morrill, C. 1989. The management of managers: Disputing in a managerial hierarchy. *Sociological Forum* 4:387-408.

Nader, L., and H. F. Todd. 1978. *The disputing process: Law in ten societies.* New York: Columbia University Press.

Silberman, M. 1985. *The civil justice process: A sequential model of the mobilization of law.* Orlando, Fla.: Academic Press.

Stevens, M. 1981. *The Big Eight.* New York: Harcourt Brace.

Strauss, A. 1978. *Negotiations.* San Francisco: Jossey-Bass.

Strauss, A., L. Schatzman, D. Ehrlich, R. Bucher, and M. Sabshin. 1963. The hospital and its negotiated order. In *The hospital in modern society*, ed. E. Freidson. New York: Free Press.

Turner, V. W. 1957. *Schism and continuity in an African society: A study of Ndembu Village Life.* Manchester, England: Manchester University Press.

5

The Role of Conflict in a
Second Order Change Attempt

JEAN M. BARTUNEK
ROBIN D. REID

In the past few years, there has been considerable interest in second order organizational change (e.g., Bartunek 1984; Levy and Merry 1986; Moch and Bartunek 1990). As opposed to first order change (incremental modifications that make sense within the organization's already accepted perspectives or frameworks for understanding), second order change involves qualitative, discontinuous shifts in the frameworks themselves, in the way organizational members understand significant dimensions of the organization and its work.

Empirical descriptions of processes through which second order changes occur and/or are impeded (e.g., Bartunek 1984; Child and Smith 1987; Hinings and Greenwood 1988; Moch and Bartunek 1990) suggest that these changes are typically initiated when major environmental shifts lead powerful organizational members to perceive the organization's already established frameworks or perspectives as inadequate. These members develop alternative frameworks of understanding, and this development in turn leads to conflict between organizational members espousing old and new frameworks. Second

AUTHORS' NOTE: We thank Dennis Gioia and Deborah M. Kolb for their helpful comments on earlier drafts of this chapter and Boston College for its financial support for the research.

116

order changes, when they occur, are typically the outcome of this conflict: the development of a new perspective that transcends either the original one or its proposed alternate. For example, a second order change in the educational mission of a religious order centered on interaction and conflict between groups of order members operating out of two perspectives. According to the original perspective, the order's educational mission was best expressed in work in the order's schools. Holders of the new perspective saw this mission more in terms of work for social justice. There was considerable conflict between proponents of the two perspectives that led to modifications in both of them and, eventually, to the educational mission of the order being understood in a way that reconciled and transcended the differences in the two approaches (Bartunek 1984; Bartunek and Ringuest 1989).

Sometimes conflict between perspectives inhibits, rather than fosters, second order change. For example, Moch and Bartunek (1990) found that union and management officials participating in a Quality of Work Life project interpreted participation in decision making very differently than organization development (OD) consultants to the project. While the OD consultants understood participation as shared responsibility for decisions between union and management, local union and management officials understood participation to mean that employees asked for amenities and management decided whether to provide them. The different groups were never aware that they "saw" participation in two very different ways. As a result, the differences between their perspectives were not surfaced in such a way that the groups could address each other's views, and this was one reason the project eventually failed. In these cases, as in others, the processes by which conflicts between perspectives are surfaced and handled has a significant impact on the outcomes of second order change processes.

The conceptual framework that emerges from these studies emphasizes that, when differing perspectives are present, it is through their dialectical interaction (implying both conflict between them and their simultaneous validity) that qualitative changes in shared frameworks can best evolve (Bartunek 1988). When the different perspectives remain separated, their differences neither recognized nor confronted, however, the change process is impeded. Further, while conflict is necessary for changes in perspective to occur, the empirical findings have shown that the experience of conflict is likely to be uncomfortable and difficult for the organizational members involved. Thus conflict may be avoided, inhibiting significant change in frameworks (Hinings and Greenwood 1988). To gain a more adequate understanding of factors affecting second order change, it is necessary to appreciate the role of conflict in this process.

Research has not addressed several dimensions that are crucial for an understanding of conflict during second order change. A more complete understanding of conflict during this process must include descriptions of (a) how conflicts regarding perspectives are expressed by organizational members involved in the change process, (b) how these conflicts are understood, and (c) how conflict-handling processes constrain and/or facilitate change. With the exception of an awareness that underlying conflicts must be surfaced to foster change, there is not, at this point, a well-developed understanding of these issues. In this chapter, we explore conflicts that occurred in an organization undergoing an attempted second order change and then articulate an understanding of how conflict might operate during this type of change.

Conceptual Context for the Study

Research on organizations' frameworks or perspectives indicates that organizational members are often not conscious of the shared perspectives that undergird their actions (e.g., Bartunek 1984; Moch and Bartunek 1990). The introduction of new perspectives during attempted second order change may make people more conscious of their original understanding than previously; however, they still may not fully appreciate newly developing perspectives or the relationship between perspectives and actions.

Rather than experiencing differences between perspectives for what they are, organizational members are likely to identify particular perspectives with the people and groups who espouse them and, when conflict between perspectives occurs, to displace these differences in perspectives onto personality conflicts. This occurs in part because most Americans are reared on a "psychology of the individual" (Sarason 1971) and so have difficulty appreciating the impacts of social systems. When someone acts out of a perspective that is different than their own and in so doing frustrates their aims, they will attribute their frustration to the person rather than the perspective (Sproull and Hofmeister 1986). Related to this, several years' worth of attribution research suggests that the "fundamental attributional bias" is to attribute causality to personal rather than situational factors, even when there are clear situational causes for events (Ross 1977). As a consequence, conflicts that appear to outside observers to be caused by structural factors are often experienced as due to personality traits by the actors involved (Kolb 1987). Thus apparent personality conflicts between individual organizational members may mask more central but also more hidden conflicts regarding differences in perspectives (see Smith, Simmons, and Thames 1989). The first purpose of this study is to identify how organizational members involved in an attempted second order change experience and interpret conflicts associated with differing perspectives.

The second and third purposes are to address ways these conflicts are handled and affect the course of change. Black (1990) describes several forms of conflict handling: self-help, avoidance, negotiation, settlement, and toleration. He proposes that most social situations are characterized primarily by one of these conflict-handling modes as opposed to others. Further, he suggests that the particular conflict-handling mode most likely to be present in a particular situation will be isomorphic with the social or organizational framework—the shared perspectives of actors in the situation. That is, conflict patterns are some of the ways already established perspectives are expressed in action. One implication of Black's argument is that, if second order change attempts are to succeed, the ways conflicts are handled probably have to "break" from the organization's typical pattern of conflict handling. The use of already established conflict-handling patterns should lead the original perspective to become more entrenched rather than less.

One way conflict-handling modes may differ from the modes that are isomorphic with the organization's original perspective is by enabling dialectical interaction between the original and new perspectives (Bartunek 1988). This type of interaction has been labeled "paradoxical" (Smith and Berg 1987), in that people using it are recognizing and accepting the concurrent validity of two or more apparently contradictory frameworks. Dialectical interaction involves a kind of negotiation between holders of the different perspectives that is aimed not at compromise between them or victory of one perspective over the other but at the development of a new shared understanding that transcends either of the original perspectives (see Cameron 1986).

In contrast to dialectical interaction, many conflict-handling modes "split" competing perspectives, acknowledging the validity of only one of them rather than of both (Smith and Berg 1987). The acknowledgment of the potential validity of more than one perspective typically causes considerable cognitive and emotional discomfort. Consequently, Smith and Berg (1987) suggest that groups and, by extension, organizations tend not to establish conditions that foster dialectical interaction between differing perspectives. They more frequently attempt to "extinguish" one or another of them, to set them in a competition in which one clearly wins over the other. Or they avoid the conflict in such a way that a new perspective never has the chance to enter into dialogue with the original one. As a consequence, underlying conflicts between perspectives often become displaced onto other conflicts, particularly onto personality conflicts, which then become the focus of attention. The displacement sometimes results in organizational members feeling "paralyzed," unable to make or implement decisions on issues related to the underlying conflict (Smith and Berg 1987). It clearly impedes second order change.

In the following pages, we describe conflicts that occurred during an attempted second order change at a private school. The stated aim of the change was to introduce a perspective that valued coordination among academic units into a situation that strongly favored the autonomy of these units. The new perspective was to be introduced structurally, through the implementation of a new administrative position. We describe the conflicts that occurred in the situation, how they were expressed and understood, and how they affected the course of change.

The Study

The study took place during the 1987-88 school year at the McLaughlin School (a pseudonym), a private school located in Ohio. The school, which enrolls about 550 students, is organized into three main administrative units, a lower school (K-4), middle school (5-8), and upper school (9-12). The primary change was the introduction of a new "academic director" position. This position, which replaced a previously established "curriculum coordinator" role, was aimed at achieving greatly increased coordination of curriculum among the different academic units (schools and departments) at McLaughlin. A detailed case description of several of the events that took place during the 1987-88 school year is available in Bartunek (1991).

McLaughlin had had difficulty for the previous 15 years with the curriculum coordinator position. As one of the administrators said in May 1987, the school had "eaten curriculum coordinators over the years." Turnover in the position had been high, and the people who held the role felt they had not succeeded. They attributed their lack of success in part to a pervasive sense in the school that the various academic units were autonomous, independent of each other and of the administration. For example, on a self-administered questionnaire in 1983 (part of the preparation for a 1984 accreditation evaluation), faculty and administration at McLaughlin had referred to communication between schools, between departments, and between the administration and faculty as the aspect of the school "most needing improvement." According to McLaughlin's principal, the autonomy of the different units had led to significant problems. For example, it was not unusual for upper school students to spend "all-nighters" on their assignments, largely because the departments opposed coordination regarding homework assignments and tests. The principal hoped to achieve increased coordination at McLaughlin.

As the principal had designed the position in 1987, the academic director would have much more responsibility for coordinating curriculum across the three schools than the curriculum coordinators had had. For example, the department chairs of physical education and fine arts would report to the academic director because the activities of these departments encompassed the entire school. The academic director would also have other responsibilities that had not been assigned to the curriculum coordinators, such as taking charge of textbook ordering in the entire school, serving as the school's liaison to the educational subcommittee of the board of trustees, and organizing preparation for an accrediting evaluation to take place in April 1988.

During spring 1987, the principal discussed this new position with the administration and gained their apparent approval. She also informally described the position to the faculty. The position was formally implemented in the fall.

The first author (hereafter called "the researcher") visited McLaughlin in May 1987 and approximately every three weeks during the 1987-88 school year. She interviewed the academic director on each visit, the principal on all but two visits, the heads of schools four times, the department chairs twice, and other administration and faculty members involved with the new role one or more times. She also contacted and interviewed three of the former curriculum coordinators. In addition, she conducted occasional telephone interviews with the academic director and principal and sat in on some meetings and other events at the school.

The interviewees discussed a large number of conflicts with the academic director, with the previous curriculum coordinators, and with other administrators. Even if the researcher did not bring up such conflicts, they were repeatedly mentioned.

The two authors recorded all of the conflicts encountered at the school or described by someone there during the course of the study. We categorized each conflict according to how it was handled (or described as handled) and used this categorization to determine the predominant understandings of conflict, patterns of conflict handling, and their impacts in the school that year and in previous interactions with the curriculum coordinators.

In the following pages, after introducing McLaughlin's administration and department chairs, we present the results of our analysis. We describe conflictual patterns at McLaughlin both before and during the year the academic director position was implemented. First, we describe conflict patterns prior to the implementation of the position and some effects these patterns had on the various curriculum coordinators as well as on administration and faculty perceptions of McLaughlin. These serve as background for our description of the conflict patterns present during the 1987-88 school year.

The Administration and Faculty at McLaughlin

In spring 1987, there were five administration members whose positions were directly concerned with the academic life of the school. A chart listing the administrators (all names are disguised) and their tenure at McLaughlin is shown in Table 5.1. The principal was Mary Anne Walters. The upper school head was Carol Rooney, who was described by some administrators and faculty as very competent at individual counseling relationships with students but far less competent in developing curriculum. The middle school head was Karen Kerns, who had come to McLaughlin as a lower school teacher in 1975 and had been middle school head since 1981. Mary Anne and Karen were good friends, and Mary Anne was widely viewed as Karen's mentor. The lower school head was Judy Gallagher. She had been at McLaughlin longer than any other administrator. The curriculum coordinator was Janice Luebbe, who had just accepted a

Table 5.1 Administrators at McLaughlin School During the 1987-88 School Year

1987-88 Position	Name	Tenure at the School
		(as of September 1987)
Principal	Mary Anne Walters	6 years
Upper School head	Carol Rooney	16 years
Middle School head	Claudia Lindhorst	3 years
Lower School head	Judy Gallagher	18 years
Academic director	Karen Kerns	12 years
Former curriculum coordinator	Janice Luebbe	(at McLaughlin 3 years)

position for the next year as principal at another school. When Mary Anne decided to create the academic director position, she also decided to appoint Karen Kerns to it. Mary Anne knew that Karen was very familiar with the problems the curriculum coordinators had encountered. In addition, she believed that the job description for the academic director position "fit Karen's expertise" very well and was a natural progression in the development of Karen's administrative skills. In May 1987, Karen described herself as effective at selling new ideas to people and as quite capable of fighting for ideas she considered important. She said she felt comfortable with conflict, a capacity that would help in her new role. Karen would be replaced as middle school head by Claudia Lindhorst, who was a teacher in the middle school.

In addition to the administrators, there were seven department chairs, for science, social science, English, foreign languages, physical education, fine arts, and mathematics. On the average, the department chairs had been at McLaughlin for 12 years, with the range from 8 years to 18. The physical education and fine arts departments extended from kindergarten to grade 12. All of the other departments were primarily in the upper school.

As is evident from Table 5.1, there was very little turnover among administrators and department chairs other than the curriculum coordinators. One of the effects of this low turnover rate was that all but one of the administrators and all of the department chairs had been at McLaughlin longer than the principal.

The low turnover rate appeared to be due to the fact that, with the exception of issues surrounding coordination of curriculum, faculty and administration experienced relationships at the school as warm and supportive. The school's 1983 self-administered questionnaire supports these perceptions. In it, the faculty and administration rated a sense of family and a supportive atmosphere as the strongest aspects of the school. This supportive climate may have made the problems surrounding the curriculum coordinator role stand out more than they would in other settings.

**The Principal's Perceptions of the
School and Actions to Achieve Coordination**

From the time she had arrived at the school in 1981, Mary Anne had perceived a high degree of autonomy between the different departments and schools and had viewed it as detrimental to the students' overall development. She described her initial reaction as follows:

> My picture of the school in 1981 was a series of dots not connected in any way. . . . No one has an overview of what happens to each student. Then I got the distinct impression that hostility arises about treading on people's turf. . . . The department chairs were all separate when I arrived. . . . The upper school faculty refused to be advisors, and they didn't want me at faculty meetings.

Prior to 1987, Mary Anne had already made several attempts to change the ways faculty and administration coordinated with each other for the students' well-being. Shortly after she came to the school, she had insisted, against the upper school faculty members' considerable opposition, that they serve as academic advisers, so they would have a sense of the "whole" student rather than only in terms of activities related to their own discipline. She had significantly upgraded the student affairs staff, both in personnel and in activities, to achieve more holistic education. She had also redesigned the curriculum coordinator role twice. As of May 1987, three different people had served in some version of that position since 1981. The first person, who had been at the school prior to Mary Anne's arrival and had primarily acted as a guidance counselor, had resigned the position for personal reasons in 1981. Mary Anne described aspects of the position since then as follows:

> In 1982 I got Toni Druffel to pull the curriculum together. It didn't work. . . . At the most she was a coordinator of advisers, but that's stretching it. . . . Toni decided to go to another school. The next year we [had] no one doing curriculum. The accrediting evaluation was in 1984. They said, "You need a

curriculum coordinator." . . . I interviewed Janice Luebbe, and she said she would come. . . . It ended up in 1984-1985 with Carol Rooney and Janice Luebbe and (two student affairs staff members) as a team. . . . Carol could always follow up kids with problems. She is not gifted at long-range planning or at new educational ideas. . . . Janice had agreed to stay for two years; she stayed three.

The curriculum coordinators had focused most of their work on the upper school, although they had been expected to carry out some coordinating activities in the other schools as well. Mary Anne felt that these efforts had had some positive effects. Neither Mary Anne nor the past curriculum coordinators, however, felt they had achieved a sense of coordination that would provide the faculty with a comprehensive overview of each student's academic, psychological, and physical well-being.

Patterns of Conflict Prior to 1987

Well-established, recurring patterns for dealing with conflicts regarding curriculum were present at McLaughlin. When an administrator asked someone else to coordinate work, reactions to the request most frequently took a form that several school personnel labeled *passive resistance.* Behaviorally, passive resistance meant that school personnel continued to operate as they pleased when coordination requests were made: They ignored the requests or obstructed changes by dragging their feet. Sometimes department chairs responded to the administration's coordination attempts through *active resistance,* that is, explicit refusals to comply with a request, occasionally including threatening reprisals unless the request were withdrawn.

All three curriculum coordinators said they had been able to accomplish far less than they hoped in their jobs as a result of the pervasive resistance they encountered. For example, when asked to reflect on her efforts to coordinate grading forms, one said "All I remember is resistance." Another reported, "We didn't make great strides in unifying the curriculum. What we tried to do was blocked." The conflictual patterns that occurred most often were between (a) the administration (especially the upper school head) and the department chairs, (b) the department chairs and the curriculum coordinators, and (c) the lower and upper school heads and the curriculum coordinator.

Administration and department chairs. There were regular conflicts between individual departments and the administration, especially the upper school head, regarding grading policy. In these conflicts, the predominant pattern was for the administration to make a proposal, for a department to resist it, and for the administration to back down. In one situation, for example, a social studies teacher failed a majority of students in her class. Carol challenged the teacher about this, saying that the students couldn't all have failed. The teacher threatened Mary Anne that she would quit unless Carol backed down. Carol apologized to her. The next year, the social studies department administered exams that took only 15 minutes for some of the students to complete and gave an inordinately large number of "A" grades.

This pattern can be traced to an implicit contract established between Carol and the department chairs in the mid-1970s. Due to problems with the school's enrollment and external reputation at that time, the principal (Mary Anne's predecessor) had concentrated primarily on McLaughlin's external constituencies. Thus, as Carol said, "I was the only [administrator] here in the upper school. So to get the upper school going I delegated autonomy [to the department chairs]." As part of this delegation, Carol had given the department chairs responsibility for a wide variety of functions, including departmental curriculum and hiring. As a result, the department chairs had come to feel entitled to a high degree of autonomy over these and related areas.

The department chairs and the curriculum coordinator. The typical reaction from the department chairs to the curriculum coordinators' efforts was passive resistance. When a new coordinating activity or policy was initiated, the department chairs' most common response seemed to be to ignore it and operate as they pleased. As one former curriculum coordinator put it, "The art of passive resistance is well developed by a number of key people at McLaughlin. . . . They can wait out changes in personnel and job titles. When the dust settles . . . they will still be there doing things pretty much their own way." She reported that the response to her coordination attempts seemed like "shadow boxing . . . never like active resistance."

School heads and curriculum coordinator. Conflictual patterns also existed between both the lower and the upper school heads and the curriculum coordinator. The lower school head did not encourage the curriculum coordinator's involvement in the lower school. One of the curriculum coordinators reported that "Judy Gallagher ran a tight little school into which outsiders didn't get." Apparently, Judy's resistance to their efforts made the curriculum coordinators feel sufficiently unwelcome that they did not attempt to intervene in the lower school.

The relationship between the upper school head and the curriculum coordinators was quite different than the relationship between the upper school head and the department chairs. The curriculum coordinators perceived Carol as threatened by any attempts they made to coordinate curriculum. They said she would make it difficult for them to achieve their purpose, frequently by becoming angry and withdrawn or by accusing them of overstepping their reach. The curriculum coordinators would eventually back down. For example, one curriculum coordinator said she tried at first to "relate to her as an equal," but Carol was "defensive and obstructive," so this curriculum coordinator decided to back down and act as if she were reporting to Carol. After that, their relationship was smoother. This curriculum coordinator, however, then felt unable to accomplish the objectives of her job. Instead, she said, "My job had little identifiable domain beyond what a good secretary or registrar could do." Another former curriculum coordinator said, "Carol wouldn't let you do it [i.e., coordinate the curriculum], and she couldn't do it."

Effects of Autonomy and of the Conflict Patterns

The department chairs' autonomy in relation to the administration had a significant impact on the school. In May 1987, four of the school's administrators used the following phrases to describe the different units at McLaughlin: "Each school is a fiefdom"; "The biggest problem is the departments who think they're queens of the world"; "Each department is its own fiefdom"; and "Each department is a fortress unto its own." During the fall of 1987, various department chairs said that individual faculty members in different departments didn't know what the others were doing or that there was no communication between the departments and the administration. One described department chair-administration relationships as a form of "guerrilla warfare," and another described the departments as "little fiefdoms." Mary Anne was very frustrated by this separation between academic units. She (and other administrators) felt that too many disparate demands were placed on the students, impairing their overall development as "whole persons."

The strong opposition faced by the curriculum coordinators had negative effects on them as well. All of the curriculum coordinators felt that they had been blocked by the upper and lower school heads and department chairs. All felt that they lacked authority and decision-making power. All felt they failed to achieve the goals of the job. It is not surprising that two of the three said they did not like the job at all.

The Implementation of the
Academic Director Position

Two events that occurred near the beginning of the implementation of the academic director position in 1987 indicated that the already established patterns would not automatically cease with the introduction of the new position. During the summer, Mary Anne asked each of the current administrators as well as the incoming academic director to draw up job descriptions, which they discussed at their planning meeting in August. At this meeting, Judy Gallagher said she disagreed with the duties assigned to the academic director. She said that she, Judy, and not the academic director should coordinate curriculum in the lower school. Karen and the other administrators were very upset at Judy's reaction: They thought the academic director job duties had already been agreed upon by all the administration. Consequently, there was, as Carol later described it, "a huge conflict in terms of what Karen should be doing." When the school year began, this conflict had not been settled.

At the orientation session for the faculty at the opening of the school year, Mary Anne formally introduced the academic director job to the faculty. She said:

> Karen's role is a curricular growth role. She'll be working on curriculum programs K-12, and will be working on professional growth with the individual department chairs. Work with her so she can get to know the total curriculum as much as possible. If you're doing an overview, tell her. She's not the one who solves problems related to faculty, students, and parents. So if someone is failing math, go to the head of the school. And she *doesn't* write the faculty evaluation.

One of the faculty told Karen later that day that Mary Anne had said "more what the job doesn't entail than what it does." As a result, Karen was concerned that the faculty wouldn't have a clear understanding of what the functions of the role really were.

During the early weeks of the school year, Karen devoted her attention first to matters regarding textbook ordering and then to initiating preparation for the accrediting evaluation to take place in the spring. She said she was unsure about what she should try to accomplish and hesitant about taking authority after Judy's reaction to her at administration meetings. In October, following prompting and support from Mary Anne, who told Karen to visit lower school classrooms and told

Judy she was telling Karen to do so, Karen became more assertive about taking action and becoming involved in decisions she felt were part of her role. Her attempts, however, met with considerable resistance.

Conflict Patterns Related to the Academic Director Position

Much of the conflict related to the academic director position came in the form of passive resistance to coordination attempts, the same pattern the curriculum coordinators had experienced. This pattern operated as follows. Administrators or department chairs would discuss issues or make decisions in which Karen felt she should have been involved because, from her perspective, they concerned curriculum. She would insist to those involved that she should participate in the discussion and/or decision. The typical response would be that that decision was not her job. Mary Anne would reinforce the others' authority over Karen's, saying frequently that a particular decision Karen thought was part of her domain was "the heads' job."

For example, early in the school year, Karen learned that the math department had made a decision in which she felt she should have been involved. She complained to Mary Anne that she was being shut out of departmental decisions. Mary Anne, however, told her that she herself often learned about decisions via hearsay. The school's business manager said after this that Karen was "more gloomy than she should be; she's finding a passive resistance in that she doesn't get included in things. People are not interested in having her tread on their turf."

A similar example took place during an administration meeting in November. Carol brought in a proposal from the science department for money for new equipment. As Karen recounted it, "I thought [the proposal] should go through me. . . . Carol asked Mary Anne if the equipment goes in the regular budget. They just kept talking. I tried to get in the conversation. Mary Anne gave it back to Carol. . . . Mary Anne said later she'd made the right decision [about who should be in on the discussion]. I said Mary Anne should have had Carol and me decide. I didn't get a satisfactory response from her."

Breakdown in the relationship between Karen and Mary Anne. Events like these caused a gradual breakdown in Mary Anne's and Karen's personal and professional relationships. During the previous six years, they had enjoyed a close friendship. Both of them, however, felt the friendship become strained shortly after Karen took on the new job and then deteriorate throughout the school year.

From Karen's point of view, the cause of the breakdown was Mary Anne's lack of support. Her perception was that the following type of pattern would occur. She would carry out an activity that she felt had gone well or would initiate a coordinating activity she felt was in her domain. She would experience Mary Anne as unsupportive at best, critical at worst, and never giving her positive feedback on her attempts regardless of how well they went. For example, in January, Karen organized the first in a series of meetings of the department chairs to discuss ways of coordinating the curriculum. This was the first such meeting at McLaughlin since the mid-1970s. Mary Anne and Carol both attended it, but Karen's impression of their participation was less than enthusiastic. Karen said that "Carol and Mary Anne sat in the back and whispered to each other. . . . Mary Anne came late and left early." Karen felt a lot had been accomplished at the meeting but, when she asked Mary Anne her reaction, Mary Anne had told her only that "that was a department chair meeting, not a curricular meeting."

Karen felt misled by Mary Anne. From her perspective, Mary Anne not only failed to support Karen's coordination efforts but also participated in "end runs" around her. For example, as part of Karen's job responsibilities, she was to give input on faculty hiring decisions, including significant job changes. During spring 1988, Karen heard that Mary Anne and Carol had approached one of the department heads, who reported to Karen, about becoming director of student affairs, but without consulting her. On another occasion, Mary Anne arranged for a middle school faculty candidate to interview with both Karen and the middle school head but told an upper school candidate to interview only with Carol. Karen said, "I signed up to do a job and thought there were certain rules and someone changed them without telling me. This isn't the job I signed up to do. I want to implement my vision, but I have to buck Mary Anne sometimes."

From Mary Anne's point of view, the breakdown in her and Karen's relationship was due primarily to Karen's developing excessive demands for personal affirmation. Karen would frequently complain to Mary Anne that Mary Anne wasn't supporting her enough. Mary Anne said in January that

> I may have the wrong personality in the job. . . . The present person is getting very unhappy, even though a lot of the job is getting done. . . . To make the situation

worse, I'm a problem in her life . . . there's an overdependence. . . . She's so desperate to make the job work . . . she really wants affirmation . . . it's almost as if she's had a severe attack of lack of confidence . . . she has succeeded in [several] things. As she succeeds she gets more and more miserable.

As the year progressed, due to Karen's constant complaining, Mary Anne found herself increasingly unable to respond to Karen. She started to avoid discussions with Karen and would find herself "clamming up" if they did talk.

Karen's attempts to get support from other sources. As Karen became more frustrated at her inability to gain affirmation from Mary Anne, she started turning to other school personnel to take her side in opposition to Mary Anne. This kind of action was prominent during the intense preparation for the evaluation during the winter and spring and affected the course of the preparation.

Early in December, when committees working on the self-study for the accrediting visit reported on how their work was going, they said that several upper school faculty members had expressed the belief that there were serious problems of alienation, isolation, and lack of trust between the upper school faculty and the administration. The committees agreed that these issues should be addressed as part of the preparation for the evaluation. Consequently, Karen designed a format for addressing them, and they were discussed at the next preparation meeting, which took place in January.

The self-study report to be sent to the accrediting team was due to be submitted by early March. All of the school heads were expected to make sure that the sections discussing their schools were written. As far as Karen could tell, however, as of late February, Carol hadn't begun to write the upper school report. Consequently, one Sunday, Karen and three members of the school's student affairs staff who were friends of hers spent the day at the school and wrote a draft of this report. In it they included the issues of alienation and mistrust that had been discussed at the January meeting. They didn't tell Mary Anne what they were doing. While they were working on the draft, Karen confided in the others about her worsening relationship with Mary Anne. They expressed their sympathy for her, agreeing she wasn't getting the support she needed. Karen eventually gave a copy of the draft they produced to Carol for revision.

In early March, Karen gave a draft copy of the upper school evaluation report to the upper school faculty. It included discussion of alienation and mistrust, because those had been a focus of the committee meetings. The next day, there was a faculty meeting to discuss the report. Some of the faculty challenged it, saying trust wasn't an issue. All those who had helped write the report were afraid to say they had been involved and so didn't say anything during the meeting. Consequently, discussion of mistrust and alienation was dropped almost entirely from the report. A few days later, Mary Anne learned that the student affairs staff had helped Karen write the report and that Karen had told them about their problems in dealing with each other. Mary Anne felt Karen was turning people against her.

About this time, Karen started telling a large number of people—not only the student affairs staff but also several administrators, department chairs, and other faculty members—about the problems she and Mary Anne were having. Some of these people started complaining to Mary Anne that she wasn't supporting Karen enough. Consequently, Mary Anne felt caught in a dilemma about how to deal with Karen. Sh⁻ said,

> If I should ask her today how her job is coming that's interpreted as pressure. If I don't ask her it's interpreted that I don't care. . . . I know now that she's talking with everybody about the fact that I'm not supporting her. She's putting me in a very, very difficult position. . . . I'm sure more needs to be done with the evaluation report. One section hadn't been pulled together from last week's meeting. Karen had taken it after the meeting, but wasn't telling anybody where it was. But I'm gun-shy.

The report eventually was finished and sent to the accrediting committee several weeks late. Its preparation had been slowed down considerably by disagreements such as the ones described here.

Conflict between Karen and Mary Anne during the evaluation. The conflict between Karen and Mary Anne came to a head during McLaughlin's evaluation, which took place in April. On the Sunday night the evaluation began, the accrediting team met with the school's administration to discuss how it would proceed and to plan the process for a faculty meeting that would take place during it. The accrediting team suggested a plan for the faculty meeting that was a little different than the school's typical procedure. Most of the administration favored the plan, but Karen, with some support from Judy, violently objected. The discussion became very heated. The accrediting team reluctantly went along with Karen's proposed alternate plan, which required Karen to develop a question to guide faculty discussion at the faculty meeting. On Monday morning, when the accrediting team was introduced to the school as a whole, chairs were set up for the accrediting team, Mary Anne, and the school heads. Karen complained about this, saying that because she had been in charge of preparing the evaluation, she should sit in the front of the room with the others. During that day, she tried to develop a question to guide the faculty discussion but couldn't do it. Mary Anne said she would help her, so on Monday night Karen and Mary Anne met to discuss the question. During that meeting, Mary Anne asked Karen why she was so upset. Karen told her that "everyone had a place to go with the accrediting team but me. . . . I felt like a fifth wheel."

Karen was so tired that at the next morning's accrediting teamadministration meeting someone asked her a question and she started crying. As a result of these types of events, the accrediting team kept asking Mary Anne about Karen's role. Although they reaccredited the school, they made a strong recommendation that Karen's role be clarified by the following September.

After the evaluation ended, Mary Anne said she was disappointed that the accrediting team had focused almost entirely on the academic director job and had missed the rest of the school. She added, "I know you [the researcher] have talked with some people about the academic director position. The evaluation team interviewed the whole school on this position. *Everyone . . .*"

Shortly after the evaluation, following up on the accrediting team's recommendation, Mary Anne told Karen that her job description and Mary Anne's overlapped and that where they overlapped Karen's would have to change. She told the researcher, "I'd like Karen to come to grips with the fact that this is a service job. . . . She's accountable to the heads for things in their schools . . . and [she needs to] understand the job in relation to the principal and then, having come to grips with that, decide whether she'd like to do the job."

Effects of the Conflicts on the Academic Director

Sense that patterns had not changed. Karen started to feel unable to accomplish what she believed were the primary objects of her job. In fact, she began to realize that the underlying patterns had not changed with the introduction of her role. She said, for example, that "the job [title] might have changed from curriculum coordinator to academic director, but the communication patterns didn't."

Sense of lack of authority leading to "paralysis." In December, Karen began describing herself as "paralyzed," a term she used frequently throughout the rest of the year. This issue was intricately linked with her sense that she lacked authority in her role: "Do I have the authority or do I have to win it? I'm not given it . . . I'm forced to wrest it out of the hands of others in a manipulative way."

Sense of isolation. In February, Karen began expressing feelings of extreme isolation. She said, "Sometimes I feel that no one is on my side."

Changed sense of herself. The year also had a strong impact on Karen's sense of her own competence. After the evaluation, she said that she was "feeling borderline stupid. I've made a jerk of myself." She felt she had "betrayed" Mary Anne at the evaluation. She added, "I've changed the way I look at myself 2000% this year. . . . I see things in a whole other perspective. It's a very tumultuous and confusing time."

Giving up attempts to coordinate. After a month of intense difficulty following the evaluation, when efforts to sort things out with Mary Anne were failing and her role description was being reduced to a service position, Karen virtually gave up trying to achieve the goals of her job. She said, "When I'm at an administration meeting I don't say much, because if I make a mistake and talk about the wrong thing, it's unforgivable."

Effects of the Conflicts on Others' Perceptions of the Academic Director

The evaluation had a strong impact on other administrators' sense of Karen. They started to describe her as overly concerned about power. For example, Judy Gallagher said, "Sometimes Mary Anne thinks Karen's trying to take over. At times I see where Karen might give that impression." Carol said she was upset that Karen was spending too much time focusing on the upper school when the academic director was supposed to focus on all three schools. Carol wondered what the faculty were thinking about who was in control in the upper school.

Effects of the Conflicts on Administrative Perceptions

In June 1988, the researcher made a preliminary report on her observations during the study to the members of the administration. At this meeting, several of the administrators said that, at least to this point, the implementation of the academic director role had had very little impact on coordination among the schools or departments. In fact, Mary Anne, Karen, and Carol each commented during the feedback meeting or shortly after it that nothing had changed with respect to coordination among the schools and departments. During that year, in their minds, the implementation of the position did not achieve its primary aim.

Analysis of the Conflict Patterns

Mary Anne designed the academic director position as a structural means of increasing coordination in a situation characterized by autonomy. The position was a public, formal role in the school. The conflicts surrounding it, however, operated on less formal and less public levels.

Expressions and Understandings of Conflict

Expressions of conflict. As our presentation indicates, repetitive patterns for conflict handling had developed long before the implementation of the new role—in fact, before Mary Anne had become McLaughlin's principal—and these continued to manifest themselves throughout implementation of the new position. The most frequent pattern was passive resistance to the curriculum coordinators' or the academic director's initiatives concerning coordination of curriculum. During the 1987-88 school year, this pattern was implemented most frequently (although not only) by the lower school head and by the upper school head, with the latter typically supported by the principal.

This repetitive pattern may best be described as a strong passive resistance "script" (e.g., Gioia and Manz 1985; Gioia and Poole 1984; Schank and Abelson 1977) that school personnel had, albeit unknowingly, been operating from since the 1970s. This script derived from the shared perspective that emphasized and valued the autonomy of the different academic units. The means for implementing it during the 1987-88 school year included school personnel ignoring the academic director and calling decisions "the heads' job." Some of these means, especially ignoring the academic director, were essentially private activities that were difficult for Karen (or anyone else) to confront publicly. The script seemed to be evoked and applied virtually every time decisions related to coordination of curriculum were to be made. Because of it, school personnel did not have to deal publicly with issues of coordination. Their almost instinctive response of passive resistance sufficed as a way of subverting the introduction of the new perspective.

The enactment of the passive resistance script caused the academic director to become more and more frustrated in her attempts to have an impact through formal channels such as administration meetings. Consequently, she began to take informal actions: She increasingly resorted to telling others about how unsupported she felt, first the principal and then other faculty, administration, and staff. She also tried to have her position recognized as powerful at the school's accrediting evaluation. Her strategy was unsuccessful, however; it focused others' attention on her personal difficulties, led the principal to redesign the position in a way that reduced its power, contributed to her sense of failure, and fostered a breakdown in her friendship with the principal.

Understandings. While some school personnel used the term passive resistance to describe some conflicts, it was clear that that term did not describe their perception of the central events of the year. Rather, the conflict that assumed central importance during the year for Mary Anne, Karen, and other school personnel was an interpersonal, primarily private one between Mary Anne and Karen. As one dimension of this conflict, both Mary Anne and Karen made personal attributions about the other. Karen said Mary Anne was personally unsupportive, and Mary Anne came to see Karen as overdependent and, possibly, "the wrong personality" for the academic director position. Other people made personal attributions about Karen as well. For example, the business manager said Karen was more gloomy than she should be and, after the evaluation, Carol and Judy began to describe Karen as personally overconcerned with power. Karen eventually came to view herself as "borderline stupid" and as having made a jerk of herself.

Relationship Between Patterns of
Conflict Handling and Change

We have suggested a way conflict may constrain second order change. The manner in which conflict is handled may reinforce the already established perspective (see Black 1990) and, in the process, "split" the original and new perspectives (Smith and Berg 1987) rather than enabling dialectical interaction between them. These events happened at McLaughlin.

Even though the academic director's job description included a different type of role and more formal power than the curriculum coordinators', the informal passive resistance script evoked in response to other coordination attempts virtually reproduced the conflict-handling patterns that had been established before. These in turn clearly reinforced the autonomy perspective (see Black 1990). The academic director initially responded somewhat more aggressively to this pattern than the curriculum coordinators had. Nevertheless, in her responses, she focused on her personal difficulties in her role (e.g., she emphasized the lack of support she was receiving). Because several curriculum coordinators had already been "defeated" by the patterns of passive resistance, it is likely that other school personnel viewed her experiences as consistent with those of her predecessors, not as a serious challenge to their autonomy. Thus her responses likely reinforced the passive resistance script even as they obstensibly challenged it.

The conflict-handling mode implied by passive resistance is a kind of avoidance of conflict in that grievances are dealt with by the curtailment of interaction (Black 1990). Brown (1983) notes that avoidance often promotes isolation of the conflicting parties, supporting their autonomy but certainly constraining change in the direction of greater coordination. Avoidance of conflict was manifested in many ways. For example, the upper school and lower school heads, the principal, and the department chairs simply made curriculum decisions independent of the academic director. Conflicts that did occur were rarely openly discussed. Indeed, as tensions between the principal and academic director mounted, their meetings and discussions decreased in frequency.

The establishment of the academic director position was, in and of itself, a controversial move on the principal's part; it publicly and formally acknowledged the need for coordination across schools and departments. The principal introduced the position somewhat obliquely, however. When the faculty and administration met to begin the school year in September 1987, she said little about the new position and what she did say referred as much to what the academic director would not do as to what she *would* do. In this way, the principal raised the issue of coordination but in an understated way that avoided a public confrontation between coordination and autonomy perspectives.

Personnel at McLaughlin also "split" the autonomy and coordination perspectives. For example, the upper and lower school heads and department chairs all tended to take the side of autonomy as opposed to coordination when disagreement related to these perspectives arose. Although the principal had supported the coordination perspective when she designed the academic director position, her actions during the school year were also more consistent with the autonomy perspective when coordination was challenged.

Smith and Berg (1987) suggest that splitting different perspectives veils the real underlying dynamic below an apparent conflict, thereby causing group members to feel "paralyzed." These events occurred. The ostensible conflict became an interpersonal one between Karen and Mary Anne, with autonomy remaining unchallenged. Further, both Karen and Mary Anne experienced a sense of being "stuck": Karen perceived herself as "paralyzed," and Mary Anne "clammed up" and became "gun-shy" in attempts to deal with Karen. The original objective of the academic director position—to increase coordination for the sake of increased innovation and a more holistic education—was certainly not realized during the school year. Instead, the primary change that occurred was in Karen's and Mary Anne's relationship and in perceptions of Karen, especially Karen's perceptions of herself.

Discussion

In the study reported here, the process conflict took interfered with, rather than fostered, the course of second order change. Consequently, this discussion will focus on ways of understanding negative relationships between conflict and change, especially changes aimed at increasing coordination.

Schools have an almost legendary reputation as settings in which it is hard to achieve particular proposed changes (e.g., Rossman, Corbett, and Firestone 1988; Sarason 1971). Established patterns in schools are very difficult to alter.

Schools' difficulties in implementing change have been attributed to a number of factors. For example, Sarason (1971) suggested that schools typically develop behavioral and programmatic "regularities" (what have come to be called "scripts") for enacting shared perspectives. These behavioral regularities are overlearned by school personnel and often not addressed by people who propose changes. Difficulties in achieving change also result from the loosely coupled structure of schools, wherein the different elements of schools are tied together weakly or infrequently

(Weick 1976). This type of structure leads influence and coordination attempts to be diminished as they move through the system.

Our exploration has yielded findings that are consistent with these arguments but suggest additional, interrelated dimensions. At McLaughlin, there was indeed loose coupling between different departments and schools. This structure was supported by a well-developed passive resistance script that effectively avoided coordination of curriculum and that was able to channel potential threats regarding coordination to other organizational locations. The combination of structure, script, and understanding was expressed by various administrators and department chairs in the metaphor of "fiefdoms," a term that accurately communicated the collective view and emotional reality of the school (see Srivastva and Barrett 1988). The combination suggests why the conflict patterns emerged as they did: Avoidance and passive resistance do not imply any "active" confrontation between conflicting parties. Passive resistance is thus an appropriate conflict-handling mechanism for maintaining a culture that is largely autonomous.

The Relationship Between Conflict and Change

In situations in which structures and conflict patterns are mutually supportive of autonomy, achievement of shifts in perspective in the direction of coordination is extremely difficult. This study showed how pervasively conflict patterns could reinforce autonomy, even when attempts were made to challenge it.

Actually, several methods by which administrators and managers might achieve coordination in autonomous settings have been proposed. For example, Morgan (1981) and Weick (1982) suggest that organizations may counter autonomy by exercising control over the selection and training of organizational members so they share common norms and by trying to design systems so that functional interdependence among units inhibits autonomy of the parts.

While these proposals suggest some important means of strengthening coordination, they all avoid overt confrontations between autonomy and coordination as well as the possibility of organizational members considering both autonomy and coordination as simultaneously valid concerns (Feldman 1989). Moreover, they fail to consider how conflict-handling patterns that are already established in an organization may support autonomy, even if attempts are made to introduce another perspective. Consequently, they are likely to reinforce perceptions of coordination as imposed by management rather than as the shared concern of a variety of organizational members.

There is no magic formula for achieving second order change in general or changes in perspective away from autonomy and toward a perspective that encompasses autonomy and coordination in particular. Our results are consistent, however, with the notion that one necessary element for achieving such change, in addition to the surfacing of differing perspectives, is change in the patterns or scripts for handling conflict. Means of changing scripts are less well known than ways of reinforcing them. At least two ideas that are relevant to this issue have been suggested, however. One involves the development of situations or events (especially crises) so drastically different than the usual situation at the organization that they short-circuit the enactment of typically applied scripts, because no one knows how to deal with them (e.g., all the students do poorly on standardized tests; see Gioia and Poole 1984; Rossman, Corbett, and Firestone 1988). Another is the development of models or exemplars of new types of behavior for responding to the stimulus that evokes the script (e.g., the principal demands that the academic director and the school heads publicly negotiate disagreements between them regarding curriculum; see Gioia and Manz 1985). Even these changes are unlikely to be adequate unless they are accompanied by clear introductions of an alternative perspective and, perhaps, structural change that expresses this perspective (Moch and Bartunek 1990).

Methods such as instigating script changes, which may need to be applied strongly and consistently if movement toward new perspectives is to be accomplished, require that organizational change agents—formal change agents and others, such as managers—are able to see particular organizational events as reflecting repetitive patterns of interactions and not only being indicative of individuals' personality characteristics (see Sproull and Hofmeister 1986). Such methods also require that change agents are able to diagnose organizational perspectives and their expressions in scripted activities such as conflict handling and imagine ways of acting that short-circuit or are inconsistent with these patterns. As our results indicate, this type of awareness is very difficult to achieve. Increasing change agents' consciousness of shared perspectives and conflict patterns that express them, however, may begin to make the task a little easier.

Conclusion

Literature regarding second order organizational change has focused on the need to surface differences in perspectives and to allow different perspectives to interact with each other in a dialectical pattern (e.g., Moch and Bartunek 1990). As we have demonstrated in this chapter, achievement of this type of interaction is often likely to be difficult, in part because of the ways conflict mechanisms operate. These mechanisms may enable organizational members to avoid conflict on the level of perspective and instead focus their attention on conflicts somewhat removed from the original source. Full understanding of ways of achieving second order change requires appreciation of the intricacies of mutually reinforcing structures, perspectives, and conflict patterns as well as ways of modifying all of these simultaneously. There is still a considerable amount to be learned about effective means of achieving such change.

References

Bartunek, J. M. 1984. Changing interpretive schemes and organizational restructuring: The example of a religious order. *Administrative Science Quarterly* 29:355-72.
—1988. The dynamics of personal and organizational reframing. In *Paradox and transformation: Towards a theory of change in organization and management,* ed. R. E. Quinn and K. S. Cameron, 137-62. Cambridge, Mass.: Ballinger.
—1991. McLaughlin School. In *Cases in organization development,* ed. A. M. Glassman and T. G. Cummings, 396-414. Homewood, Ill.: Irwin.
Bartunek, J. M., and J. L. Ringuest. 1989. Enacting new perspectives through work activities during organizational transformation. *Journal of Management Studies* 26:541-60.
Black, D. 1990. The elementary forms of conflict management. In *New Directions in the study of justice, law, and social control,* ed. Arizona School of Justice Studies, Arizona State University, 43-69. New York: Plenum.
Brown, L. D. 1983. *Managing conflict at organizational interfaces.* Reading, Mass.: Addison-Wesley.
Cameron, K. S. 1986. Effectiveness as paradox: Consensus and conflict in conceptions of organizational effectiveness. *Management Science* 32:539-53.
Child, J., and C. Smith. 1987. The context and process of organizational transformation: Cadbury Limited in its sector. *Journal of Management Studies* 24:565-93.
Feldman, S. P. 1989. The broken wheel: The inseparability of autonomy and control in innovation within organizations. *Journal of Management Studies* 26:83-102.
Gioia, D. A., and C. C. Manz. 1985. Linking cognition and behavior: A script processing interpretation of vicarious learning. *Academy of Management Review* 10:527-35.

Gioia, D. A., and P. P. Poole. 1984. Scripts in organizational behavior. *Academy of Management Review* 9:449-59.

Hinings, C. R., and R. Greenwood. 1988. *The dynamics of strategic change.* Oxford: Basil Blackwell.

Kolb, D. M. 1987. Who are organizational third parties, and what do they do? In *Research on negotiation in organizations.* Vol. 1, ed. R. S. Lewicki, B. H. Sheppard, and M. H. Bazerman, 207-27. Greenwich, Conn.: JAI.

Levy, A., and U. Merry. 1986. *Organizational transformation.* New York: Praeger.

Moch, M. K., and J. M. Bartunek. 1990. *Creating alternative realities at work: The quality of work life experiment at FoodCom.* New York: Harper Business.

Morgan, G. 1981. The schismatic metaphor and its implications for organizational analysis. *Organization Studies* 2:23-44.

Pettigrew, A. M. 1973. *The politics of organizational decision-making.* London: Tavistock.

Ross, L. 1977. The intuitive psychologist and his shortcomings: Distortions in the attribution process. In *Advances in experimental social psychology.* Vol. 10, ed. L. Berkowitz, 337-400. New York: Academic Press.

Rossman, G. B., H. D. Corbett, and W. A. Firestone. 1988. *Change and effectiveness in schools: A cultural perspective.* Albany: State University of New York Press.

Sarason, S. B. 1971. *The culture of the school and the problem of change.* Boston: Allyn & Bacon.

Schank, R. C., & R. P. Abelson. 1977. *Scripts, plans, goals and understanding.* Hillsdale, N.J.: Lawrence Erlbaum.

Smith, K. K., and D. N. Berg. 1987. *Paradoxes of group life.* San Francisco: Jossey-Bass.

Smith, K. K., V. M. Simmons, and T. B. Thames. 1989. "Fix the women": An intervention into organizational conflict based on parallel process thinking. *Journal of Applied Behavioral Science* 25:11-30.

Sproull, L. S., and K. R. Hofmeister. 1986. Thinking about implementation. *Journal of Management* 12:43-60.

Srivastva, S., and F. J. Barrett. 1988. The transforming nature of metaphors in group development: A study in group theory. *Human Relations* 41:31-64.

Weick, K. E. 1976. Educational organizations as loosely coupled systems. *Administrative Science Quarterly* 21:1-19.

—1982. Management of organizational change among loosely coupled elements. In *Change in organizations,* ed. P. S. Goodman, 375-408. San Francisco: Jossey-Bass.

6

The Culture of Mediation

Private Understandings in the
Context of Public Conflict

RAYMOND A. FRIEDMAN

Organizations and interorganizational fields (Warren 1967) are made up of subunits that have conflicting interests and conflicting points of view. These differences are essential for organizational functioning: They allow specialized talents and perspectives to develop (Follett 1942) and provide members with strategies of action (Swidler 1986), values (Bartunek 1984), and identities (Louis 1980). But the different groups, with their different identities and perspectives, need to be coordinated as well (Lawrence and Lorsch 1967). Conflict and cooperation are both essential.

Too often, we see intergroup relations in and among organizations as either conflictual (Raelin 1985) *or* cooperative (Peters and Waterman

AUTHOR'S NOTE: Earlier versions of this chapter were presented at the annual meeting of the American Sociological Association, August 1987, and at a session of the labor relations seminar at the Sloan School of Management at MIT, May 1988. I would like to thank Jean M. Bartunek, Bob Eccles, Wendy Griswold, Deborah M. Kolb, Ed Laumann, and John Van Maanen for their comments and suggestions on this chapter, and the UAW, International Harvester, and Barbara Marsh for their help in conducting the research. This research was funded by the Kaiser Foundation of the Reuther Archives at Wayne State University, the Harper Fellowship at the University of Chicago, and the division of research at Harvard Business School.

1982). In fact, conflict and cooperation occur simultaneously. On a public and collective level, intergroup differences are created and reinforced as essential ingredients to support in-group culture and identity. On a more private and interpersonal level, subgroups develop that are specialized in connecting opposing groups. These subgroups function as translators, conveying and receiving meaning across cultural divides. They also function as buffers between the conflicting groups, protecting the integrity and reproduction of the separate conflicting cultural systems and limiting direct confrontation between them. These groups serve both to *link* opposing groups and to provide a *buffer* between them—both to bypass and to maintain differences and conflict.

To act as interstitial conveyors of meaning, members of this subgroup develop rules of interaction that are distinct and apart from those of the constituent groups. A social space is created that allows commonalities to be discovered, relationships to be established, and trust to be developed among members of these subgroups, all within the context of public conflict. A specialized subculture forms that supports their collective function as a mediating[1] force between publicly opposing groups. The subculture of this interstitial group is called a "culture of mediation."

In this chapter, I will describe the culture of mediation and use that concept to analyze labor-management conflict, contract negotiations, and the 1979 strike of International Harvester by the UAW. The findings are based on archival research and extensive interviews with all negotiators and top executives for both the company and the union as well as a sample of local leaders, managers, and workers. The case study is reported in full in Friedman (1987).

The Culture of Mediation

For organizations and groups to function, they have to manage external relations, gaining resources, support, and information (Thompson 1967; Ancona 1990). The people who make those connections are responsible for both understanding the ideas and positions of their members (which they convey externally) and understanding the ideas and positions of external groups (which they convey internally). As Adams (1976, 1177) put it:

Effective transactions require that BRPs [i.e., "boundary role persons"] have knowledge of and be sensitive to the preferences, needs, beliefs, attitudes, norms, and aspirations of the external organization with which they are dealing. Without this, successful impression management, negotiation and bargaining are, at best, made difficult or a matter of chance since successful transactions must, in the long run at least, be successful from the point of view of both a BRP's organization and the external organization.

But, to develop the kind of mutual understanding that Adams implies, boundary spanners from the different organizations or groups have to be able to trust one another enough to be open and frank when they meet. This, in turn, depends on the development of relationships, trust in reputations, the existence of a common symbol system among these boundary spanners, and mechanisms to produce status equality between the parties during interaction. All of these factors, though, run in the face of constituent worries that the boundary spanner cannot be trusted because she or he is spending too much time with outsiders, sees things from the opponent's point of view, and represents the opponent in discussions with constituents. If trust develops across boundaries (i.e., between opposing boundary spanners), it cannot be displayed too publicly.[2]

Because representatives of different groups cannot publicly acknowledge cooperation, it becomes difficult to formally institutionalize trust relations. They must depend, by contrast, on *unwritten* rules of interaction that are known and followed among boundary spanners. These trust-supporting behavioral norms are reinforced by implied moral judgments (Garfinkel 1967), and the anger that violations of those norms produce, not by formalized legal rules.[3] In this sense, boundary spanners, considered together as a collective unit, operate according to a distinct subculture: one that provides strategies for action and norms of interaction that facilitate trust and enable parties to be open and honest but in a way that is not blatantly visible to constituents.

This boundary spanning group, supported by its unique subculture, serves two functions. First, by providing a context where representatives from opposing organizations can interact in an open and trusting way with each other, and learn how the other organization views the world, each organization develops personnel who have the capacity to understand how the organization and its actions are viewed by others.[4] Second, by isolating that capacity for understanding in a separate subunit—by mediating the contact between the two organizations—the boundary spanning group protects the opposing groups from direct confrontation with each other. The mediating group serves as both cultural translator and cultural buffer between opposing groups. It provides a mechanism through which groups and organizations can coordinate action while still retaining independence as distinct entities. It supports intergroup integration while simultaneously protecting the integrity of the separate groups.

The Labor-Management Cultural Opposition

The relationship between labor and management is one example of intergroup relations in organizations (and, given the fact that most unions in the United States exist as independent bodies outside of particular organizations, it is also an example of interorganizational relations). Labor and management have different worldviews, which support their group identities and protect their interests. These world views, as exhibited by International Harvester (IH) and the UAW in the 1970s, and described in analyses of managerial ideology in the postwar era, can be summarized as three sets of opposing ideals.

The first opposition is between the future orientation of the company and the historical focus of the union. Comparing UAW publications and IH annual reports, the UAW makes great efforts to remind its membership of their history, including their past struggles and accomplishments (which many members have come to take for granted), while IH looks to the past only as a way of focusing on the future—they emphasize new products and future growth.

The second opposition is between the union's "logic of rights" and the company's "logic of efficiency." A fundamental premise of much of the UAW's literature is that workers have rights, that the company violates them, and that the union's role is to guarantee that those rights are not violated. By contrast, a fundamental premise of the "American business creed" (Sutton et al. 1956)—and one that is represented in IH's annual reports—is that all actions can be justified in terms of the efficiency that results. Efficiency takes on a moral imperative for management because it guarantees greater material comfort for all as well as greater profits for shareholders.

Union	Management
Logic of Rights	Logic of Efficiency
Heritage of Memory	Future-Oriented
Ideal of Equality	Ideal of Control

Figure 6.1. Union-Management Conceptual Oppositions

And, third, the union's "ideal of equality" is opposed to the company's "ideal of control." For the union, group solidarity, mutual assistance, and equality are basic premises that guide union behavior. Equality is an ideal—not only within the union but between workers and management. For management, by contrast, the ideal is control over resources—including labor. As Sutton et al. (1956) pointed out, the very fact that management is not secure in its control over the factors that influence business (e.g., interest rates and consumers) makes it that much more important to imagine oneself to be in control of the few things that are within reach of management, including labor. Harrison (1982, 8) supports this point:

> Labor relations problems were particularly able to probe the sensitive spots in the businessman's psyche, because they challenged his justifications of his own authority, privilege, and power. They presented a real threat to his interests too, of course. But his reactions were not purely cool and rational.

These three conceptual oppositions are shown in Figure 6.1. They are rooted in the particular differences between IH and the UAW in the 1970s, but could be considered a fair representation of the differences between labor and management generally.

The conflict between labor and management at IH and elsewhere is composed, then, of a basic difference in worldview, identity, and behavioral expectations. Conflict is not over the defense of material interests alone but also over the defense of concepts of life. For both the union and management, their respective worldviews have inherent value—they do not exist merely to serve instrumental purposes or underlying "interests." There exists for unions, "value commitments which are ideologically opposed to the values which underlie the [business] organization's procedural norms" (Fox 1971, 49).

Bridging the Gap: The Culture of Mediation and
Contract Negotiations at International Harvester

Labor and management at IH were deeply divided ideologically in
the 1970s, but they also worked together, coordinated their actions, and
solved problems when they arose. This occurred during work every
day, in grievance meetings or joint committees, and during contract negotiations. In each of these cases, mechanisms existed to bridge the gap
between the two sides. In the rest of this chapter, I will look at that
mechanism for one point of contact between these two sides: contract
negotiations. The analysis is based on individual and group interviews
with approximately 100 union officials, executives, workers, and managers in 1985.[5] They were asked to explain (a) what generally occurs
in negotiations and (b) what actually happened in the negotiations that
resulted in a six-month strike in 1979 and 1980. The first part—what
they generally expected in negotiations—is reported in this section.

Negotiations, in most cases, are semipublic events. Because of that,
they can function not only to create an agreement but also to display
and reinforce the values, ideals, and cohesion of each side. Negotiation
includes public ritual that carries symbolic meaning. It is also a situation where public bluffs can be of strategic importance (Schelling
1960). For both of these reasons, there is a great deal of "show" in labor
negotiations.

Union negotiators at International Harvester refer to the company's
typical opening presentation as, in the words of one union pro, the "dog
and pony show":

> The company told us that they had to get competitive. We call it the dog and pony
> show because we see the same thing, not identical, from all the companies.
> Sometimes we get a movie, sometimes we get a slide presentation.

They view the union's own demands in a similar light. The union presents a
"laundry list" of demands to the company, explained a union team member:
"Obviously, in negotiations, you went in there and threw a 10-pound list of
demands across the table."

While this "show" is important, taking it "too seriously" would in-
terfere with the process of finding an agreement. The initial presentation of a laundry list of demands is, explained the union pro quoted
above, a starting point in negotiations—"everybody understands that."

"In the meantime," this pro explained, "responsible people are taking a look at these things and deciding where to go and then a time comes to get a settlement." Company negotiators, he added, "obviously knew that you weren't serious about every one [of the demands], that you would settle for a fraction of the items."

This expectation that the company negotiators knew the rituals of negotiations was met by negotiators on the company side. They explained that one of the primary responsibilities of their job was to interpret the union's statements: "I'd evaluate, first, how much of it was 100% or how much of it was 50% or how much of it was 25% for effect, and then we'd discuss it in our negotiations committee meeting," explained one company pro. Another company pro added:

> You learn the body language, the sign language, the inflection in the voice. And I think it was probably accurate to say that both sides could read a lot into something that was said, the order in which it was said, the time devoted to it, the body language while it's going on. Clearly an indication was: "Well, that can go to subcommittee." That would just tell you something. It wouldn't tell you it was unimportant; it would just tell you that it should be resolved to both parties' satisfaction without coming to the main table.

These negotiators worry that, if you take the rhetoric seriously—if, as the first company pro quoted above added, you "don't understand the rituals, [and instead] see trivia as serious—you can make some very big mistakes."

Such mistakes were avoided through knowledge of the people with whom one was negotiating and knowledge of the process of negotiation. Experienced negotiators on both sides expected that, during certain stages of the negotiations, unreasonable demands would be made to test the waters or to please constituents. But they also knew that over time many of those demands would "fall off the table" and negotiations would become more intimate. Interpretations were calibrated to this expected routine. Interpretations were also calibrated to people. The second company pro explained:

> There are high stakes. It's a very intense time. It can be a marathon time on occasions and people do and say things that they'd rather not have said. If that is taken to heart, and the environment is not taken into consideration, and there's no solid basis to bump it against—like, "Gee, I know that guy, he can't mean that, I know he said it but he can't mean it because I know him and he wouldn't do that"—if you don't have that kind of a base to bump it against, it can cause some serious problems.

These personal ties, and the trust they engendered, also helped negotiators meet out of the public eye. A third company pro explained:

> You learn to assess who you can get a signal from off the record and who you can't,
> and who's giving you b.s., and who's not telling you the whole story. There is some
> of that conversation that goes on and that comes from long relationships.

It was not expected that negotiators would reveal their secrets during these
"sidebar" contacts but that these contacts would provide a mechanism to clear
up potential misunderstandings. This company negotiator continued:

> You're not going to get a clear signal that says, "Hey, the union's ready to move
> on mandatory overtime." What you're going to get is, "Hey, why don't you try this
> kind of approach." And it may be nothing more than a way to start the conversation
> going. Or, the message might be, "Why did you present the issue that way? You
> really screwed up." "Well, how did we screw up?" "Well, did you know that Bill
> at Louisville feels this way about it and he's got a particular issue?" Sometimes
> how you present things can either turn them on or turn them off.

In addition to these mechanisms of signaling and sidebar discussions,
more direct and open communication was facilitated by the tendency to
shrink the size of the negotiating teams over time. Toward the end of
bargaining, explained another company pro,

> your committees get smaller and smaller and instead of having a circus with a
> hundred people in the room you get down to small committees of 8 or 10 and then
> at some point in time maybe only four of you. [At this point] both sides could try
> to be as honest and frank as you could in negotiations: "Look, this isn't going to
> go away. We can't do that."

This process of small group negotiating creates some tensions within the
union, but it was largely accepted as a necessary evil. A union local president
and member of the bargaining council[6] explained that the council would
"bitch and moan" about the meetings, but, he added, "it was accepted as a
way of life. I presume it's probably a lot easier for the company and the union
to operate that way. Don't have the whole mass meeting there."

When this system of personal ties and common expectations among
negotiators was in place, company and union negotiators were able to
work together relatively well. One of the company pros quoted above
explained:

Pat Greathouse [the UAW's chief negotiator at IH] had been with our company for years and years and years and knew Roscoe Batts [IH's former negotiator] extremely well. So they were able to—for better or worse—sit down and talk positions through and find out where the hot buttons were and when the settlement time was.

A similar perspective on Greathouse and Batts existed among union negotiators, one of whom explained:

They knew the process of negotiation. They knew the feelings of each other. They knew what each other's movements were going to be. They knew how far they could go with each other.

The Culture of Mediation as a
Social System: Negotiator Embeddedness

But what prevents either side from using the "inside track" to fool its opponent? In other words, what prevents tactical bluffs (Schelling 1960) and opportunistic use of private channels of information flow? The answer, I believe, is social "embeddedness." In contrast to the game theoretic view (Young 1975), negotiations are not carried out by anonymous parties making one-shot deals. Over time, despite their positions as representatives of opposing camps, negotiators at IH establish (as do many company and union negotiators) social relations with each other. In Granovetter's (1985) words, they are "embedded" in a common social network: These people (a) have dealt with each other in the past, (b) know from personal experience how the other tends to act, (c) expect to have to deal with each other in the future, and (d) have a relationship overlaid with social content. To the degree that embeddedness is sustained, there is less opportunity for misrepresentation.

The first three aspects of embeddedness focus on the continuity of interaction. The impact of this aspect of negotiations is seen most clearly in the use of "reputation." As a union negotiator at IH explained: "In this business all you've got is your own integrity, your own reputation—there isn't anything else. If you don't have that you don't have anything." These people know that their jobs depend on getting a bit of information, assistance, advice, and cooperation from various players in the labor-relations game. If you are considered untrustworthy, then you will not be given the assistance of signals and sidebar discussions, and your "word" will not hold any weight. Reputation is a critical resource to be defended if at all possible. And it is clear that trustworthiness is a highly salient attribute. People are judged to a very large degree in terms of their honesty. Given that relations are ongoing, attempts to misrepresent one's position may cost a negotiator dearly.

The fourth aspect of embeddedness is also visible in IH-UAW negotiations: Social content develops in the negotiating relationships. Despite the competitive structure of negotiations, negotiators go out for a beer together upon occasion and "talk about the kids." There is an awareness that people on each side are just doing their jobs and that statements made in negotiations are not to be taken seriously. As one negotiator put it: "Negotiations were almost a social event."

Even without beer drinking, there are mechanisms to generate a sense of commonality among negotiators. One is what Walton and McKersie (1965) call "rights of common fate." The example they use is the marathon bargaining session. By staying up all night bargaining, members on both sides share an unpleasant experience together. They are thereafter more "alike" than before. In my interviews, the marathon bargaining session was discussed as if it were a rite of passage into the fraternity of negotiators.

Another way of making negotiators seem more alike, and thereby (through the logic of balance theory) generating positive sentiments (Walton and McKersie 1965), is to minimize status differences. The marathon bargaining session can be seen in this light: After a long night of bargaining, negotiators on both sides appear equally tired, dirty, and unkempt. If there was a difference before in terms of style or dress, it is neutralized by 24 hours of bargaining and 10 cups of coffee. Going out for a beer also symbolizes status equality, as does the common use of "shop talk" and a linguistic style that includes "cussing" like a "normal guy." As one of the pros on management's bargaining committee put it:

> If you approach it in an educational arrogance kind of way, you're just wasting your time. Even though you might not know the other side of the bargaining table that well, there needs to be a credibility and an understanding and you have to respect that they know more about the nitty gritty of what goes on at the local level than you do. While we might know more about the economics of things and what some other companies are doing, their sources of information are pretty good. You just can't take an arrogant approach to it. And you really do have to recognize that there is a lot of knowledge there and a lot of ability in terms of their own situation and their own negotiation. It's not an uneven match-up by any means.

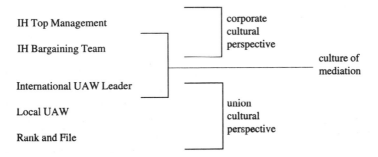

Figure 6.2. IH-UAW Cultural Overlap

To a certain degree, then, there usually develops at IH mutual trust, understanding, and even camaraderie between the two sides. They go through negotiations together; status differences are avoided; and there are moments when interaction can occur on a purely social level. To the degree that negotiators become embedded in such an ongoing social network, deceit and opportunism are greatly limited.

In sum, the group of people who interact in negotiations at IH, and at other companies, form a distinct group with its own conceptions, values, behavioral routines, and symbols—that is, its own culture. The value system emphasizes honesty and trust; the behavioral routine includes the movement toward private forms of interaction; there are common symbols used to send and read signals; and there is a clear conceptual scheme that highlights an established "script" for negotiations and an awareness of constituent pressures on negotiators.

Thus, while IH and the UAW each have separate cultural perspectives, the culture of mediation provides a third, connective cultural system. Schematically, the pattern looks as shown in Figure 6.2.

Traditionally, the negotiation process at IH was directed and managed by negotiating pros who shared the understandings and expectations of this culture of mediation. These understandings allowed them, as a group, to shape an agreement while still protecting both sides from having to publicly "compromise their ideals." The particular cultural understandings of this interstitial group helped to buffer the two sides from direct contact and confrontation while also providing a system for conveying information and meaning between the two sides.

The 1979 Negotiations at International Harvester:
Choosing to Bypass the Culture of Mediation

Bargaining in 1979 began, for International Harvester, as an attempt to regain control over the plants and especially to make some changes in work rules that management thought were too costly. Management thought they would provoke a strike (perhaps even a long one—a month or two) but were surprised to find themselves in a bitter, six-month-long, protracted battle where some workers were antagonized to the point of being self-destructive. The company lost over $200 million, by their own estimates, and those losses contributed greatly to the virtual collapse of the company in the ensuing years.

The labor-relations strategy that produced this strike was part of a larger project by IH management to revive a company that at the time was seen as a slumbering giant. Since its formation in 1902, IH was not just a company—it was an institution. It was the largest producer of agricultural implements and trucks in the country in the 1940s, achieved sales of more than $1 billion by 1950, and was seen as among the most stable and prestigious companies to work for in the Midwest. But that same strength turned to overconfidence, which in turn led to over-expansion, the creation of a bloated bureaucracy, and a lack of financial controls (Marsh 1985). These problems were finally addressed in the early 1970s. The solution was to replace much of top management with new people who would not reproduce the company's old bad habits. This "fresh blood" would break from tradition and revitalize the company. One part of this process would be to make changes in the way that labor relations were handled.

That goal was accomplished by wrenching control over bargaining away from old-hand bargaining pros and putting it the hands of the new chief executive officer (CEO), Archie McCardell, and the company's new vice-president of human resources, Grant Chandler. Although some pros remained, they were fewer, were kept out of leadership positions, and were largely ignored.[7] The new leaders, who had little labor relations experience and none with the UAW or heavy manufacturing, would take a very different approach than that taken by the pros: Instead of a "laundry list" of demands, the company immediately identified only seven demands and stuck with them; on the first day of negotiations, the company's spokesman openly acknowledged that IH would "match the pattern" set in Detroit for economic issues (thereby lessening the union's ability to appear to have "gained" those pay levels), and negotiations were moved out of the social atmosphere of the Drake Hotel and into the more formal atmosphere of the company's meeting rooms. Sidebar discussions were minimized, and symbolic issues were ignored by the company's new negotiators (the company's lead bargainer was ridiculed by union leaders, for example, for wearing silk suits during negotiations and even an ascot on one weekend).

In sum, they staffed negotiations with people who did not know or understand the cultural prescriptions that had governed the interactions of negotiators. They did not enact the behavior patterns that were expected (including sidebar discussions, the use of signaling, and the development of social ties across the table), so that private understandings among the pros could not occur. This had two effects: it (a) disempowered the union's negotiating pros and (b) forced contact between the company and the union to occur only on a public level.

Disempowering the Pros:
The Loss of Private Understanding

For both union and company pros (i.e., the ones who had been embedded in social relations with each other and knew the culture of mediation), the company's bargaining strategy was disturbing because it eliminated their ability to establish channels of communication across the bargaining table and thus their ability to develop the private understandings needed to manage and guide the negotiations.

On the union side, negotiations were directed by three top union officials (Pat Greathouse, Art Shy, and Horace Williams) who were highly experienced and knew the rituals and expectations of negotiations. These people were frustrated at the "incompetence" of the company's negotiators (especially their lead negotiators). Williams explained:

> They offered us everything. They weren't trying any back to work movement, they weren't trying to bust the union. They weren't trying to do any of these things, they just felt that before they'd do all the other things, they had to have [their demands]. But the most stupid thing was then telling people all that: "Sure, you can have all these things, but now here's the things that we have to have."

The company's negotiators did not understand the importance of conveying information in a more private fashion through signals; nor were the company's negotiators able to read the signals that the union sent.

Moreover, Shy complained, company negotiators were unwilling to meet in sidebar discussions: "You couldn't meet with them. When we ended the strike with them, it was right at the bargaining table." There was no sense that the company negotiators had the capacity to understand the industry, the union's positions, or the politics that these leaders faced; neither were these negotiators truly free to develop that understanding. According to Greathouse, Chandler was "a transmission guy from the guys upstairs that were making raw pronouncements back down to the bargaining table."

On the company side, there were negotiating pros on the bargaining team (albeit not in a position to influence negotiations) who knew the rituals and culture of bargaining. They, like their union counterparts, complained about the inexperience of the company's lead bargainer. Chandler, they thought, did not know how to speak to union officials or relate to their problems. According to one pro, Chandler

> might say something in a term that was not the same [as the union used]. It was not important, but simple usage of the words. He might say it wrong, which would then be cause for ridicule on the other side of the table—"Obviously, he doesn't even understand our problem."

While Greathouse and the UAW, he added, needed to be able to deal with a "rough and tumble, up from the bottom labor negotiator" who was more socially equivalent to them, Chandler "had never been in our plants, had not worked in our plants, didn't understand the psyche of our employees. He and Greathouse just couldn't talk."

This lack of understanding, they felt, bothered the union, but it also lessened the company's ability to accurately interpret the union's real positions. Members of the company's team who were new to bargaining, they pointed out, "were *surprised* that there could be this organization within the UAW that could resist as long and as hard and as well as they did—I mean the local leadership and the formal or informal communication channels that they set up for themselves." Even more worrisome, they argued, was the fact that the company's new top management thought that all they had to do to win the strike was to "tell the people and they will come to the party." McCardell, one negotiator explained, was

> convinced that it was the international union driving the strike and not the rank and file. So all you had to do was to tell the rank and file what the story was and they'd

understand. Not true. It was a rank and file driven strike and that's something McCardell never understood. He never did understand it. And primarily because of the attacks on the seniority system and the personal rights issue. He never understood that.

For old hands on both sides of the table, the problem was not simply what the company was trying to accomplish but the fact that the established ground rules were not followed, social relations were not developed, and the translation of understandings between the two sides did not occur. By breaching the cultural understandings of the negotiating group, this mediating force was neutralized. Without mechanisms for developing private understanding, the union lost, as one company negotiator put it, "the tools" that the union's bargainers used to direct negotiations and control their constituents. What drove the strike thereafter was not the lead bargainers on the union side but local leaders and the rank and file membership.

Unmediated Labor-Management Interaction:
Heightened Public Conflict

While the response from the negotiating pros was frustration, the response from workers, local labor leaders, and IH management was anger. Without the buffering and translation that the culture of mediation usually provided, each side was left to interpret the actions of the other side in terms of its own distinct worldview. Motivations were misunderstood, and their differences were highlighted and reinforced. Opposing cultural systems came into direct contact and conflict.

On the union side, local leaders (who attended bargaining but were not as experienced as the International staff in bargaining and were not in the lead negotiating positions) interpreted management's strategy quite differently than the negotiating pros did. The company's request for mandatory overtime, they thought, was intended as a means of control, not cost savings. "I think they wanted the thumb on us," explained one local chairman. "They wanted to be able to dictate to the people what they were going to do; they wanted control; they wanted us under their thumb."

Gambits for management control were seen not only in the content of their proposals but also in the bargaining process they imposed. In the eyes of one union team member, the company was "arrogant":

Any time you've got demands and you just take a hard stand, "We're going to get these or else," that, to me, is arrogant. There's no room for adjustment. From the very beginning that's just what they told us.

This "attitude" of control was also conveyed by cultural symbols of superiority: Anderson described how "one guy on their side come in with an ascot, so the guys, after they left, some of them were putting the napkins in so they could have their little ascots on. It looked like some of these guys come out of the yacht club or something to meet with us."

Local leaders who were team members saw the union itself as a target of the company's actions. The company did not "respect the unions," explained one union leader: "They felt that they could just do anything that they wanted to do and didn't figure that our people would back us." According to another, "it was like they were slapping us in the face." They felt that the company's negotiators were more than just disrespectful of the union, they wanted to destroy it: "We felt after a while that they were just trying to kill us, destroy us." The anger they showed was bitter and personal: "We didn't think it was management or the company, we thought it was Hayford and McCardell and Chandler." In an unusual expression of vindictiveness, one local leader commented that, when a company spokesman had a heart attack a short way into the strike, "Nothing did more to lift our spirits. No sympathy. Nothing. It was a bitter one."

These local union leaders, angered by the "attitude" of the company and observing the confusion of their top negotiators, rallied the rank and file. They depicted the company's position as "take-aways" of "things that it took us 30 years to get," talked about the union's work rules as "rights," and tried to "keep the spirit alive and the strike active." This included rallies, blockades, and targeting the company's CEO: "We zeroed in on McCardell—we picked him as the goat."

On the rank and file level, the anger focused almost completely on one individual: Archie McCardell. According to one worker:

Look what Archie did to Xerox—bankrupt 'em. Archie wanted to do one thing. Bust the union. He didn't care how he did it. The guys down here are like spit on his shoes.

Stories and rumors (such as this inaccurate statement that McCardell bankrupted Xerox) became social facts among IH union members, and their understanding of the intentions of the company were far from what the company intended.

Beyond McCardell himself, rank and file anger focused on the issue of mandatory overtime. One worker explained: "There were wage and concession things—we could have given that. But mandatory overtime—it's like abortion to some people." Because these company demands were so completely illegitimate in the eyes of workers, the company, they figured, must have *intended* to put them out "on the streets." The anger they felt built up to the point that, as another worker put it,

> I had the feeling—it's like grabbing something by the neck and taking it under water and drowning it and, if I got to drown with them, I'll go with them. We were going to win or we were both going to lose.

On the company side, top management was just as misinformed about union members as union members were about top management. McCardell pinned the blame for the union's intransigence on one particular militant leader from Louisville (at the Harvester Council meeting in Chicago on March 20, this leader headed the opposition to Greathouse's attempt to settle the strike) rather than on widespread anger. McCardell was also misinformed about what the union bargainers "understood" about the company's position. He felt that "everyone knew" that his bargaining demands were negotiable:

> We started off with seven or eight [issues and took] a strong position, just as the union takes a strong position. But the negotiation process is such that everybody knows that some of those are really up for grabs. But I don't think that the UAW particularly, the international UAW, ever had the feeling that we were going to stick with every one of those seven or even every one of the last four.

Union pros and team members, by contrast, had exactly the opposite understanding: These positions, they thought, were not negotiable. Another mistaken perception among IH top management was that the *way* they negotiated was insignificant: Chandler called them "mechanics." In his view, only the content of negotiations, not the process, made a difference.

Old-hand company bargaining pros had a vastly different view of the union's situation: As these managers saw the situation, process was important, the company appeared intransigent to the union, and the presence of union radicals was nothing new or significant—it was only because of the company's public appearance of intransigence and

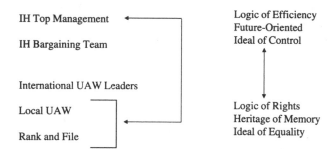

Figure 6.3. IH-UAW Cultural Conflict

arrogance that the union leaders could not, in this case, control those radicals. This level of understanding, ironically, reinforced the isolation of these pros. They (and even Chandler, as he gained more experience) were not trusted by McCardell, both because he did not know them well personally and because their "understanding" of the union could lead the company away from new ideas and back to established practices. McCardell retained personal control over negotiations.

In 1979, channels of communication between the bargaining committee (especially Chandler) and the union were weak, and those between the bargaining committee and top management were even weaker. As negotiations progressed, the gulf between top management and the bargaining team widened. The company's pros (and Chandler) became increasingly aware of the severity of union and rank and file resistance, but top management thought that this was just another case of the old hands giving in.

The mediating group was continually bypassed in these negotiations, and the cultural system that had guided negotiations was ignored. Management went directly to the full bargaining team and the union membership, without signaling, without sidebar discussions, and, at times, without the union leadership. They presented their case, convinced of its logic and truth: The company would have to look to the future, focus on efficiency, and maintain control. In the process, their proposals and their way of presenting their proposals were deemed by union members to be an arrogant attempt to assert dominance over the union and its members, violating the union's ideal of equality and ignoring the union's concept of rights and history. The battle that resulted was especially bitter because it was as much about the confrontation of ideals as it was about the particular policy changes over which they fought. Such cultural confrontations, we know, are hard to contain and especially bitter.[8] Schematically, the unmediated interaction between labor and management in this case looked more like Figure 6.3 than Figure 6.2.

Conclusion

Labor and management represent different people who each have a role to play in contributing to organizational performance. They also have distinct identities, values, and perceptions (as well as different material interests), which are reinforced and played out in public confrontations such as contract negotiations. In private, however, understanding is developed between the two sides, and agreements are reached based largely on personal ties across the bargaining table and the exchange of information that those ties facilitate. Those who interact across the table and form those personal ties do so based on a set of expectations and understandings that are unique to those in a mediating position. This culture of mediation enables private understandings to develop in spite of public conflict. When this group and its sustaining culture is bypassed or ignored, as in the case of the 1979 contract negotiations at International Harvester, interaction between constituent groups is likely to be more public and direct, and driven by the more radical members of the constituent groups who represent and act upon their pure cultural ideals. Such direct confrontation between opposing groups and ideals can lead to bitter conflict and disastrous results.

This type of mediating culture is found not only in collective bargaining but also in relationships between supervisors and stewards on the shop floor (Sayles and Strauss 1953), in plea bargaining (Sudnow 1965), in relationships between street cops and police administration (Reuss-Ianni 1983), and in relationships between utility companies and the government (Ritti and Silver 1986). In each of these cases, there exists a public order that demands conformity to a structured opposition between different groups, while in private people who were in direct and ongoing contact between the two groups develop private understandings of the other side and of how the conflicts between them should be settled. In this way, stalemate is avoided while the public oppositional order is preserved.

The *lack* of a culture of mediation has consequences in other cases as well: The Public Broadcasting System is a much less stable institution than book publishing because, unlike the latter, it lacks an overlapping subculture to integrate it with its environment (Powell 1988); and, in negotiations where the bargainers are not "pros" who know the rules of interaction, third party mediators are more likely to have to do the actual deal-making for them (Kolb 1984).

Mediating groups, guided by their particular cultural systems, are essential for maintaining private understanding in the context of public conflict: These informed groups facilitate coordination between constituent groups and organizations that have conflicting world view—ones that they would like, for technical, political, or identity reasons, to preserve and reinforce.

Notes

1. In the world of labor negotiations, *mediation* is typically used to refer to the actions of outside professionals (often on the staff of the Federal Mediation and Conciliation Service) or other individual third parties. When I use the word *mediate*, I am referring to the original, broader meaning of the word: "to resolve or settle differences by acting as an intermediary agent between two or more parties; to serve as a vehicle for bringing about (a result) or conveying (information) to others" (*American Heritage Dictionary*). My point is that the negotiators, as a whole, serve a mediating function between the two sides.

2. Such visible signs of "collusion," Adams argues, trigger intensified monitoring by constituents, which decreases the boundary person's freedom to build trust with opponents and thus decreases his or her ability to produce better outcomes, which further reduces trust in the boundary person.

3. Zucker (1986) argues that it is exactly because of the difficulty that people have enforcing trustworthy behavior in economic exchange that trust is institutionalized. Laws demand trustworthy behaviors by establishing, for example, the fiduciary responsibility of directors of firms, or agencies that monitor stockbroker behaviors. But these controls only help to correct, after the fact, the most egregious violations of trust. In labor relations, trust is institutionalized by the very existence of the union and the labor laws that ensure fair representation. But, within that context, problem solving would be totally stymied if there were no more immediate (i.e., interpersonal) basis for trust.

4. This capacity is equivalent to Mead's concept of a "me" but extended from the interpersonal level to the intergroup or interorganizational level.

5. The people at the negotiating table who were experienced negotiators will be referred to as the negotiating *pros*; others at the table will be called *team members*; those who remained behind the scenes will be called *workers* or *managers*.

6. The bargaining council included all local union chairmen within IH (about 100 people). They did not attend negotiations but helped set the bargaining goals and controlled whether a contract would be sent to the rank and file for voting.

7. There were negotiating pros on the bargaining committee but they were only allowed to enact the strategy set by McCardell and Chandler. The company's spokesman at the table had been with the company for a long time but had never negotiated before. He was replaced in the middle of bargaining due to an illness, but the replacement (who had a great deal of bargaining experience) was still not allowed to affect the bargaining strategy.

8. In his analysis of social conflict, Oberschall (1973) argues that conflict is more intense if it cannot be calculated, if the outcomes are indivisible and irreversible, and if they are zero-sum—all of which are characteristics of conflicts over symbols or principles.

References

Adams, J. S. 1976. The structure and dynamics of behavior in organizational boundary roles. In *Handbook of industrial and organizational psychology,* ed. M. D. Dunnette, 1175-99. Chicago: Rand McNally.

Ancona, D. G. 1990. Outward bound: Strategies for team survival in an organization. *Academy of Management Journal* 33 (2): 334-65.

Bakke, R. W. 1966. *Mutual survival: The goal of unions and management.* 2d ed. Hamden, Conn.: Archon.

Bartunek, J. M. 1984. Changing interpretive schemes and organizational restructuring: The example of a religious order. *Administrative Science Quarterly* 29:355-72.

Follett, M. P. 1942. *Dynamics of administration: Collected papers of Mary Parker Follett,* ed. H. C. Melcalf and L. Urwick. New York: Harper & Row.

Fox, A. 1971. *A sociology of work in industry.* London: Collier-MacMillan.

Friedman, R. A. 1987. Organizational change and cultural analysis: Redefining labor-relations at International Harvester. Ph.D. diss., University of Chicago.

Garfinkel, H. 1967. *Studies in ethnomethodology.* Cambridge, Mass.: Polity.

Granovetter, M. 1985. Economic action and social structure: The problem of embeddedness. *American Journal of Sociology* 91 (3): 481-510.

Harrison, H. J. 1982. *The right to manage: Industrial relations policies of American business in the 1940s.* Madison: University of Wisconsin Press.

Kolb, D. 1984. *The mediators.* Cambridge, Mass.: MIT Press.

Lawrence, P., and J. Lorsch. 1967. *Organization and environment: Managing differentiation and integration.* Boston: Harvard University, Graduate School of Business Administration.

Louis, M. R. 1980. Surprise and sense making: What newcomers experience in entering unfamiliar organizational settings. *Administrative Science Quarterly* 25:225-51.

Marsh, B. 1985. *A corporate tragedy: The agony of International Harvester Company.* New York: Doubleday.

Oberschall, A. 1973. *Social conflict and social movements.* Englewood Cliffs, N.J.: Prentice-Hall.

Peters, T. J., and R. H. Waterman, Jr. 1982. *In search of excellence: Lessons from America's best-run companies.* New York: Harper & Row.

Powell, W. W. 1988. Institutional effects on organizational structure and performance. In *Institutional patterns and organization,* ed. L. Zucker. Cambridge, Mass.: Ballinger.

Raelin, J. A. 1985. *The clash of cultures: Managers and professionals.* Boston: Harvard Business School Press.

Reuss-Ianni, E. 1983. *Two cultures of policing: Street cops and management cops.* New Brunswick, N.J.: Transaction.

Ritti, R. R., and J. H. Silver. 1986. Early processes of institutionalization: The dramaturgy of exchange in interorganizational relations. *Administrative Science Quarterly* 31:25-42.

Sayles, L., and G. Strauss. 1953. *The local union.* New York: Harper & Row.

Schelling, T. C. 1960. *The strategy of conflict.* Cambridge, Mass.: Harvard University Press.

Sudnow, D. 1965. Normal crimes: Sociological features of the penal code in a public defender's office. *Social Problems* 12:255-76.

Sutton, F. X., S. E. Harris, C. Kaysen, and J. Tobin. 1956. *The American business creed.* Cambridge, Mass.: Harvard University Press.

Swidler, A. 1986. Culture in action: Symbols and strategies. *American Sociological Review* 51 (2): 273-86.

Thompson, J. D. 1967. *Organizations in action.* New York: McGraw-Hill.

Walton, R. E., and R. B. McKersie. 1965. *A behavior theory of labor negotiations.* New York: McGraw-Hill.

Warren, R. L. 1967. The interorganizational field as a focus for investigation. *Administrative Science Quarterly* 12:396-419.

Young, O. R., ed. 1975. *Bargaining: Formal theories of negotiation.* Champaign: University of Illinois Press.

Zucker, L. 1986. Production of trust: Institutional sources of economic structure, 1840-1920. *Research in Organizational Behavior* 8:52-111.

7

The Suppression of
Gender Conflict in Organizations

JOANNE MARTIN

In spite of legal "guarantees" of equal opportunity and equal pay for
equal work, the differential between men's and women's wages (60 cents
to the dollar) has remained remarkably stable for the last three decades
(Kahn and Crosby 1985; Larwood, Gutek, and Stromberg 1985; Strober
1982; Treiman and Hartmann 1981; Waite 1981). Women in the work
force are generally clustered in gender-segregated, low-paying jobs that
have no well-established opportunities for upward mobility (Barron and
Morris 1976; Bielby and Baron 1986; Harlan and Weiss 1982; Hartmann

AUTHOR'S NOTE: A preliminary version of this chapter was presented at a symposium
titled "The Cultural Contexts of Organizational Conflict" (Deborah M. Kolb and Roy J.
Lewicki, chairs), at the annual meeting of the Academy of Management, Anaheim, California, August 1988. A more detailed version, which explains the postmodern strategy
(deconstruction) used to analyze the story, was published in *Organizational Science*. (Re-
printed by permission, "Deconstructing Organizational Taboos: The Suppression of Gender Conflict in Organizations," *Organizational Science*, Vol. 1, No. 4, November 1990,
pp. 339- 359. Copyright 1990, The Institute of Management Sciences, 290 Westminster
Street, Providence, RI 02903.) I owe many thanks to the faculty associated with Stanford's
Institute for Research on Women and Gender. They have introduced me to postmodern
and feminist theory and helped me think through the relevance of these ideas to organi-
zational theory and practice. I am especially grateful for helpful comments on an earlier
draft of this chapter from Barbara Babcock, Jean M. Bartunek, Marta Calas, Reginia
Gagnier, Elizabeth Hansot, Mary Jo Hatch, Nan Keohane, Anne Klein, Deborah M. Kolb,
Rod Kramer, Barbara Levitt, Joseph McGrath, Deborah Meyerson, Diane Middlebrook,
Jeffrey Pfeffer, Pamela Pommerenke, Deborah Rhode, Maureen Scully, Linda Smircich,
Caren Siehl, and four anonymous, exceptionally helpful reviewers.

1976; Malveaux 1982). Few women enter the more lucrative occupations dominated by men, and those who do are likely to encounter gender prejudice in hiring, performance evaluation, and promotion decisions (Blum and Smith 1988; Kanter 1977; Hartmann 1976; Taylor, Fiske, Etcoff, and Ruderman 1978; Terborg and Ilgen 1975). Furthermore, within and outside the family, child care and housework are still predominantly being done by women (e.g., Berk 1985). Thus, in spite of efforts to alleviate discrimination, gender inequality at home and at work remains a serious problem.

Efforts to alleviate this inequality have made it socially, and even in some contexts legally, inappropriate to express overt gender prejudice. Of course, open and direct expressions of such prejudice do still occur. Gender conflict in organizations is more likely to be suppressed, however, so that it remains unspoken or hidden, like the more subtle forms of racial prejudice (e.g., Pettigrew and Martin 1987; Van Dijk 1987). Most organizations are controlled by men and by assumptions that in effect favor men (such as these: authority is legitimate; promotions are meritocratic). Women's interests therefore often appear as contradictions, disjunctions, disruptions, and silences—signs of suppressed conflict: "The feminine has consequently had to be deciphered as forbidden ("interdit"), in between signs, between the realized meanings, between the lines" (Irigaray 1974, 20, quote in Moi 1985, 132). Such suppressed conflict is easier to deny, harder to detect and combat, and more difficult to study.

Suppression in the Study of Conflict

Most conflict research has focused on overt forms of conflict that are resolved by formal structural mechanisms such as mediation and/or negotiation meetings. For example, conflict researchers have examined overt conflict across interdependent work units, within groups of managers or professionals, between vertically related groups such as management and labor as well as within social movements and other collectivities (e.g., Bacharach and Lawler 1980; Kochan 1986; Oberschall 1978; Pfeffer and Salancik 1978; Pondy 1986; Walton and Dutton 1969; Walton and McKersie 1965; Zald and Berger 1978). In all these studies, the parties to the conflict were relatively powerful; they had enough resources (such as sufficient numbers and resources necessary for communication) to struggle openly and often collectively for influence, control, and political change.

In contrast, disempowered people in organizations (such as women and minorities) often lack the resources that are necessary prerequisites for overt conflict. Therefore, research more relevant to gender issues focuses on suppressed, covertly expressed forms of conflict (e.g., Coch and French 1948; Kotter, Schlesinger, and Sathe 1979). For example, Bartunek and Reid (this volume), Morrill (this volume), and Van Dijk (1987) argue that some conflicts are handled with relatively little open and direct communication. Smith and Berg (1987) show how conflicts are perpetuated because they are functional, and Smith, Simmons, and Thames (1989) show how overt clashes can be incomplete and misleading indicators of deeper, hidden sources of conflict.

This chapter offers a way of studying covertly expressed forms of conflict. It explores how apparently well-intentioned organizational practices, designed to "help" women employees, can suppress gender conflict and reify, rather than alleviate, gender inequality. This chapter analyzes, from a feminist viewpoint,[1] an organizational story told by a high-ranking executive. Using a postmodern analytic strategy (deconstruction), the chapter examines what the story says, what it does not say, and what it might have said.[2]

This chapter has three parts. The first describes the context in which the story was told. The second part shows how the story reifies, then transgresses, an alleged dichotomy between the public world of work and the private domain of the family. In the third part of the chapter, the conflicts revealed by this analysis are iteratively eased, offering increasingly emancipatory visions of how work and child care might be organized. This part of the analysis shows why relatively minor changes in organizational practices will fail to alleviate gender inequalities. Instead, major changes in the organization of work and family lives are required.

Telling the Cesarean Story

The schools of business, law, education, and medicine at a major university recently sponsored a conference focusing on the ways that individuals, businesses, and other organizations can help solve societal problems. Students and faculty from the university as well as the press and members of the surrounding community came to hear an anchorman from NBC nightly news interview several panelists. One of those panelists was the president and chief executive officer of a very large, multinational corporation. This company has an unusual reputation for being deeply concerned, in a humanitarian fashion, about the personal well-being of its employees. In response to a question about the company's concern for the well-being of women employees with children, the president told the following story:

> We have a young woman who is extraordinarily important to the launching of a major new [product]. We will be talking about it next Tuesday in its first worldwide introduction. She has arranged to have her cesarean yesterday in order to be prepared for this event, so you—We have insisted that she stay home and this is going to be televised in a closed circuit television, so we're having this done by TV for her and she is staying home three months and we are finding ways of filling in to create this void for us because we think it's an important thing for her to do.

The feminist analysis of this story offered below is only one of the myriad story interpretations possible. It should not be construed as the single "correct" way to view the story, and it may well not be the interpretation that the teller of the story intended to communicate.

Analyzing the Story

Dismantling the Public/Private Dichotomy

There is a dichotomy that is so central to the cesarean story's unstated, fundamental assumptions that it can serve as a fulcrum point for prying open deeply embedded alternate interpretations of this text. This is the public/private dichotomy that contrasts with the public domain of the marketplace, the political arena, and the legal system with the "closed and exclusive sphere of intimacy, sexuality, and affection characterizing the modern nuclear family" (Benhabib and Cornell 1988, 6-7).[3]

This alleged dichotomy between the public and private spheres of influence is a false distinction. Concerns and behaviors said to be characteristic of the public arena (particularly the marketplace) are evident within the family (e.g., Berk 1985). For example, one feminist analysis concludes:

> [Modern nuclear families] are sites of egocentric, strategic and instrumental calculation as well as sites of usually exploitative exchanges of services, labor,

cash and sex, not to mention sites, frequently, of coercion and violence. (Fraser 1988, 37)

In addition, concerns supposedly relegated to the private domain of the family also surface in organizational contexts. For example, the needs of children and other family members are inseparable from the demands of the workplace (Frug 1984; Olsen 1983). Because most women carry a disproportionate share of these family responsibilities, they must somehow find time during working hours to take a sick family member to the doctor, meet with a teacher, and so on (Berk 1985; Hess and Ferree 1987). Unless adequate forms of child care are consistently available, and unless work is restructured to allow family members' needs to be met, these conflicts take time away from work, forcing many women to operate at a competitive disadvantage with comparable men. In these and other ways, concerns associated with the private domain are constantly intertwined with life at work.[4] If this dichotomy is indeed so problematic, why is it reified and perpetuated?

Woman Is to Private as Man Is to Public?

This public/private dichotomy is associated with gender. Supposedly, the public world of politics, economics, and organizations is territory dominated by men, while women watch over the private sphere, where children are conceived and family members are nurtured. This gendered characterization of the dichotomy, like the dichotomy itself, is oversimplified:

> This characterization [of the public/private split] tends to exaggerate the differences and occlude the similarities between them. For example, it directs attention away from the fact that the household, like the paid workplace, is a site of labor, albeit unremunerated and often unrecognized labor. Likewise, it does not make visible the fact that in the paid workplace, as in the household, women are assigned to, indeed ghettoized in, distinctly feminine, service-oriented and often sexualized occupations. Finally, it fails to focalize the fact that in both spheres women are subordinated to men. (Fraser 1988, 37)

When work is conceptualized as separate from family concerns, the conflicts encountered by working mothers are defined as private problems that must be solved individually; the corporation is not responsible.

As documented in the introduction to this chapter, working women are likely to be occupationally segregated, unfairly evaluated, and paid less than men. This gender inequality is explained and legitimated as an inevitable aftereffect of the alleged distinction between men's public and women's private priorities. Emphasis on individual solutions to "private" family problems further defuses the potential for collective action by women. This may explain, in part, why the problematic public/private dichotomy is reified and perpetuated—it provides a rationale for gender discrimination:

> "The separation of public and private," namely the separation of the official economic sphere from the domestic sphere and the enclaving of childrearing from the rest of social labor . . . [is] an institutional arrangement that is widely held to be one, if not the, linchpin of modern women's subordination. (Fraser 1988, 39)

A Partial Acknowledgment of the Interconnections

The management of some organizations, such as the corporation described in the cesarean story, partially acknowledges the inevitable intersections of work and family lives, expressing holistic concern for employee well-being as well as the usual desire for productivity at work. In addition, as in the cesarean story, some organizations have instituted a series of ostensibly humanistic policies designed to "help women." These policies are congruent with human relations theories that advocate "humanitarian" philosophies of management (Hackman et al. 1975; Katz and Kahn 1978; Leavitt 1972; Likert 1967; McGregor 1960). Similarly, advocates of "strong" organizational cultures, employee involvement strategies (such as quality circles), and "high-commitment" organizations encourage participatory decision making, value consensus, and the development of a "family feeling" at work (Dertouzos, Lester, and Solow 1989; Kanter 1986; Lawler 1986; Mohrman and Cummings 1989; Ouchi 1981). This ostensibly humanitarian research partially acknowledges interconnections between the public and private concerns, both as an end in itself and as a means of increasing productivity and efficiency.

Critics have argued that some of these theories mask conflicts of interest between employers and employees with an apparently benign, humanitarian facade (Bailyn in press; Braverman 1974; Clawson 1980; Nord 1974; Perrow 1986). Below, I make a similar argument about the kinds of policies and values implicit in the cesarean story.

Who Is in Control of the Private Domain?

The cesarean story begins with the phrase, "We have a young woman . . .," rather than "A young woman works for us." This phrase situates the text at the juncture between the public and the private domains and offers a redefinition of the usual employment contract. Such a contract is generally conceived of as an exchange. Employees surrender, within some ill-defined limits, control of their behavior at work. In exchange, the employees are guaranteed pay, benefits, and certain explicit and implicit rights.

This standard conception of an employment contract implicitly attempts to separate an employee's public and private lives, giving the employer extensive control over the employee's behavior at work. In contrast, the possessive language of the cesarean text (e.g., "having") suggests that the company has access to the whole of the woman—her health and her home life—as well as her work. The usual boundaries between the public and the private have been transgressed to an unusual degree—far in excess of the usual understandings of what is implicitly and explicitly entailed in an employment contract.

The choice and timing of the cesarean operation is also problematic. A cesarean operation is painful, its timing can be crucially important, and current medical practice questions its necessity or helpfulness in many cases. The sentence, "She arranged to have her cesarean yesterday in order to be prepared for this event," suggests that the employee may have let the choice of this treatment, or its timing, be influenced by the company's product introduction schedule. Because the employee agreed to the cesarean operation and "she arranged" its timing, it is not clear whether the company forced her, or encouraged her, to make these choices. Either way, the text implies that the product's introduction schedule affected the timing of the baby's birth.

It would be highly unusual if such a serious operation were not followed by some period of recuperation away from work. Such phrases as "We insisted she stay home . . ." indicate that the corporate "we" took responsibility for making decisions that are usually the responsibility of a doctor and a patient—not an employer. This use of "we," as in the first sentence of the text, lends the authority of a group to the words of an individual (in this case, the president) while absolving that individual speaker, to some extent, of personal responsibility.

The placement of the closed circuit television in the employee's bedroom was also apparently an initiative of the company: "so we're having this done by TV for her." The employee seems to have lost control over decisions about what goes in her bedroom. Of course, she may have appreciated the chance to keep in touch with her work, perhaps as a welcome distraction from pain. It is also possible that she resented the placement of the closed circuit television in her bedroom. Arguably, had she actually chosen to have the television transmissions, the invasion into her privacy could be seen as even greater than if this intrusion occurred against her expressed will. Because the story is not told from the employee's point of view, it includes no mention of how the employee reacted to these events.

Whether she acquiesced to these decisions with alacrity or felt she had little choice, the silences and absences of this text are eloquent, documenting a corporation that has, to an unusual degree, taken control of aspects of an employee's life usually considered "private." Next, I ask who benefits from this attempt to "help" a working mother.

Costs, Benefits, and Conflicts of Interest

The hidden ideology of a text is revealed at those places where the text is disrupted, where a contradiction or a glimpse of meaninglessness reveals a subtext that may be inconsistent with the text's apparent message. The most obvious disruption in the cesarean text is this: "we are finding ways of filling in to create this void for us." This incoherence surfaces precisely at the point where the organizational costs of the arrangements described in the text are addressed. The contradiction, evident in simultaneously "filling" and "creating" this void, reflects the organization's ambivalence about the extent to which the organization and the employee benefit from this acknowledgment of the interconnections between the public and private spheres.

The text suggests that the employer was willing to invest in having the television brought to the sickroom, so that this important employee could keep up to date concerning her work responsibilities. In this regard, the benefits to the company were clear. The employee's need to take an extended leave of absence, however, was of less obvious direct benefit to the company. When the text's words become jumbled and contradictory, ambivalence about entailing these latter costs is evident.

To summarize, beneath the surface of the company's apparently benign concern with the employee's well-being are a series of silences, discomforts, and contradictions. These difficulties arise because the cesarean operation exposes conflicts of interest between the organization (for example, to have the product released on time, to have the employee perform her job) and the individual employee (such as to rest and let her incision heal). Although the president ostensibly was claiming holistic concern for the employee's well-being, the text's disruptions reveal that concern is expressed not as an end in itself but as a means of maintaining some level of employee involvement and productivity during a leave. The primary beneficiary of this company's attempt to "help" a working woman is the company, not the woman.

At this point, it is essential to acknowledge that none of the observations offered so far is gender specific. An employee by definition has entered an unequal power relationship with the employer. In a roughly comparable surgical situation, the interests of a man might well be similarly subordinated to those of the employing organization. Below, this possibility is explored in some detail.

Bypassing the Heart

One way to approach this problem is to rewrite the cesarean story, making the employee a man. Because men do not have cesarean operations, the nature of the surgery must also be altered. Changing then only the sex of the protagonist and the type of operation, the rewritten story is as follows:

> We have a young man who is extraordinarily important to the launching of a major new [product]. We will be talking about it next Tuesday in its first worldwide introduction. He has arranged to have his coronary bypass operation yesterday in order to be prepared for this event, so you—We have insisted that he stay home and this is going to be televised in a closed circuit television, so we're having this done by TV for him, and he is staying home three months and we are finding ways of filling in to create this void for us because we think it's an important thing for him to do.

No surgical procedure, of course, is strictly comparable to a cesarean, but a coronary bypass operation is similar in some important ways. Like a cesarean operation, a bypass operation is painful. Current medical practice questions the necessity and helpfulness of both operations in many cases. In addition, the timing of both operations is crucial. The need for bypass surgery is sometimes unexpected and is usually dictated by a doctor, with the permission of the patient. Similarly, the need for a cesarean can arise unexpectedly and a doctor's advice about timing is generally followed.

One might argue that an organization has more right to exercise control over a woman having a cesarean, in contrast to a man having a bypass operation, because a women has control over the timing of a pregnancy and a cesarean birth. This is not the case. Assuming her doctor concurs, a woman can control the timing of a cesarean only within a very small range of days—a degree of latitude often available to bypass candidates. Of course, a woman can take steps to avoid the change of cesarean by avoiding pregnancy, but birth control techniques do fail and, short of abstinence or abortion, the tick of the biological clock (menopause) is an uncontrollable factor for women who wish to bear children.

Again, the bypass operation is not dissimilar. A person can choose to abstain from smoking, reduce intake of high cholesterol foods, and exercise with fanaticism. Nevertheless, the effects of the biological clock may still be impossible to counteract; a bypass may still be necessary. Thus both a woman having a cesarean and a man having a bypass operation have little—sometimes no—control over the long-term need for and timing of the surgery.

When the original cesarean and the rewritten bypass stories are compared, some similarities are evident. In both stories, the corporate "we" apparently made choices that would, under most circumstances, be made by the employee and the doctor—such as whether and when to have an operation, where and how long to recuperate, and whether to have a closed circuit television in the bedroom. As in the story about the cesarean operation, the invasion of the employee's bedroom reveals suppressed conflicts of interest between the employer (for example, to have the product released on time, to have the employee present to perform his job) and the employee (such as to rest and to heal). In both stories, the alleged public/private dichotomy is bypassed.

The Product-Baby Trade-Off: A Cesarean Birth

Although these two operations do have salient similarities, the dissimilarities are even more important, as they reveal gender-specific aspects of this conflict of interest between employer and employee. Whereas bypass surgery places one life in jeopardy, both a mother and an infant are involved in a cesarean birth. Although both operations are painful, heart disease is an illness to be endured or cured, while, in spite of the pain, childbirth usually brings a welcome addition to life. A bypass operation literally bypasses a weak heart, the realm of intimate emotions, while a Caesarian brings a baby, a focus of these emotions, into the world. These differences between the two operations point to some aspects of the cesarean story that are gender specific.

The choice and timing of a cesarean operation would usually be dictated by the progress of the infant's gestation and the mother's labor. The cesarean story suggests that the mother may have jeopardized her child, or at least altered the timing of his or her birth, to fit the schedule of a product introduction. When a product introduction influences the timing of a bypass operation, only the employee is affected. When a product introduction influences the timing of a cesarean operation, two lives are affected and only one of them is an employee.

The gender-specific aspects of the cesarean story, however, go deeper than a simple conflict between the interests of the organization and the mother and her child. The fact that the employee in the cesarean story is pregnant exposes intersections between the public and private spheres and reveals a series of sexual organizational taboos.

Gender at the Juncture of Public and Private

A pregnant employee is an alien element in an organizational context dominated by men. When an employee becomes visibly pregnant, it becomes impossible to ignore her gender. The usual ways of doing business, insofar as they reflect norms that are more comfortable for men rather than women, come into question. Pregnancy caries connotations of nurturance and intimacy—emotions that seldom characterize board meetings or the usual business lunch.

A pregnant employee also is a walking contradiction to the unstated sexual ideology that undergirds current norms of organizational functioning. She is sexually active but (usually) has not chosen an employee. This act fits none of the usual sexual stereotypes. To use Kanter's (1977) gender stereotype labels, the competent and dispassionate Iron Maiden is revealed as sexually active. The nurturant Mother or Sister is not sexually innocent. The Seductress is plying her talents outside the firm. This, then, is the sexual taboo that a pregnant employee violates: Sex is happening and the high-ranking male employee is getting none of it. This breaking of the sexuality taboo is particularly problematic, as can be seen with further analysis of the "double entendres" in the cesarean story.

The Sexual Subtext:
Who Does What to the Void?

Since Freud exposed the power of the unconscious and, in particular, the pervasiveness of suppressed/repressed sexuality, many psychologists have found exploration of these hidden elements to be potentially informative. That acceptance, however, has seldom extended to organizational theory, where the explicit examination of sexual issues has usually remained as taboo as in actual organizations. Below, sexuality is discussed in an overt manner quite alien to the usual forms of organizational discourse. Readers uncomfortable with this approach may find their resistance a useful source of insight into the ways sexual taboos operate in an organizational context.

When the man's bypass surgery becomes a woman's cesarean operation, suppressed sexuality emerges in the undertones and double entendres of the president's speech. For example, the phrase, "We have a young woman" is a double entendre. The heterosexual meaning of "having a woman" enters the text.

In the context of the cesarean story, the disruption of the president's language also has sexual undertones. "We are finding ways of filling in to create this void for us" carries sexual meanings. In addition to the void at the office created by the employee's absence, there was a void in the woman's body. That void, once filled by a man, and then by the child, was emptied by the cesarean. These interpretations have the linguistic effect of making the woman sexually accessible ("filling in" her void, "having" her). No wonder then that the president's language was disrupted ("filling in to create this void") at this particular point in the text.

The corporate "we" of the cesarean text is masculine because it is (usually) a man who has a woman, and it is a man who fills the void. To explore what is left out here, the relationship between reproduction and production must be examined. Traditionally, reproductive capacities are the aspects of womanhood that have been associated with the private domain. Supposedly, a woman provides physical and emotional nurturance for her family, thereby freeing her husband to devote his energies to the workplace and the broader public domain. Because women experience sexual pleasure independently of reproduction and production, this gendered way of attempting to separate public from private effaces—by ignoring—a woman's potential for sexual pleasure (Spivak 1987).

Thus the sexual double entendres in the cesarean story presume a masculine perspective that, in effect, supports men's dominance of production in the public arena, reinforces women's responsibilities for reproduction and nurturance in the private domain, and excludes consideration of a woman's need for sexual pleasure. Such attempts to reify a gendered public/private dichotomy mask the ways organizations structure child care and sexuality by making the birth process, children's needs for nurturance, and some aspects of female sexuality taboo in organizational contexts. These are ways the public/private dichotomy serves as a linchpin of gender discrimination.

Although awareness of the interconnections between work and family life is the first step to dismantling this false dichotomy, a deeper acknowledgment of these interconnections could deeply disrupt and transform the language, premises, and objectives of organizational discourse. How this might be done is the topic of the next section of this chapter.

Rewriting the Story

In this section of the chapter, the cesarean story is rewritten in an attempt to articulate what would have to be changed to alleviate the problems discussed above. Staying close to the story text, only a few phrases will be altered at a time. These small changes cause other, adjacent phrases in the story to seem inappropriate. Iteratively, this process reveals unanticipated consequences of each small step in a major change effort.

Why a Product Can Be Launched and a Baby Cannot

The cesarean story partially acknowledges interconnections between the public and private spheres, but it does so in a way that gives precedence to the public rather than the private, the product rather than the baby. Below, this precedence is reversed, changing nothing else:

We have a young woman who is extraordinarily important to the launching of a major new child. We will be talking about her baby next Tuesday in its first worldwide introduction. She arranged to have her product introduced early yesterday in order to be prepared for this birth.

Although both products and babies are delivered—and, in both cases, it is good to deliver on time—the metaphor of "launching a baby" does not work. Babies are "brought into" the world with more pain and a different kind of trajectory than is suggested by the metaphor of "launching." The *Concise Oxford Dictionary* (1964, 683) defines *launching* in terms of hurling, discharging, sending forth, and bursting—all images that have the male sexual connotations of ejaculation. The language of the public domain, in this case, "launching a product," often has male sexual undertones that make it inappropriate for describing women-related issues such as birth (Derrida 1976; Spivak 1987).

The Unnatural

Other word combinations in this first rewriting of the story seem awkward or "unnatural," a condition that can signal a hidden assumption:

> The hegemonic orientation prevails not by overt domination or resigned acceptance, but by naturalization, by a general recognition that "this is the way things are, and they cannot be any other way." (Calas 1987, 209)

Although all babies, even at birth, are not created equal, it does not seem "natural" to say "a major new" baby. A new product may be considered "major," but a mother's investment in producing a baby cannot easily make it "major," except in the eyes of the baby's family. Similarly, a "worldwide introduction" seems inappropriate, except possibly for a baby with royal or celebrity parents. For these few babies, birth is a transition from the private world of the womb into, quite literally, the public domain. Only in these instances does the language of a product introduction become a "natural" substitute for discussing issues of reproduction and nurturance, usually relegated to the private domain.

Furthermore, it does not seem "natural" that an organization would see a baby as so important. It would indeed be costly to devote this much attention to the babies of even a few employees. And, given the organization's tendency to give precedence to its own interests rather than the interests of the family, parents might well fear having their baby be so important to an organization.

Altering Who Does What Where

The next step of this rewriting alters the mother's behavior. In the president's version of the story, the company *"insisted she stay home."* Suppose instead that she insisted on coming in to the office—with her baby, so that her attention would be split between work and the infant. The public and private elements in this rewritten story have not yet been symmetrically merged. The office location suggests that work will be given priority most of the time, as organizations are not generally accustomed to accommodating the needs of parents working with children present. Furthermore, the concluding sentence in this rewriting of the story (*". . . she thinks it's an important thing for her to do"*) makes it seem as if the corporation does not share her perception of the importance of her child care activities.

Experimental Organizational Forms:
A Failure to Thrive

Some might argue that such conflicts of interest between working parents and their employers are inevitable. Other judgments, however, are possible. In the next version of the story, the choice to merge work and child care remains in the hands of the woman, but the organization sees itself as benefiting as well:

> She has insisted that she come to work and this new baby is going to be brought to the office, so she's having this done for us, and she is working for three months. We are finding ways to create this void for us because we think it's an important thing for us to do.

At this point, the limitations of small-scale changes become evident. If an organization really wanted to take responsibility for helping men and women live comfortably with the interconnections between the public and private realms of their lives, then a wide range of organizational policies would have to change. For example, such an organization might have on-site pediatricians and sick care available, flexible hours, and comfortable, safe, and supervised places for children to play near where their parents work. In contrast to some of the "humanitarian" theories of management discussed above, the objective of these policies would not be to increase parent's productivity, although this might well happen. The organization would be doing this to provide a more humane place for adults and children to work and play.

Here the research on experimental organizational forms becomes relevant. Some organizations and social movements have attempted to institutionalize variants on the ideas described in the rewritings above, providing a place where work and family, public and private, can be merged (Ferguson 1984; Kanter 1972; Kreiger 1982; Rothschild-Witt 1979; Smelser 1962; Swidler 1979; Zald and Berger 1978). These organizations usually allow flexible working hours and permit employees/owners to divide their time between child care and work. To avoid the power inequalities inherent in hierarchy, many of these organizations have refrained from using clearly defined job descriptions or long-term divisions of labor. For similar reasons, many of these organizations prefer consensual decision making. Sanctions for nonperformance are sometimes avoided.

These innovations have costs that make it difficult, but not impossible, for experimental organizations to survive in the long term (Kanter 1972; Riger 1984; Rothschild-Witt 1979; Swidler 1979). For example, the development of consensus is time-consuming. Tasks sometimes do not get done. Split attention can mean decreased productivity on the job. As a result of these "inefficiencies," these new organizational forms often take more time than conventional organizations to do the same amount of work.

The long-term benefits of these practices might well outweigh the costs of their "inefficiency," if it were not for the competitive markets characteristic of a capitalist economy. (This is not an observation unique to profit-seeking firms. Organizations also fail to survive in the nonprofit/governmental sectors.) As long as an experimental organization has to compete with organizations that are more productive, its long-term chances of survival will not be good.

Mandating Nurture

It is not enough, therefore, to create an innovative organizational form. Change in the broader public realm is also necessary. An experimental organizational form may seem to be a viable alternative, but it may well fail to survive unless enough organizations change in the same way at the same time. This is a big *unless*—one that requires governmental intervention.

The necessity of this broader scope of change can be argued from a different starting point. Rather than changing the way work is organized, imagine changing child care. One way to do this is to bring in a person not yet mentioned in the cesarean story: the baby's father. If he were willing to stay home and care for the baby (without the immunogenic advantages of breast-feeding), the woman could go back to work as soon as her cesarean incision healed, with minimal disruption for the company.

As long as the father is willing to take the parenting role traditionally assigned to the mother, the organization does not have to change its ways. Such a "resolution" simply reverses gender roles. It is insufficient because it leaves the public/private dichotomy intact. To show this, I must again go beyond the text.

Because a man generally earns considerably more than a woman, many families would find it a financial strain to substitute a woman's salary for that earned by her husband. It is possible, of course, to legislate equal pay for men and women, perhaps in the form of a comparable worth law. In that case, the man might still not want to stay at home with his child because he fears subsequent maltreatment when he returns to work. Again, this could be forbidden by legislation.

A man might still not want to be at home, however, perhaps because of the traditional devaluation of housework and child care as opposed to paid labor. Again, legislation might be helpful. In Sweden, for example, so few men have taken advantage of opportunities for parental leave that some have suggested the leaves be made mandatory (Olsen 1983, 1559).

In each of these examples, change in the private domain of the family's child care arrangements requires governmental intervention as well as new organizational policies. This analysis of policy alternatives reveals that the gendered aspects of the public/private dichotomy are critical to the current structure of our organizational, familial, and governmental systems. The eradication of gender discrimination within an organization would require change in all these realms (Frug 1984; Olsen 1983).

Why Gender Discrimination Is so Persistent

This chapter examines gender conflicts suppressed between the lines of a story about a cesarean operation. This story was told by a corporation president as evidence of his firm's humanitarian concern for the well-being of women employees with children.[5] The analysis revealed that the primary beneficiary of this apparently well-intentioned effort to "help" was the corporation—not the woman or her child. A comparison of the cesarean operation with coronary bypass surgery was used to separate gender-specific difficulties from the problems inherent in other unequal power relationships.

Some of these gender-specific issues included the organizational taboos that make life at work difficult for a pregnant woman. Her visible pregnancy, capacity for sexual pleasure, and involvement with intimate emotions and nurturance all become evident in an organizational context where such aspects of life are considered "inappropriate." In this part of the chapter, the analysis revealed how apparently well-intentioned efforts to alleviate gender inequality can mask gender conflict, forcing it to surface elsewhere in more subtle and pernicious forms. Because women are usually relegated to relatively less powerful positions in organizations, gender conflicts may generally tend to be suppressed and displaced so that they surface in the covert and indirect forms studied by such researchers as Smith, Simmons, and Thames (1989), Morrill (this volume), and Bartunek and Reid (this volume).

In the third section of this chapter, the rewritings of the cesarean story explored ways to renegotiate the usual social contract between employer and employees, merging and transforming personal and organizational life. Analysis of the unexpected ramifications of a series of these rewritings demonstrated the inadequacy of small-scale organizational reforms. The public/private dichotomy was revealed to be a linchpin supporting discrimination against women. The gender segregation of tasks, paid and unpaid, made it impossible to discuss changing gender discrimination in organizations without changing gender roles within the family. These could not be changed without a fundamental realignment of government policies concerning both the family and the marketplace.

Given the scope of the needed changes outlined in this last section of the chapter, it is no wonder that gender-based pay inequality and occupational segregation have been so difficult to eradicate. Small-scale organizational reforms—however well intentioned—reify, rather than alleviate, gender inequality and suppress, rather than resolve, gender conflict. This is a policy domain where "small wins" won't win.

Notes

1. Feminist research reveals how female interests have been subordinated to those of males, with the ultimate goal of eradicating that subordination and transforming relations between men and women.

2. Analyzing what is not said requires interpreting silences. This chapter uses deconstruction, an analytic strategy developed by philosophers and literary critics, to systematically analyze the silences, contradictions, and double entendres in a story text (see Moi 1985 and Weedon 1987 for introductions to this approach; organizational applications include Calas 1987; Calas and Smircich in press; Kilduff 1981). Deconstruction is able to reveal ideological assumptions in a manner that is particularly sensitive to the suppressed interests of members of disempowered, marginalized groups. In a text, dominant ideologies suppress conflict by eliding conflicts of interest and denying the existence of points of view that could be disruptive of existing power relationships. Deconstruction peels away the layers of theoretical obscuration, exposing conflicts that have been suppressed; the devalued "other" is made visible.

3. Habermas (1984) delineates a second version of the public/private dichotomy, contrasting some shared conception of the public good with the private interests of both individuals and profit-seeking organizations. This second version of the dichotomy is not the focus of this chapter.

4. The second version of the public/private dichotomy is also a false distinction (Frug 1984; Olsen 1983). For example, government regulations often constrain the behavior of firms in the private sector, requiring them to hire women, refrain from hiring children, or treat pregnancy like any other short-term disability. Conversely, the private sector has an enormous impact on governmental functioning. For example, business interests influence who gets elected, what bills get written and passed, and which laws are enforced.

5. In the original version of this chapter, the limitations of this analysis are discussed, including the biases inherent in focusing on high-ranking women and heterosexuality.

References

Bacharach, S. B., and E. J. Lawler. 1980. *Power in politics.* San Francisco: Jossey-Bass.
Bailyn, L. In press. Changing the conditions of work: Responding to increasing work force diversity and new family patterns. In *Transforming organizations,* ed. T. Kochan and M. Useem. New York: Oxford University Press.
Barron, R. D., and G. M. Morris. 1976. Sexual divisions and the dual labor market. In *Dependence and exploitation in work and marriage,* ed. D. Barker and S. Allen. New York: Longman.
Benhabib, S., and D. Cornell, eds. 1988. *Feminism as critique.* Menasha: Banta.
Berk, S. 1985. *The gender factory: The appointment of working American households.* New York: Plenum.
Bielby, W., and J. Baron. 1986. Men and women at work: Sex segregation and statistical discrimination. *American Journal of Sociology* 91 (4): 759-99.
Blum, L., and V. Smith. 1988. Women's mobility in the corporation: A critique of the politics of optimism. *Signs* 13 (3): 528-45.
Braverman, H. 1974. *Labor and monopoly capital.* New York: Monthly Review.

Calas, M. 1987. Organizational science/fiction: The postmodern in the management disciplines. Ph.D. diss., University of Massachusetts, Amherst.

Calas, M., and L. Smircich. In press. *Postmodernism and the management disciplines.*

Clawson, D. 1980. *Bureaucracy and the labor process.* New York: Monthly Review.

Coch, L., and J. P. French. 1948. Overcoming resistance to change. *Human Relations* 11 (August): 512-32.

Concise Oxford Dictionary. 1964. London, England: Oxford University Press.

Derrida, J. 1976. *Speech and phenomenon.* Evanston, Ill.: Northwestern University Press.

Dertouzos, M. L., R. K. Lester, and R. M. Solow. 1989. *Made in America: Regaining the productive edge.* Cambridge, Mass.: MIT Press.

Ferguson, K. E. 1984. *The feminist case against bureaucracy.* Philadelphia: Temple University Press.

Fraser, N. 1988. What's critical about critical theory? The case of Habermas and gender. In *Feminism as critique,* ed. S. Benhabib and D. Cornell. Menasha: Banta.

Frug, G. 1984. The ideology of bureaucracy in American law. *Harvard Law Review* 97 (4): 1276-1388.

Habermas, J. 1984. *The theory of communicative action.* Boston: Beacon.

Hackman, R. J., G. Oldham, R. Janson, and K. Purdy. 1975. An new strategy for job enrichment. *California Management Review* 17 (4): 57-71.

Harlan, A., and C. Weiss. 1982. Sex differences in factors affecting managerial career advancement. In *Women in the workplace,* ed. P. Wallace. Boston: Auburn House.

Hartmann, H. 1976. Capitalism, patriarchy, and job segregation by sex. In *Women and the workplace,* ed. M. Blaxall and B. Reagan. Chicago: University of Chicago Press.

Hess, B. B., and M. M. Ferree, eds. 1987. *Analyzing gender: A handbook of social science research.* Newbury Park, Cal.: Sage.

Irigaray, L. 1974. *Speculum de l'autre femme.* Paris: Editions de Minuit.

Kahn, W. A., and F. Crosby. 1985. Discriminating between attitudes and discriminatory behavior: Change and stasis. In *Women and work: An annual review.* Vol. 1, ed. L. Larwood, B. A. Gutek, and A. H. Stromberg. Newbury Park, Cal.: Sage.

Kanter, R. M. 1972. *Commitment and community.* Cambridge, Mass.: Harvard University Press.

—1977. *Men and women of the corporation.* New York: Anchor.

—1986. The new workforce meets the changing workplace: Strains, dilemmas, and contradictions in attempts to implement participative and entrepreneurial management. *Human Resource Management* 25 (4): 515-37.

Katz, D., and R. Kahn. 1978. *The social psychology of organizations.* 2d ed. Toronto: John Wiley.

Kilduff, M. 1981. Deconstructing organizations. Paper presented at the annual meeting of the Academy of Management, New Orleans.

Kochan, T. 1986. *Collective bargaining and industrial relations.* Homewood, Ill.: Irwin.

Kotter, J. P., L. Schlesinger, and V. Sathe. 1979. *Organization.* Homewood, Ill.: Irwin.

Kreiger, S. 1982. *Mirror dance: Identity in a women's community.* Philadelphia: Temple University Press.

Larwood, L., B. A. Gutek, and A. H. Stromberg, eds. 1985. *Women and work: An annual review.* Vol. 3. Newbury Park, Cal.: Sage.

Lawler, E. E. 1986. *High involvement management: Participative strategies for improving organizational performance.* San Francisco: Jossey-Bass.

Leavitt, H. 1972. *Managerial psychology.* Vol. 1. Chicago: University of Chicago Press.

Likert, R. 1967. *The human organization.* New York: McGraw-Hill.

Malveaux, J. 1982. Moving forward, standing still: Woman in white collar jobs. In *Women in the workplace*, ed. P. Wallace. Boston: Auburn House.

McGregor, D. 1960. *The human side of enterprise*. New York: McGraw-Hill.

Mohrman, S. A., and T. G. Cummings. 1989. *Self-designing organizations: Learning how to create high performance*. Reading, Mass.: Addison-Wesley.

Moi, T. 1985. *Sexual/textual politics: Feminist literary theory*. New York: Methuen.

Nord, W. 1974. The failure of current applied behavioral sciences: A Marxian perspective. *Journal of Applied Behavioral Science* 10 (4): 557-78.

Oberschall, A. 1978. Theories of social conflict. *Annual Review of Sociology* 4:291-315.

Olsen, F. 1983. The family and the market: A study of ideology and legal reform. *Harvard Law Review* 96 (7): 1497-1578.

Ouchi, W. 1981. *Theory Z*. Reading, Mass.: Addison-Wesley.

Perrow, C. 1986. *Complex organizations: A critical essay*. New York: Random House.

Pettigrew, T., and J. Martin. 1987. Shaping the organizational context for black American inclusion. *Journal of Social Issues* 43 (1): 41-78.

Pfeffer, J., and G. Salancik. 1978. *The external control of organizations*. New York: Harper & Row.

Pleck, J. 1985. *Working wives/working husbands*. Newbury Park, Cal.: Sage.

Pondy, L. R. 1989. Reflections on organizational conflict. *Journal of Organizational Change Management* 2 (2): 94-98.

Riger, S. 1984. Vehicles for empowerment: The case of the feminist movement. In *Studies in empowerment*, ed. J. Rappaport and R. Hess. New York: Haworth.

Rothschild-Witt, J. 1979. The collectivist organization: An alternative to rational-bureaucratic models. *American Sociology Review* 44:509-27.

Smelser, N. J. 1962. *Theory of collective behavior*. New York: Free Press.

Smith, K. K., and D. N. Berg. 1987. *Paradoxes of group life*. San Francisco: Jossey-Bass.

Smith, K. K., V. M. Simmons, and T. B. Thames. 1989. Fix the women: An intervention into an organizational conflict based on parallel process thinking. *Journal of Applied Behavioral Sciences* 5 (1): 11-29.

Spivak, G. C. 1987. *In other worlds: Essays in cultural politics*. New York: Routledge.

Strober, M. 1982. The MBA: Same passport to success for women and men? In *Women in the workplace*, ed. P. Wallace. Boston: Auburn House.

Swidler, A. 1979. *Organization with authority: Dilemmas of social control in free schools*. Cambridge, Mass.: Harvard University Press.

Taylor, S., S. Fiske, N. Etcoff, and A. Ruderman. 1978. Categorical and contextual bases of person memory and stereotyping. *Journal of Personality and Social Psychology* 36 (7): 778-93.

Terborg, J. R., and D. R. Ilgen. 1975. A theoretical approach to sex discrimination in traditionally masculine occupations. *Occupational Behavior and Human Performance* 13:352-76.

Treiman, D. J., and H. I. Hartmann. 1981. *Women, work, and wages: Equal pay for jobs of equal value*. Washington, DC: National Academy Press.

Van Dijk, T. A. 1987. *Communicating racism*. Newbury Park, Cal.: Sage.

Waite, L. J. 1981. U.S. women at work. In *Population Bulletin*. Vol. 36, No. 2. Washington, DC: Population Reference Bureau.

Walton, R. E., and J. M. Dutton. 1969. The management of interdepartmental conflict: A model and review. *Administrative Science Quarterly* 14:73-84.

Walton, R. E., and R. B. McKersie. 1965. *A behavioral theory of labor negotiations.* New York: McGraw-Hill.

Weedon, C. 1987. *Feminist practice and poststructuralist theory.* New York: Basil Blackwell.

Zald, M., and M. Berger. 1978. Social movement in organizations: Coup d'etat, insurgency, and mass movements. *American Journal of Sociology* 83 (4): 823-61.

8

Culture and Conflict

The Cultural Roots of Discord

FRANK A. DUBINSKAS

Conflicts have a nasty habit of reappearing in organizations even when they have been "resolved" through a formal negotiation process. Public agreements to compromise may be based on trade-offs or optimizations that settle a dispute for the moment, but other similar conflicts often arise between the same parties again later. Does some hidden viper of ill will lie behind the public curtain of commitment to strike down the unwary cooperator? Is there some inscrutable or irrational force at work disrupting concord? Or is there something about the way we try to deconstruct opposing arguments that blinds us to a fundamentally dialectic interpretive process? If we try to reduce all argument to a single, hegemonic rational framework, we will lose sight of an essentially *native* process of interpretation (and misinterpretation) going on in conflicts.

Any interpretative process is rooted in the culture of the interpreters. In a dialectic of discord, the cultural systems of two conflicting groups provide fundamentally disjunct ways of understanding what is happening. Differing cultural systems create different and often opposing orientations to basic issues of life, work, goals, and values of the antagonists. Because the concept of culture provides a rubric for understanding persistent differences between groups, it also provides a foundation for understanding the generation of conflict. But cultural patterns are often invisible to their own members, and it is the very obviousness of culture that sometimes hides it from analysis. Culture is largely constituted out of the taken-for-granted, seldom articulated patterns of everyday action and belief. To the parties in an organizational conflict, their own cultural patterns simply constitute the "natural" way to do things. Each group's particular way of working and understanding their work becomes normalized and turned into a sort of commonsense backdrop to everyday life. While some guiding principles are articulated and embodied in mottoes, stories, or slogans, culture is enacted mostly in the little commonplace, everyday, unanalyzed actions that weave together into a coherent life or career. Rather than being hidden, these acts are everywhere to be seen; but their commonsensical character makes them uncommonly impervious to questioning (Geertz 1983). Fish may be keenly aware of sharks, competitors, and food, but they don't talk about *water*—they just swim in it. And life in organizations often has this peculiar, taken-for-granted flavor to it.

Ethnography provides research tools for investigating the complexities of everyday work life and its meaning. By looking at the details of particular events in the context of persistent patterns of action, ethnographic analysis can help uncover the consistencies and coherence in a cultural system. Understanding these consistencies implies a process of interpretation, and the interpretation of culture means translating the members' "native" point of view into a text that is both accessible to the reader yet still true to the natives' own understandings as well (Geertz 1973b; Ricoeur 1970; Taylor 1971). This chapter will take an ethnographic look at conflict in a small biotechnology firm and then interpret the roots of this conflict in terms of a cultural chasm separating the two major groups of antagonists: R&D scientists and senior executives.

In contemporary organizations, the sources of conflict often lie in the cultural patterns that distinguish and differentiate functional specialties from one another. The legacy of mechanistic approaches to administration in advanced industrial societies has created a surfeit of bureaucratic organizations whose internal departments stand like separate fiefdoms in a realm of arcane medieval complexity. Worse, however, is the historically emergent tendency to treat all problems of complexity as opportunities for the infinite subdivision of labor and the creation of yet narrower technical specialties. A Taylorist or mechanistic subdivision of work and responsibility has become an almost naturalized response to complexity for American managers since the 1950s, forming a cultural system of expectations about the "natural" way to manage.[1] Internal bureaucratic separations, combined with career paths along narrow tracks of expertise, promote deepening divisions of goals and interests within the organization and set the stage for conflict. Particularly vexing in a contemporary era of increasing worldwide competition are those conflicts that impede the coordination and integration of complex technical[2] projects. The pressures of rapidly bringing high-quality new products to market have increased managerial awareness that cross-functional integration is necessary to success. The problem of cross-functional *discord,* however, remains a common and often intractable one in many organizations. Overcoming the relative isolation of specialists and turning conflict into cooperation is a problem whose roots lie partly hidden in the isolation of separate and "naturalized" cultures within organizations and their intransigence to understanding another's perspective.

Conflicts emerge through a process of interaction and dialogue between groups, which includes a process of each group interpreting the other. The problem is that groups use their own naturalized cultural standards to appraise the actions of the Other, and these are not the standards by which the Others guide themselves. Cross-functional discord is thus partly a series of interpretations based upon a false premise: that everyone in an organization does (or ought to) understand things and act the same way that oneself does. Then the further unfolding of conflict is the dialectic process of interpretation between the antagonists, who gradually create a resolution through a mutual understanding of the issue at hand. Of course, power and structural factors also constrain and shape conflict resolution; and solutions may be as transient and ephemeral as the partial understandings and misinterpretations on which they are based. But the process itself is nonetheless a dialogue of native interpretations.

The task of the analyst is twofold. First, a cultural interpretation must present both of the contrasting native cultural systems to the reader so that they are both comprehensible and compelling as worldviews in themselves. Then the analyst must illuminate the contrasting native interpretations of each group by the other and show how these differences contribute to the generation of conflict. This chapter presents a cultural interpretation of a conflict arising out of cross-functional interaction both to elucidate this model and to shed light on a particular example

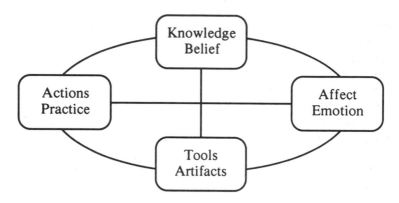

Figure 8.1. A Model of the Cultural System

of culturally rooted discord. The case of scientists and executives in start-up biotechnology firms considers differences based in widely divergent professional socialization and experience. Their social roots are nourished by disparate cultures of practical activity in a high-technology industry, and they grow into branches with internally coherent but externally competing worldviews. My goal is to show how conflicts and their expression in arguments are based in the fundamentally different cultures of work and self-definition of the antagonists.[3]

The importance of the concept of culture to this argument requires that it be defined more precisely, particularly to distinguish my usage from a number of competing contemporary models. By *cultural system*, I mean a coherent pattern of understanding built from the reciprocal relationships among four focal components. In summary, these are (a) knowledge or beliefs (the shared cognitive or conceptual understandings of what or how things are), (b) patterns of practice (both the models for doing and the model-guided, habituated actions of everyday practice), (c) tools and artifacts (the means and ends of practical action), and (d) patterns of affect that embody the compelling force of culturally appropriate models.

At the core of the culture concept is the relationship between knowledge and action: "[a] group's shared and coherent (if loosely structured) ways of interpreting their worlds, and their patterned processes of verbal and other interaction" (Dubinskas 1988, 171). "Pattern" and "process" are closely linked in this model. Whatever coherence or pattern is discernible in domains of knowledge and expertise, or belief and understanding, this same coherence is also manifested in the group's patterns of activity—in their daily enacted processes of living and working.

In essence, culture is never a strictly intellectual or cognitive category but one that is intimately tied to the ways people do things. The relationship between knowledge and practice in the culture model has two important implications, and "patterns of culture" (Benedict 1961) embody practice in two interrelated ways. First, cultural patterns are not just models *of* reality; they are also models *for* acting in the world and *for* creating that social reality through patterned actions (Geertz 1973a). A monastic rule for rituals of prayer and fasting and a company's manual of Standard Operating Procedures (SOPs) are similarly guides to right (if not always righteous) conduct. The second way that belief and practice are linked is through the daily process by which engagement in actions according to these guides makes the world envisioned in those guides both believable and compelling. The continuous reiteration of everyday practice—according to patterns or guides—reinforces the sense of coherence and validity of a model of reality. Practice habituates us to that simultaneous model *of* and *for* reality and, in the process, helps construct a coherent meaning world (Weber 1949; Schutz 1967; Taylor 1981). Cultural pattern and coherence is thus a continuous loop of interaction between what is understood and what is done.

The third component of the culture model has to do with *how* things are done. If patterns of culture are manifest in the everyday activities of technical work, then the means or "tools" by which people do this work must be part of cultural analysis as well. These tools may be intellectual, like the theories and models of scientists and financiers, or they may be material, like the electrophoresis gels of the biologist and the spreadsheet of the accountant.[4] The tools we use color and condition the ways we see and understand the world around us, and tools are themselves part of our habituated ways of practice. Tools are shaped *by* culture—they are cultural artifacts that reflect or embody understanding—and tools shape cultural practices—they mediate human activities in pursuit of all human goals.

Finally, the affective component of culture is crucial for understanding how a cultural system is experienced or *felt* as compelling by its members. People identify strongly with their own cultures; and anthropologists have consistently argued that culture is constitutive of personhood as well as of group identity (Rosaldo 1980; Shweder and Levine 1984). To say that "I *am* a biologist" or "I *am* an executive" is making a stronger claim to systematic inclusion and self-identity than simply saying "I *do* engineering or executive work." The intimacy of this strong self-definition and self-to-group identification helps make culture pervasive, persistent, and difficult to change. A comfortable intimacy grows from the familiarity of patterned daily practice; and, in this instance, we might say that "familiarity breeds *content*." Likewise, things that are "out of place" (Douglas 1966), outside the rules, or uncertain are often a source of affective disruption: anger, upset, or antipathy. This affective component is the fourth cornerstone of the cultural model. A patterned system of actions guided by understanding and mediated by tools and other objects creates a feeling in actors of positive affective association with the "right" (culturally appropriate) way to be and to do things. It is thus not surprising that encounters with those who see or do things quite differently can arouse the passions, aside from any rational calculation of "interests" in conflict. With these four components linked together and mutually influencing one another, the cultural system provides us with a multifocal intellectual lens for examining conflict and discord in organizational life.

In organizations, cultural systems may not have the depth of history that anthropologists of the farther world are wont to encounter; but organizational members and cohorts often have long personal histories of experience as members of their profession, department, or work group. And, even if they can freely exchange their work identity with other ones like mother or musician, parishioner or politician, in other contexts, they are fully immersed in the practical culture of doing things at work for nearly half their waking lives. This continuous everyday practice is certainly enough to inculcate a group ethos (Bateson 1958, 1972, 1979), a "naturalized" way of looking at and acting in the world. And the dedicated professionals of high-tech start-up firms are perhaps even more likely than many to embody a special culture of their professions. This "naturalization" of everyday practices is part of what we call "common sense," but this common sense is itself a cultural system (Geertz 1983). And common sense is a system particularly intractable to argument, discussion, or compromise. It comprises tacit as well as explicit assumptions, "automatic" as well as reasoned actions, and it engages emotion, too. Common sense may be less accessible to verbal articulation and argument, but it is no less intimately constitutive of a group's culture and worldview. It is also closely bound up in those technical, economic, political, and social activities through which organizational tasks are conducted and goals are accomplished.

With our more elaborated model of culture, we may ask again: "How is culture related to conflict in organizations?" Culture is a way of understanding both the constitution of a group with a distinctive identity and the fundamental grounds upon which groups differentiate or distinguish themselves from one another. When disparate groups in an organization encounter each other with a strong need[5] to coordinate their actions, the drive to collaborate may be stymied by a fundamental disjuncture or clash between cultural systems. Cross-functional integration is not as simple as exchanging information—like tossing the ball crisply to the next player. It is often more like standing with a baseball mitt in hand while some big fellow in a kilt prepares to toss a caber.[6] The difficulty is not just unclear "messages" but fundamental unpreparedness to receive what the sender is sending. The dilemma for participants is interpreting from a different language, with different ground rules and procedures and with different perspectives on a task.[7]

To make these concepts concrete, I will present a sketch of a conflict rooted in basic differences in worldview between two groups of antagonistic collaborators across two interacting functional specialties in the same firm. The conflict is between research scientists and financial executives over product and project planning in a young biotechnology firm. The discussion is based on ethnographic field research conducted in the early to mid-1980s in two dozen young genetic engineering firms and in their academic training grounds. (See also Dubinskas 1985, 1988.) Many of these new businesses were founded in a pressure cooker of high economic expectations and intense professional hubris by partners from the worlds of academic molecular biology and high-risk new-venture finance. As their disparate professional cultures were melded into a single organization, the new firms often experienced conflict over what research goals to pursue and how the choice should be made. Their two competing cultural logics—that of "science" and that of "business/economics"—clashed. I use "time" or "temporal order" as a key symbolic nexus in each of their cultures as a medium for exploring the grounds of conflict; and I trace temporal culture patterns across their professional careers and life cycles as well as through their everyday technical work.

Biotechnology Start-Ups:
Cancer Cures Versus Doggie Diagnostics

Many of the biotechnology start-up companies of the 1980s had two major internal constituencies: biological scientists who directed and performed R&D work and nonscientists from the business world who filled executive, financial management, and other staff positions. On the R&D side, start-up firms initially copied the structure and style of university research laboratories. Top university postdoctoral fellows and a few junior faculty were recruited as R&D directors and bench scientists. Biologists were commonly offered two to four times their university pay, a splendidly equipped lab, and an equity position in the firm. By contrast, many of the early management teams were headed by nonscientists with little background in the biology upon which their firms are based. They came from the ranks of professional entrepreneurial managers—managers who specialize in high-technology start-ups—or from the venture capital firms that had organized initial financing for the companies. Their primary expertise was in dealing with the *outside* financial world of investors rather than the *internal* management of research and development operations. The managers and scientists of these young companies saw themselves as being "in"—and "from"—different "worlds."

On the one hand, their work and future success seemed securely in the hands of research biologists, and, on the other, control of the finances and business operations of the firms usually rested in the hands of nonscientist executives. Like the two-faced god Janus of Roman mythology, these groups seemed to talk about and see their organizational world from radically different perspectives. They clashed especially over how to integrate the scientists' style of long-term, open-ended research with a business perspective geared to short-term returns for investors. On the surface, these clashes seem linked to a simple divergence in attitudes toward time: Scientists have the long-term view and managers, the short range. With further examination, however, we shall see how these different temporal planning orientations grow out of rich and complex cultural systems where the temporal ranges in planning are intimately interwoven with other significant aspects of their professional work and careers.

One illustrative argument from my field notes exemplifies the more drastic planning conflicts. A new company had been formed with the fairly general aim of exploiting the new technology of "monoclonal antibodies." The technology was part of the revolution in the "new biology" of the late 1970s that made it possible to easily create multiple exact copies (clones) of a single antibody to some particular biological substance. This monoclonal antibody (MAb) could be used as a marker for the presence of that biological substance, making it a highly specific diagnostic tool for diseases. The monoclonal antibody would attach itself to some specific disease product in a body fluid, and the linked antibody-antigen couple could be easily detected by a simple chemical assay. The CEO of "Histo-Compatibility Technologies, Inc."[8] (HiT) saw a tremendous potential market for medical diagnostics from this new technology. A recent Harvard MBA, "Wanda's" business strategy was to develop easy-to-use monoclonal antibody test kits for related families of diseases. She saw scientific expertise as key to the endeavor and wanted to attract the best scientific talent to HiT.

The company's chief scientist and R&D director, "Waldo," was a rising star in MAb research who had left a junior faculty position to join HiT. The firm's lure was the full-time pursuit of research at twice his faculty salary, with the best equipment available, and without the distractions of teaching and grant applications. As well as knowing the new monoclonal antibody technology, he was particularly interested in the "magic bullet" concept for cancer therapy. Waldo pressed me with enthusiastic details of the concept's medical promise:

> The problem with cancer chemotherapies is that the drugs are almost as bad as the disease. We flood the body with poison indiscriminately when we treat the patient. It's a delicate balancing act to get just the right amount of toxin to kill the cancer without making the patient too sick from the cure. Monoclonal antibodies will be our answer! We can use MAbs to deliver a really toxic drug directly to the cancer cell, without having it diffuse through the whole body, attacking other cells and making someone sick.

> It works like this: cancer cells have characteristic protein molecules on their cell surfaces which are different from any other proteins in the body. All we have to do is identify and isolate one of these "surface antigens" and its companion antibody. In the lab, we can clone up a whole armada of exact copies—monoclonal antibodies. Then we chemically attach a toxin to each MAb. These MAb molecules will now seek out and stick to the surface antigen on a cancer cell, and the attached drug will poison the cell. The monoclonal antibodies will deliver the drug precisely and only to the site of the cancer.

It's like a magic bullet to kill the cancer cell without any of the dangerous side effects of traditional chemotherapy!

In the beginning, the CEO and Waldo agreed that they would have a two-pronged strategy. They would split the laboratory work between some easier-to-accomplish diagnostics projects and the longer-range "magic bullet" research. The diagnostic products would generate short-term gains to fund the more complex project. Waldo's excitement was contagious; and, in the first six months of the company, he seemed to be making great progress toward his goals. If the magic bullet project worked, he would be a sure candidate for an eventual Nobel prize. He had gathered a group of postdocs and technicians through his academic networks, and their lab was bustling with energy. The medical diagnostics projects were less challenging, so they received a little less attention from Waldo himself; he left them primarily to the postdocs.

Soon, he and Wanda began to realize that they had different expectations for their collaboration. Wanda had raised nearly $7 million in two rounds of venture capital and R&D partnership funding, but the firm's capital burn rate was much higher than she initially anticipated. Waldo's lab was making progress, but even the isolation of their first antibody-antigen system for cancer was proving elusive. Wanda pressed the scientists for some signs of progress: markers or milestones they could point to on the path to their product. Much of their "progress" seemed to be eliminating failed alternatives. Now they were talking about starting work on a different kind of cancer cell whose surface proteins had already been characterized. This seemed to Wanda (and the board of directors) like a step backward. HiT would have to go back to the well for more funds, and they couldn't even show a concrete sign of progress to investors. At the same time, Wanda was unhappy that Waldo had delegated most of the diagnostics work to more junior scientists in whose hands it seemed to languish while attention was lavished on the magic bullet.

As weeks went by, the CEO and directors became increasingly frustrated with the seeming inability of the scientists to respond to their pleas for more measurable progress. They began to suspect that real effort wasn't even going into the diagnostics projects because the scientists weren't really interested in them. The marketing group, CFO, and CEO met to devise a new product strategy that they could take to the funding markets to keep the firm afloat. The plan they came up with was to temporarily dampen the magic bullet project, leave the medical diagnostics project intact (with some additional senior attention), and move the top scientific talent to a new project. The new project was a multitest monoclonal antibody diagnostic for veterinary diseases. Their market research showed them that canine disease diagnosis was a huge market in the United States. Americans will pay a lot to treat their sick pets, but it is hard to diagnose illness because dogs can't speak to describe their pains. An MAb diagnostic was a 100% certain test for diseases. Unlike human drugs or diagnostics, animal diagnostics didn't require extensive testing; and the field was not blocked by stringent government regulation. Test animals were easy to get, and test procedures could be noninvasive: no needles, jut dip a stick in a sample of feces and then swirl it in the provided test tube of buffer solution. The diagnostic MAbs are coated onto another dipstick; and this too is swirled in the test tube. A color change on the dipstick indicates the presence of a disease by-product. The planners were ecstatic about this rapid-fire way to gear up a product from expertise they already had available. Time-to-market could be an order of magnitude shorter than their current projections for magic bullets; and this was a market niche that no other "new biology" firm had entered yet.

Waldo described their reaction when he and the other scientists first heard the plan from the strategizers:

> It was the doggie-doo dipstick debacle![9] We were shocked and insulted that they wanted us to give up the very thing that had lured us to HiT in the first place. This was some little garbage project designed to scrape up a few more bucks—which we needed, for sure; but raising money was supposed to be *their* job. They were the finance experts! . . . Yet they were going to waste their best scientific resources on some mindless "dogshit" product, when we could be making a great breakthrough in the war against cancer. And now we're supposed to defeat canine heartworm? We were up in arms against it. . . .

It seemed drastically short-sighted to Waldo and his laboratory colleagues to set aside a project that would make them all rich and famous for life. The scientists argued that HiT was throwing away its future by dropping cancer research for a short-term money fix. But the business strategists retorted that "if they didn't do something for the short run, there wouldn't be any long run left!"

The two groups argued for weeks about how to balance their long-term versus short-term needs. The business plan proponents argued that the scientists had demonstrated an unwillingness even to work seriously on diagnostics as long as the "sexier" magic bullet project was in the air. They said that the company would fold if they didn't begin to generate revenue soon or at least show a clear, staged plan with definitive stages and milestones to reach the goal. Wanda argued that all of the company's scientific resources had to be dedicated to this urgent task immediately. The scientists, led by Waldo, objected strongly to killing the bullet project; but, in the end, they were forced by the power of the purse strings to start work on veterinary diagnostics. In companies like HiT, similar arguments have sometimes led to the departure of senior scientists back to academe; Nobel prize winner Walter Gilbert's exit from Biogen is an oft-noted example. But, after a few years in industry, many postdocs and technicians could not easily return to their former university bases; the status gap was too wide. Most of the HiT scientists grudgingly (and a few willingly) acknowledged the necessity of planning for near-term market winners and buckled down to the new project. As a compromise, a small but diminishing amount of resources was put aside to keep the magic bullet project alive but "on ice" until the future.

During the course of argument, however, Waldo persisted in his view of scientific work that carried over to the veterinary diagnostics: that it was inherently impossible for the biologists to promise a project with fixed dates at scheduled times. Even a doggie-doo dipstick had uncertainties about it that could not be beaten into a schedule, because aspects of the problem were hidden by Nature itself. He imaged that discovery process as one of guided iterations—with many false starts and returns, like the magic bullet project. Waldo argued that every scientific project was inherently exploratory and uncertain and that they would never be able to please the business planners with the certitude Wanda seemed to demand.

Time and Conflict

The clash between scientists and managers in HiT epitomizes the conflict between cultures that was common to those nascent industrial organizations.[10] The central ordering principle of "time" can illuminate the gulf that separates the planning styles of the two groups. Each group has a different culturally constructed sense of how their daily actions and life courses are ordered in time. Two separate domains of time are particularly important to this contrast, and I define them as planning time and developmental time. *Planning time* is the temporal patterning of social action—the order, place, and schedule of activities—in the future. There is a major contrast between the executives' "short-" or "near-term" perspectives versus the scientists' "long-range" or "long-term" view. Making schedules and doing the work according to plan are continuing sources of conflict. This temporal contrast draws most closely on the first two components of the culture model: *knowledge* and *action*, although technical knowledge tools like scientific theories and financial models certainly figure in these contrasts as well. A second domain of time addresses contrasting images of the self that each group holds. That contrast turns on disparate models of the life course and professional career: continuous movement for scientists versus maturation for managers. *Developmental time* is my general gloss for these images of a growing or maturing person, following a culturally *qua* professionally appropriate path. *Maturation* and *development* both evoke natural and social processes simultaneously. Developmental time is keyed closely to the *affective* component of the culture model, because issues of self-definition evoke a passionate commitment to the rightness (or righteousness) of one's own way of being, but it also draws again on both *belief* and *practice*—living the "right" life. Both "planning time" and "developmental time" are key symbolic nexes (Ortner 1972; Traweek 1988a, 1988b) around which important images coalesce of how the company world works and who populates it. These two symbols provide two significant interpretive lenses through which we can view the cultural roots of conflict.

Years of formal education (especially for the scientists) and practical learning have socialized each cohort to be appropriate members of their profession—knowing how to be and how to do their particular professional work. Their differences are rooted in distinctive knowledge bases and in the character and conduct of everyday work—its technical detail. The description that follows summarizes material from ethnographic fieldwork both on the respective groups' formal educational processes as well as on the working contexts of their company lives. While space does not permit much of that detail here, a thicker description is presented elsewhere (in "Janus Organizations," Dubinskas 1988a). That ethnographic context is synthesized below and organized as the dialectic of images of the Self and the Other that each group constructs in the native process of interpretation.

The dispute over magic bullets or doggie diagnostics highlights the clash of temporal relativities in a concrete argument. The basic contrast is between "long-" and "short-term" planning, and this difference also maps onto a difference between "open-ended" and "closed" plans and schedules. Planning time will thus provide us with the first cultural lens for viewing the conflict.

First, managers see themselves as quite capable of both long- and short-range planning, yet they often complain that they have "no time" to do long-range or strategic planning. They stress that immediate concerns like quarterly financial reports must take precedence over more "distant" ones such as five-year plans. They speak of this as an aspect of their native managerial "realism" (especially in contrasting themselves with their scientists). The *next* milestone, the *next* contract, and the *next* stockholders' report are the "real" near-term subjects that a manager must always address; and managers' self-images as "hard-nosed realists" emphasize their association with that immediacy. The stages on a milestone chart are also fixed points in a predictably unfolding sequence of events. They have a punctuated regularity, which fixes events in the future to a definitive schedule and defines goals and outcomes precisely along the way. An important aspect of these goals and outcomes is monetary or financial—either money spent or profit gained—and realism to the executive is linked to an economic reality that guides and impinges upon events with concrete and measured force.

Managers see their compatriot scientists as never quite having an end in sight. The time range for scientists' plans, if they are even "plans" at all to the manager, is too long, and encompasses a seemingly infinite profusion of possible branches and paths into an indistinct future. The scientists can't be easily pinned down to fixed stages and milestones, and they measure progress in the knowledge gained—a rather insubstantial sum to most executives. Furthermore, money spent on the quest seems not to bother the scientists very much. This "open-ended" approach to planning (or a struggle to keep projects open-ended) is viewed by manager as unrealistic, in terms where "realism" has necessarily to do with short terms, clearly defined processes, and finite economic goals.

But, from the opposite perspective of the interpretive dialectic, scientists have quite a different way of characterizing themselves. They say that they can "set their sights" on far-distant, visionary, and indistinct goals. They construe their open-ended temporal frames as appropriate and necessary for professional scientific work. They argue that science is drawn continually forward by the questions posed to it by Nature; there can be no fixed end in view. Their work is *prospective in its practice and planning*, an exploration and discovery process whose specific results are still hidden by Nature at the outset of planning. Thus, they argue, management demands for "milestones" on research projects—definite stages of *completed* work toward a fixed, specific end result—*contradict* the very essence of their work toward "discovery." The scientists' facts or answers are in Nature, so that marking out every stage of their discovery path in advance is futile. Scientists thus claim to have the long view but deny that they can plan and schedule work along it in the regular style that their managers require.

In striking contrast to their own self-image, the scientists see their executive partners as mired in short-range business concerns and limited by shortsightedness. As one of the senior scientists described his marketing managers:

> It's the marketing people . . . who don't understand how the *process* of science works. . . . Their sense of the world of [scientific] possibilities is too superficial. The scientists are looking five years ahead at what is being or *will* be developed, while marketing people are . . . rooted in the existing present state of perceived needs. They're just always stuck in the present. (Field note cited in Dubinskas 1988, 197)

Producing scientific *knowledge* is the primary and most valued goal of the scientists, and this professional worldview conversely devalues purely economic aims. This is not unusual in a field like human biology, where many professionals were attracted at least partly to the notion of contributing to general human welfare. There is also an aesthetics of scientific work that values broad, open-ended discovery research over the smaller refinements to established theory. This aesthetics rates exploratory science as much more personally pleasing and "elegant" (not to mention better regarded professionally) than the accomplishments of business projects motivated by short-run economic goals. This ranking of scientific work is reinforced through professional socialization, which elevates to guru status those scientists who have made the most striking leaps into the unknown and returned with new knowledge. Nobel prizes and cancer cures have much more panache to them than veterinary diagnostics. When business executives complain that they have no time for long-range planning, scientists accuse them of a fundamental incapacity, turning the observed trait into a generic character aspect of managers rather than a learned necessity of their economic role.

Moving from the planning arena per se, our scope of vision is broadened by a second symbolic lens for seeing difference: the trope of "developmental time." Underlying the conflict over how to build plans is a more fundamental difference of self-definition: contrasting images of the self as either continuously growing (the scientists) or adult and mature (the managers). This sense of developmental time overlaps with our interpretation of planning time, particularly through the image of the "open-endedness" of professional careers for scientists versus the "complete adult persons" for managers' careers. Again, the paragraphs below present a distillation of the interpretive dialectic between the two groups.

First, the managers see themselves as rather unproblematically adult and fully formed human beings. Their careers may continue to "advance" throughout their lives, but their essential nature as "complete" people is certainly accomplished by the time they achieve their first responsible managerial position. Growth in time is complete, at least in the sense of any further evolving transformation. Career advances mean getting relatively more of what they have finally achieved—positions with responsibility, authority, prestige, and financial reward—rather than a fundamental transformation in character. Managers often speak of scientists, though, as "immature" or "adolescent" in their attitudes or "not grown up." Managers connect their own maturity with their definition of the real world—one that is full of finite economic and productive activity. Productivity, for them, is measured in milestones met, schedules completed, goods delivered, and measurable wealth created rather than insubstantial and "unreal(ized)" ideas. Their finite goals contrast with the scientists' *in*finite knowledge expansion.

By contrast, biologists characterize their own developmental processes as continuous evolution. This includes progressive stages in their education as undergraduates, graduate students, and postdocs. A first faculty position in a research university then begins the long march through promotions, the tenure process, and gradually increasing administrative responsibilities. Finally, at the height of one's (ideal) career[11] come institute directorships, deanships, and "spokesperson for a field" status. Eventually a senior scientist is elevated to near-guru status, where he or she is seen as a progenitor of a scientific field or subfield.

This growth should never come to "completion" or static maturity. The locus of continuous growth is the intellectual realm of productive ideas. Scientists are taught to privilege "intellectual" concerns and knowledge building over economic, emotional, and social concerns; and intellectual growth often stands for growth in general to them. Their professional image of science as a unilinear, infinite, progressive movement of knowledge is replicated in the model of their own *self-image* as continually growing or developing people. This is a patterned synergy between a model of the self, of the primary technical work of their profession, and of the nature of reality itself—all of which are informed by a common image of continuous growth and movement, primarily in the intellectual realm. Managers, in a contrasting set of models, cast their self-images as completed adults in the same mold as their own model of work: a finite, finishable, and productive reality. Scientists then cast a jaundiced eye on this image and consider managers not as "finished adults" but as cases of arrested or frozen development.

It is no wonder, in the end, that the collaborations of scientists and managers often founder on the rocks of discord. Their images of the Other seem almost caricatures in the height of argument:

> The complete adult realist managers, in their struggles with immediate economic necessity, must contend with immature scientist-dreamers; while from the other side of the table, the far-sighted progressive scientists must protect their work—the bases of the firm's wealth—from myopic and developmentally retarded managers! (Dubinskas 1988a, 201)

Continuously recurring disagreement and conflict seemed endemic in many science-heavy biotech start-ups. The kinds of arguments that I recorded in the field are not just peculiar to biotech firms; similar divisions have long been discussed in the literature of R&D management. For all this scholarly attention, however, the conflicts in biotech have not all been erased by a decade of intraorganizational experience. And the 1980s are littered with the detritus of failed ventures or merged ones that could not create their strategic syncretism of science and business in time. Looking at the foundations of their conflicts through the lens of culture allows a deeper unity of explanation. When the fundamental disparities between the self-images, the temporal structure of work, and the nature of reality itself are compared with one another as internally coherent cultural systems, the question of explaining conflict pales beside the query: How do these people ever manage to get along at all? Their naturalized, but unspoken everyday cultural constructs can continually reemerge to undermine cooperation as they underpin conflict.

Discussion and Implications

Seeing the roots of conflict in culturally constructed differences gives us a unified platform for understanding the persistence and intensity of discord. For the biologists and executives of biotech start-ups, conflicts can be understood as disparities in cultural notions of temporal reality and the construction of selfhood. The model of each culture includes belief and action, affect and artifact, in a reciprocal system of meaning construction. The disjunctions between these clashing cultural systems underlie the political and personal conflicts that are occasioned by some specific historical circumstances, like funding some particular drug research. This concept of culture both encompasses and provides a synthetic interpretive framework for understanding historically specific conflicts without erasing the explanatory power of other theories and models to also explore the dynamics of a situation. Culture thus provides a platform for interpretation across many specific occasions of conflict for the same or similar groups of actors.

The bounds of "similarity"—the breadth of the social context of relevance for a cultural pattern or system—is an issue to be explored and discovered, not assumed a priori. The limitations of the culture model include the sense in which any given cultural system is tied to its specific communities of actors. That is, the culture model creates synthetic interpretive models for some particular group—not "humanity" as a whole. This, however, may not be a weakness when American scholars of organization theory write as though "organizations" were a universal, worldwide phenomenon, all governed by the same sets of rules of human interaction. The culture concept requires one to explore how many contexts a theory or model fits and to see how the model is transformed beyond that boundary.

On the other hand, a neglected strength of the culture model for organizational analysis is its integrated inclusion of knowledge tools and everyday technical practice in its patterns. The magic bullet and doggie dipstick examples highlight those aspects of a cultural system rather obliquely, because I picked the research *planning* process as a focal activity. But other writers on culture and technical practice have used, for instance, physical theories of time itself (Traweek 1988a, 1988b) or the technical practice of laboratory work (Latour and Woolgar 1979) as their focal lens. While this style of argument has a long and distinguished history in traditional anthropological writing (e.g., Evans-Pritchard 1940 on cattle; Malinowski 1922 on canoes; or Bunzel 1929 on ceramics), it is less common in organizational studies. Many management writers treat "culture" primarily as stories, rituals, and "values" rather than including mundane work and common tools in their models. The expanded culture model I propose (which is more common to anthropological discourse) treats everyday technical work as the means through which significant beliefs are made real and the context in which these beliefs become important enough to argue over. Particularly in a profession like molecular biology, where the content of daily activity is highly specialized, if not esoteric, it becomes critical to understand *something* of the technical detail of work and tools in order to interpret the activity as meaningful.

I began this chapter by noting that the process of conflict could be modeled as a native interpretation process, where two antagonistic groups painted pictures of each other, but each used only the limited colors of its own culture's palette. In organizational settings where practical necessity forces the antagonists to continue to interact—for instance, when they have some joint project that must be agreed upon and completed—an unfolding dialectic of continuous interpretive movement is created.

This dialectic process of moving closer together from two poles of interpretive distance is a native process of cultural translation. (It is sometimes also, of course, a failed translation.) This model differs from a communication theory model for interaction, which treats the process as an exchange of information—a reified "object" or "message" that flows from sender to receiver. That communication model lacks an analytical ability to treat fundamental differences in the capabilities of senders and receivers (interlocutors) to interpret each other's "messages." A cultural translation model treats the interaction as a joint meaning-construction process. In a failing, conflictual process, two groups are blocked in their efforts to achieve agreement by a fundamental inability (or unwillingness) to interpret each other's position or perspective. In moving toward resolution, however, conflicting groups are actively seeking meaning in the other's actions as well as proactively trying to make their own actions understandable to that other. This dialogic process includes the *re*presentation of self *to* the other as well as an exploration of discovery *of* the other (Nielsen 1990). Through that reciprocal process, a joint edifice of meaning is built and shared by both groups.[12] This mutual construction provides the basis not for the *erasure* of differences but for the cooperation and coordination of joint efforts from a new cultural platform of mutual respect and shared understanding. This shared meaning is the product of a social interaction, likely including new symbolic tools, that creates a metaphoric bridge, middle ground, or new symbolic representation that can be grasped by both parties to a dispute.[13]

In summary, an expanded model of culture addresses the overlapping relations among four focal aspects of a meaning system: knowledge, praxis, means, and passion. By training a cultural lens on the meaning systems of antagonists in a conflict, we can illuminate the foundations of their discord. This discord is brought to light through ethnographic study of the details of conflict as it unfolds in the everyday actions of antagonists. Their own interpretations of Self and the Other provide the thick texture of data that constitutes a cultural context for understanding some particular conflict. This contextual backdrop of culture, sometimes hidden by the very fact that the antagonists take it for granted, creates the scene or arena of meaning where particular conflicts are played out.

Notes

1. This system was also widely copied around the world, especially in Europe and Japan, in the wake of America's evident industrial prowess after World War II. I develop and discuss this notion of Taylorism as a culture system further in "The Heartbeat of Productivity: Hierarchy and Transformation in American Work Relations" (Dubinskas n.d.).

2. *Technical* in the broader sense can refer to any shared special (or specialized) competence that is not widely distributed in an organization. Thus accounting or finance are technical specialties, and my example from the nascent biotech industries reflects this kind of difference—between biological scientists and financial executives.

3. My ethnographic description of these professional cultures in conflict relies heavily on the more extensive description in Dubinskas (1988) of the lives, socialization, careers, and work of executives and biologists in start-up biotechnology firms. That "thicker" ethnographic description (Geertz 1973b) is referred to in summary throughout this chapter, but the instance of conflict described here is unique to this chapter.

4. Tools may also have a more ephemeral substance as software-created images in a computerized spreadsheet program or an electronic data analysis system for scientists. In this work, the discussion of "tools" will be confined to intellectual tools, for the sake of brevity in descriptions.

5. In a large organization, the "need," of course, is often felt or expressed first by some superordinate level of the organization as a strategic or tactical goal for integration.

6. A caber toss is a Scottish sport, where logs the size of telephone poles are thrown for distance.

7. These differences of perspective qua culture often require an active, two-way translation process—a dialogue—to make them intelligible. I plan to expand and discuss this concept of "cultural translation" as a dialogic process, in contrast to the common Information Theory approach to cross-cultural communication, in a future paper.

8. "Histo-Compatibility Technologies, Inc." is a pseudonym, as are the names of the principals, "Waldo" and "Wanda."

9. The actual products in this example were disguised by the company parties involved to protect their proprietary interest in bringing this product to market first. "Magic bullet" approaches to many therapies are still currently being explored in the industry, as are human and veterinary diagnostics. The choice of disguise, however, was theirs; and its colorful (pungent?) language conveys the sense of disgust of the scientists with the business planners' alternative.

10. This kind of clash is still common in many high-tech start-up ventures, and it also permeates the attempts of established companies to integrate their bureaucratically divided functions.

11. This ideological construction, of course, ignores the fundamental reality that, at each stage of advance, only a few people are elevated to the next level. Traweek (1988a, 1988b) describes how physicists see this as a kind of "natural selection" process for the worthy and intelligent. The skeptical observer notes that there is also a self-replicating community of senior scientists that has considerable power over access to these higher states.

12. But note Anne Donnellan's work on what is shared in "shared" understanding in this context (Donnellan 1986).

13. See note 7 above regarding further development of the cultural translation model.

References

Bateson, G. 1958. *Naven.* 2d ed. Stanford, Cal.: Stanford University Press.
—1972. *Steps to an ecology of mind.* New York: Ballantine.
—1979. *Mind and nature: A necessary unity.* New York: Bantam.
Benedict, R. 1961. *Patterns of culture.* Boston: Houghton Mifflin.
Blakey, M., F. Dubinskas, S. Forman, et al., eds. n.d. *Diagnosing America: Anthropology and public engagement* (under review by the University of Michigan Press).
Bunzel, R. 1929. *The Pueblo potter.* New York: Columbia University Contributions to Anthropology (Vol. 8).
Donnellan, A. 1986. Language and communication in organizations. In *The thinking organization,* ed. H. Sims, 136-64. San Francisco: Jossey-Bass.
Douglas, M. 1966. *Purity and danger: An analysis of concepts of pollution and taboo.* Middlesex, England: Penguin.

Dubinskas, F. A. 1985. The culture chasm: Scientists and managers in genetic-engineering firms. *Technology Review* 88 (4): 24-30, 74.

—1988. Janus organizations: Scientists and managers in genetic engineering firms. In *Making time: Ethnographies of high-technology organizations*, ed. F. Dubinskas, 170-228. Philadelphia: Temple University Press.

—n.d. The heartbeat of productivity: Hierarchy and transformation in American work relations. In *Diagnosing America: Anthropology and public engagement*, ed. M. F. Blakey, F. Dubinskas, S. Forman, et al. (under review by the University of Michigan Press).

Evans-Pritchard, E. E. 1940. *The Nuer: A description of the modes of livelihood and political institutions of a Nilotic people*. Oxford, England: Clarendon.

Geertz, C. 1973a. Religion as a cultural system. In *The interpretation of cultures: Selected essays*. New York: Basic Books.

—1973b. Thick description: Toward an interpretive theory of culture. In *The interpretation of cultures: Selected essays*. New York: Basic Books.

—1983. Common sense as a cultural system. In *Local knowledge: Further essays in interpretive anthropology*. New York: Basic Books.

Latour, B., and S. Woolgar. 1979. *Laboratory life: The social construction of scientific facts*. Beverly Hills, Cal.: Sage.

Malinowski, B. 1922. *Argonauts of the Western Pacific*. New York: Dutton.

Nielsen, R. 1990. Dialogic leadership as ethics action (Praxis Method). *Journal of Business Ethics* 9:25-43.

Ortner, S. B. 1972. On key symbols. *American Anthropologist* 75:1338-46.

Ricoeur, P. 1970. *Freud and philosophy*. New Haven, Conn.: Yale University Press.

Rosaldo, M. 1980. *Knowledge and passion: Ilongot notions of self and social life*. Cambridge, Mass.: Cambridge University Press.

Schutz, A. 1967. *The phenomenology of the social world*. Boston: Northwestern University Press.

Shweder, R. A., and R. A. Levine, eds. 1984. *Culture theory: Essays on mind, self, and emotion*. Cambridge, Mass.: Cambridge University Press.

Taylor, C. 1981. Interpretation and the sciences of man. *Review of Metaphysics* 25:3-51.

Traweek, S. 1988a. *Beamtimes and lifetimes: The world of high energy physicists*. Cambridge, Mass.: Harvard University Press.

—1988b. Discovering machines: Nature in the age of its mechanical reproduction. In *Making time: Ethnographies of high-technology organizations*, ed. F. Dubinskas, 39-91. Philadelphia: Temple University Press.

Weber, M. 1949. *The methodology of the social sciences*. New York: Free Press.

9

Bringing Conflict Out From Behind the Scenes

Private, Informal, and Nonrational Dimensions of Conflict in Organizations

JEAN M. BARTUNEK
DEBORAH M. KOLB
ROY J. LEWICKI

The UIC Chancellor Decision

The year 1990-91 was an eventful political year in Illinois. Governor James Thompson, a Republican, was retiring, and, during fall 1990, James Edgar, also a Republican, was elected to succeed him. During spring 1991, Richard Daley, a Democrat and the incumbent mayor of Chicago, was running for (and eventually won) reelection.

During this school year, the University of Illinois at Chicago (UIC) conducted a search for a new chancellor. (In some U.S. universities, "chancellor" is a title roughly equivalent to president of the university.) The decision about the position was to be made in mid-March 1991 by the Board of Trustees of the University of Illinois, an elected body in the state.

AUTHORS' NOTE: We are grateful to Linda L. Putnam and Gay Spencer for their helpful comments on this chapter.

209

The chancellor selection procedure required that nominees be proposed by a 16-member search committee composed almost entirely of faculty and administrators at UIC. There were 100 candidates for the position. One was James Stukel, the acting chancellor. Stukel had held positions as a faculty member and administrator at the Urbana-Champaign and Chicago campuses of the University of Illinois. One of the other candidates was Paula Wolff, a former staff member for Governor Thompson and the head of the transition team for Governor Edgar. She had received a doctorate in political science from the University of Chicago and had been a tenured faculty member at Governors State University 14 years previously, prior to taking a position in state government in Illinois.

At the time the search process was initiated, Stanley Ikenberry, the president of the University of Illinois system, instructed the search committee to consider women and minorities as possible candidates. The job description he wrote, however, made Stukel seem the obvious choice for the position. Wolff was publicly supported by governor Edgar, former Governor Thompson, and Mayor Daley. Indeed, it was Edgar who originally recommended Wolff for the position and contacted the search committee on her behalf. Although Edgar eventually distanced himself from the process, Thompson and Daley continued to support her actively.

The search committee eventually narrowed the field to three finalists, all of whom were white and male. The finalists included Stukel but not Wolff. The search committee said that Wolff ranked about 30th of the 100 candidates, in large part because she lacked experience in university administration. Former Governor Thompson publicly denigrated the decision not to interview her (*Chicago Tribune,* 8 March, 1991).

The lobbying effort for Wolff intensified. Elected and appointed state and local government officials contacted members of the board of trustees and search committee as well as staff in various departments at UIC on her behalf. Ikenberry eventually requested on three separate occasions that the search committee interview Wolff for the position. After the third request, the committee agreed. The interview took place approximately one week before the board of trustees would make the decision. In response, approximately 300 to 400 faculty members and other personnel at UIC held a meeting to protest Wolff's interview in particular and political encroachment on academic prerogatives in general. For at least some of the faculty, this meeting evoked memories of their anti-Vietnam protests 20 years previously. A rumor went around campus that Wolff would be selected as chancellor, even though Ikenberry, shortly after the interview with Wolff, announced his support for Stukel.

Shortly after this protest, a group of women professional staff members at UIC announced their support for Wolff. Their support was based, in part, on their belief that the search committee had violated its mandate. It was supposed to make a special effort to seek out minority candidates and women but had predictably narrowed the field to white males.

On the weekend before the decision, Governor Edgar and President Ikenberry, along with the chairperson of the board of trustees and some other board members, attended a basketball game between Indiana University and the University of Illinois at Urbana-Champaign. At the game, they talked about the upcoming decision on the chancellor and especially Ikenberry's concerns about likely negative effects on UIC if Wolff were chosen. Shortly after the game, Governor Edgar said that he would be supporting Stukel. In addition, he announced that he would attend the board of trustees meeting and cast a vote for Stukel. When he called Wolff to let her know of his decision, she withdrew.

At the board of trustees meeting, Stukel received eight votes for chancellor, including Governor Edgar's. One woman on the board voted for Wolff and one woman abstained, both in protest over the search committee's exclusion of women and minorities. In a statement that he read at the meeting, Ikenberry promised to appoint a committee of faculty, board members, and administrators to review the composition of search committees (*Chicago Tribune,* 15 March, 1991).

*   *   *

The preceding section describes a highly public and publicized conflict. The process of selecting the chancellor included formal procedures for nomination and consideration of candidates and was resolved by a public vote on the basis of a rational criterion: who would be the best person for the job. One might conclude by looking at the outcome and the formal elements of the procedure that this conflict conformed to a rather traditional model of conflictual decision making (see Allison 1971; Janis 1989). Analysts might ask several questions about the decision. Was it the best and most rational one? Was it collaborative or competitive? Was it fair? And so on.

While the decision included public, formal, and rational components, much of its process and the factors that affected the final outcome were not at all public, formal, or rational. First of all, the decision was political. Behind-the-scenes lobbying of UIC personnel by state and local government officials undermined the formal procedure. The conflict involved issues of gender and (potentially) race, factors that surely confounded the selection process. Strong feelings about prerogatives, political process, and discrimination were expressed by many of the participants and took on symbolic meaning through a variety of activities. Finally, the conflict was resolved through informal discussion at a basketball game (one won, incidentally, by Indiana) and not at the board meeting. That formal meeting was merely a ratification of a decision that had already been made informally.

This story illustrates several of the themes in this book and suggests why attending to them is so important in understanding conflict. While this conflict was a highly public one, there were also a series of private and informal events in which the emotions and feelings of various groups came to the surface. Indeed, it was these informal events that took on increasing prominence as the dispute unfolded. The issue was resolved quietly—quite literally "on the sidelines"—by a few board members. Some professors became very emotional because the protest meeting reminded them of the days of protest around the Vietnam war—something that had tremendous affective and symbolic overtones for them. The professional women who supported Wolff also demonstrated strong affective reactions to the process; but, for them, the issue was gender, not the encroachment of government on the academy. Thus the UIC conflict example highlights a central argument of this book: The public, formal, and deliberate aspects of conflict frequently mask a more complex set of affective dynamics that take place informally and in private but that are critical to dispute dynamics and outcomes.

The chapters in this book elaborate a number of issues about these understudied dynamics of conflict in organizations and demonstrate the need to develop a framework that extends beyond more commonly accepted ways of discussing the topic. Indeed, several chapters in the book (Friedman offers the most dramatic example) suggest that there are often strongly negative consequences for an organization when only the public and deliberate faces of conflict are presumed to matter and when the private faces are deemed dysfunctional or irrelevant.

Our purpose in this final chapter is to tie these issues together and explore some of their implications. First, we summarize what the various chapters reveal about private, informal, and nonrational dimensions of conflict handling. Second, we describe the integral role of these conflict dimensions in many aspects of organizations, especially communication and interpretation processes, organizational structure, and organizational change. Third, we take a second brief look at the UIC chancellor decision. Finally, we suggest some next steps in the study of conflict in organizations.

The Private, Informal, and Nonrational Dimensions of Conflict

Characteristics of Private Conflict Handling

In the public spaces of organizations, as the chapters suggest, conflict is kept in check and masked through shared conventions that keep it from open view. Meetings are marked by civil discourse; personal attacks are whispered behind closed doors. As March and Simon (1958) suggested long ago, public conflicts are often treated as problems to be solved and decisions to be made, not simply disputes to be resolved. But what happens in the private spheres?

As managed in the backstage realms of action, conflict is *private,* covert, disguised within other activities, and often not labeled as "conflict" at all (Martin). It occurs off-line during time-outs and sidebar discussions (Friedman, Kolb, Van Maanen). In Van Maanen's study, the police deal privately with conflict during time-outs with a little help from a bottle. Morrill and Kolb describe some of the discussions that occur behind closed doors—spaces out of public view that provide opportunities for the expression of sentiments that cannot be voiced in public. For some, it is the absence of higher authority that frees disputants (Van Maanen); for others, it is the absence of scrutiny by colleagues (Dubinskas, Friedman, Kolb, Morrill).

In contrast, in the forums that are more or less public, expressions of conflict are often so tacit that they may not be recognized or labeled as such. Bartunek and Reid illustrate "passive resistance" in public meetings as an example of the ways that private conflict modes exist alongside public expression. Similarly, Martin describes a somewhat devious conflict-handling style presented under the guise of humanitarian concern, an initiative to coordinate the birth of a child with a new-product announcement. The visibility of this strategy is so low that even some of the people most closely involved in the controversy are barely aware of the conflict beneath it.

Finally, some of the chapters indicate that one of the benefits of private conflict handling is to enable public activities to proceed smoothly and without the appearance of apparent conflict. This had certainly been the case with labor relations at International Harvester (Friedman) prior to new management. In the cases Kolb describes, the mediators' peacemaking and coalition building behind the scenes preceded the orchestration of public presentations where the highly charged issues could be discussed relatively calmly. It thus may be that the outwardly collaborative front of much of organizational life has this appearance primarily *because* of private, behind-the-scenes conflict-handling activities (Goffman 1959).

From the previous chapters, it is clear that private dimensions of conflict do not exist independently of their public opposite. Indeed, these private actions make sense only in light of public activity. The time-outs Van Maanen describes, for example, can exist only if there are "time-ins" for daily work. During collective bargaining, public activities set the context for private conflict handling. Labor negotiators acknowledge that public performances—the "dog and pony show" and the "laundry list of complaints"—are a front for the "real work" of negotiation, which takes place in private (Friedman). In fact, both are necessary for effective dispute management, and understanding of both is necessary for adequately understanding conflict dynamics and resolution.

Characteristics of Informal Conflict Handling

The study of conflict in courts and communities alerts us to how the setting of dispute processing influences the ways conflicts are phrased and the norms that govern their expression. How neighbors act toward each other as they yell angrily across the back fence differs considerably from the demeanor they will adopt during formal case proceedings in the small claims court—so too in organizations. Norms governing the expression of a conflict when it is rehashed in the ladies' room differ from those that dominate in a formal complaint procedure.

The chapters suggest that there are several norms, or "rules," that govern these informal interactions. One characteristic is *informality*, in which formal status, position, procedure, and rules of interaction are minimized. During the pub tours, office parties, and raiding tours, for example, rank is treated less seriously; everyone is expected to act drunk, participate in the conversation, and forget about it in the morning. Everybody knows that disagreements that might be condemned in the formal setting can be addressed without consequences in informal time-outs (Van Maanen). In the informal culture of mediation that Friedman describes, "professional" negotiators develop a collegial mode of interacting with each other that differs considerably from their arm's length posture when they are across the table formally as adversaries. The new management's failure to understand these informal norms wrecked a carefully orchestrated formula between informal problem solving and formal ratification. Finally, Bartunek and Reid suggested that there were clear informal norms and rules for the way conflict was dealt with at the McLaughlin School: School personnel would ignore requests and the administration would back down.

These informal conflict-handling norms are frequently embedded in everyday organizational activities. For example, the situation Martin described was likely seen by the CEO as a relatively ordinary humanitarian decision, while the low-visibility conflicts Morrill describes are hidden in events like playing golf and advising a client.

As is evident from these descriptions, norms for informal conflict handling that develop, while well known and expected within individual organizations, do not bear much resemblance to each other across organizations. They are situational in nature, ideographic rather than nomothetic. As Dubinskas suggests about cross-culture comparisons, it is unlikely that these norms are identical across settings. Each organization or subgroup, however, as part of its culture (perhaps as an element of the patterns of practice that Dubinskas describes), appears to develop enduring informal patterns of conflict handling. As with private conflict handling during alleged public activities, these informal patterns support and often complement standard formal arrangements so that both can work in a satisfactory manner.

Characteristics of "Nonrational" Conflict Handling

In the public and formal arenas where disputes are handled, rational and calculated discourse is presumed to be the norm. In the background, and given the opportunity for informal expression, disputants are likely to express themselves differently. This aspect of conflict handling is frequently spontaneous and driven by impulses and feelings more than deliberate action—hence it is "nonrational." In the private spheres of organizational activity, people are more likely to be emotional; they get angry, they swear, they even cry. In these private spaces, personalized accounts of concrete events get told and gossip is freely exchanged. These modes of conflict expression are very common in organizations and often therapeutic. Indeed, the chapters in this book suggest that opportunities to behave nonrationally in private may make the public expression of disagreement in organizations appear more rational than it really is.

The chapters capture many of the nonrational dynamics that occur in private spaces. First, considerable *emotion* is attached to many of the activities described here. At the McLaughlin School, the rather personal dispute between the principal and academic director often became quite heated and upsetting for both (Bartunek and Reid). In other examples, tears were shed in the presence of the women peacemakers (Kolb), and officers hurled insults at each other and other police in the pubs (Van Maanen).

There are other examples of nonrational discourse as well. *Gossip* is quite common. Behind closed doors, in the intervals before the start of meetings, and over drinks, various people congregate to gossip with each other about events that bother them in the organization (Friedman, Kolb, Van Maanen). Gossip allows organizational members to hold forth and ventilate their feelings about superiors and to get support from their colleagues (Bartunek and Reid, Kolb, Van Maanen).

Organizational members also deal with differences through covert insults and veiled hostility. Executives covertly insult each other when they elaborately (and very publicly) clean and load their pipes while one of their colleagues is speaking at a meeting (Morrill). Organizational members cast unfriendly glances at each other, cut each other, fail to return phone calls, roll their eyes, murmur under their breath, and tell jokes at each other's expense.

The space to act in nonrational ways allows people to express their emotions about issues that may be very important to them. The disagreement between the scientists and managers that Dubinskas described ostensibly concerned rational business issues: how to finance research and how to prioritize research projects. Feelings ran deep on these issues, however. To be able to ventilate about the "doggie-doo dipstick debacle" enabled the scientists to engage the issue more deliberately on other occasions.

Sometimes nonrational expressions serve to permit resolution of the conflict in private spaces and prevent it from erupting publicly. In the pub tours that Van Maanen describes, many of the little grievances that arise at work are engaged and disposed of under the influence of drink. Similarly, some of the disputes that Kolb discusses are considered resolved simply because each party has had a chance to tell her story. On the other hand, the highly emotional battle that Bartunek and Reid describe seemed to have less positive outcomes. The acrimony of the relationship that developed between the principal and academic director eventually obscured the apparently rational issue of restructuring to achieve increased collaboration.

In their focus on the understudied dimensions of the ways that conflict is expressed and managed in several organizations, these chapters help us understand something about the puzzle posed by Galbraith that was presented in the opening pages of the book. Out of sight and in private spaces, where formal norms of conflict management are abandoned and where nonrational discourse dominates, members find ways to express their disagreements with each other. These means have substantial—though hidden—impacts on the course of public conflict.

The Integral Roles of Private, Informal, and Nonrational Conflict Handling in Organizations

The chapters in this volume make it evident that the ways in which conflicts are defined and handled informally and in private not only affect public and formal conflict handling but are also intertwined with other aspects of organizational functioning; conflict is part of the social fabric of organizations. Specifically, the chapters indicate that conflict handling affects and is affected by interpretation and communication, that conflict handling is also shaped by the structures and cultures within which it occurs (and in turn influences these structures and cultures), and that there is a strong relationship between conflict and organizational change.

Interpretation and Communication

While some organizational conflicts are objective, arising out of truly incompatible goals or scarcity of resources, much organizational conflict does not neatly fit into this category. Conflict is often a performance to which different audiences attach different meaning. Conflict arises and escalates, in part, from members operating out of different interpretive schemata and taking action to create and maintain their versions of reality (Moch and Bartunek 1990). Thus conflicts over the same issues can resurface many times but assume different forms, depending upon who is involved, their interpretations of what is happening, how the social drama is orchestrated, and the form taken by dispute resolution.

The chapters indicate that different parties to a conflict often comprehend the same apparent events in varying ways. For example, Dubinskas and Friedman explain how different groups (scientists and managers or "professional" and "new" negotiators) were operating out of very different logic systems regarding multiple dimensions of their work. Pub tours are one of the ways CID officers distinguish themselves and their viewpoints from the uniformed patrolmen (Van Maanen). In conflicts between groups, each group tends to focus on different dimensions of the conflictual issue (e.g., the importance of money and symbolic cues) and to ascribe its own meanings to the same issue (such as very different meanings of "time").

As Dubinskas notes, attempting to cross these interpretive divides is difficult, and the attempts themselves can escalate the conflict. The problem is further compounded because parties are often unaware that their interpretations differ from others'. It is unlikely, for example, that the managers and scientists described by Dubinskas are aware of their different images of time or human maturation. Indeed, differing interpretations may only become visible through conflict. Thus problems with normal communication and interpretation may only be seen when something happens that disrupts "normal" communication devices within and between groups (Gioia and Poole 1984).

The studies indicate that some form of translation process is often needed to bridge these interpretive divides and enable productive communication across them. They further suggest that, to be successful, such translation processes are likely to take place informally and in private and to allow nonrational expression. The chapters illustrate several of these devices. For example, Van Maanen shows that, when formal rules of communication and decorum are relaxed during time-outs, communication is eased. The drinking rituals create bonds not typically apparent on formal occasions. Kolb suggests that the translation process is often carried out by individuals (in particular, women) who mediate for individuals who differ. Friedman extends this notion, developing a "culture of mediation." He proposes that, in many organizations, union and management negotiators and other boundary spanners develop a specific culture that serves to bridge gaps between groups. When something happens that disrupts these cultural patterns, such as when disputants don't understand the necessity for informal and private conflict handling, the groups' ability to communicate with each other is substantially disrupted. The ability to bridge cultural gaps is a valuable contribution of the conflict-handling modes discussed here.

Private and informal conflict-handling processes affect this in at least three ways. First, they affect initial understandings about particular conflicts in that they enable participants to collect more "data" about disputes than they could in public and formal settings where "rational" behavior is required. These data may come in all forms—facts, events, behaviors, and actions as well as perceptions, feelings, reactions, attitudes, biases, and judgments (Friedman, Van Maanen).

They also allow parties to explore and test interpretations of a dispute in a relatively "safe" manner. In a discussion of the ways individuals respond to conditions of unfairness and injustice, Sheppard, Lewicki, and Minton (1992), building on an earlier model developed by Felstiner, Abel, and Sarat (1981), suggest that people proceed through four stages—naming (defining what the dispute is all about), blaming (assigning responsibility to certain individuals or events for "causing" the dispute), "explaining" (collectively defining and rationalizing the event so that particular courses of action may be more likely to occur), and taking action. Private conflict-handling procedures permit naming, blaming, and explaining processes to occur in a free and unfettered form. Parties can react to the dispute both intellectually and emotionally, rationally and irrationally, with hard data and with intuition; they can be as biased and subjective as they please and share their views with others without fear of criticism and disapproval, because they are "among friends" (Bartunek and Reid, Dubinskas, Friedman, Kolb, Van Maanen)

Finally, as parties to a dispute privately share their rational and non-rational perspectives, a collective consensus emerges about the appropriate naming, blaming, and explaining dynamic to fit the situation. As people share their perceptions and feelings, they test for agreement and disagreement. The desire for social support and social confirmation of one's perceptions and feelings often leads the discussion from a sharing of individual perspectives to a collective "group mind" or group definition of the conflict, its causes, and the implications for action (Van Maanen). Once collectively set, these explanations and actions are usually self-reinforcing and highly resistant to change. They can increase conflict, as in the case Van Maanen described, if the collective consciousness is entirely within the group. They can foster conflict resolution (Friedman) if the collective consciousness includes representatives of conflicting groups.

Structural Dimensions of Conflict

Most inquiry into the relationship between structure and conflict focuses primarily on structural factors that lead to the initiation of conflict (Miles 1980). The chapters in this book develop a different perspective by addressing the ongoing relationship between conflict handling and organizational structure. Two issues emerge from this work: (a) The dominant forms that conflict takes in an organization are related to the culture and structures within which it is embedded, and (b) there is a tendency for parties to ignore these organizational influences and to attribute most disputes to personal causes.

Structural and cultural causes of conflict. Structural and cultural arrangements in organizations influence patterns of conflict management and the forms these activities are likely to take. Conflict is built into organizational structures, whether they are simple, bureaucratic, or "adhocratic," and leads to public methods for dealing with disputes that are, in some sense, almost preordained (Cyert and March 1963; Mintzberg 1979). For example, especially in a bureaucracy, one expects that many disputes will be settled by executive fiat or by official procedures. Indeed, there are many organizational examples where almost all conflicts are resolved unilaterally (Dubinskas, Morrill). In the shadow of formal authority, however, private conflict handling frequently revolves around nonrational and informal means such as vengeance, avoidance, and accommodation (Black 1990).

In the settings investigated here, avoidance and accommodation are the most commonly described forms of dealing with conflict. Actors passively avoid (and sometimes even actively avoid) a dispute (Bartunek and Reid, Dubinskas, Martin, Morrill) or simply tolerate conflicts that arise (Morrill, Van Maanen). The authors provide a number of explanations that have both structural and cultural origins for the dominance of toleration and avoidance. In particular, within many of the organizations studied, the press to get on with one's work provides incentives to keep up the appearance that things are running smoothly and without apparent conflict (see Thomas 1976).

But organizational structures themselves can also explain why these forms of conflict handling predominate. In some of the organizations studied here, members operate more or less autonomously; thus they have little occasion to bump up against others with whom they might come into conflict. This independence was evident at the McLaughlin School (Bartunek and Reid), where units were described as "fiefdoms." In these organizations, the parts develop significant autonomy, accompanied by loyalty and language that supports and enhances the parts to the detriment of the organization as a whole. At the McLaughlin School, the various groups who were opposed to increased coordination found it relatively easy to avoid conflict through a strategy of passive resistance. In the accounting firm, the work structure of the professional partnership gave partners considerable leeway to choose to ignore certain people and initiatives (Morrill). Conflict avoidance preserves these independent boundaries. Indeed, studies in other settings suggest that, in the relative absence of crosscutting ties, mechanisms for peaceful resolution of conflict are slow to develop, leaving avoidance and violence the only major options available (Baumgartner 1988; Gluckman 1955).

In those settings where members interact on an ongoing basis, there are other forces that make avoidance and toleration the preferred modes (Martin). With close colleagues and friends, we may, as Simmel (1908, 47) suggests, "take a chance on discord." At International Harvester, the ongoing relationship between the union president and the manager of labor relations permitted exchanges of this sort, a situation that was later disrupted (Friedman). In other situations, where relationships are more instrumental, and where the ties that bind are relatively weak (Morrill), relationships appear to "take a more harmonious and conflictless course" (Simmel 1908, 47; Baumgartner 1988; Granovetter 1973). That is, conflicts are not openly expressed but tolerated.

The forms organizational conflict will take are also influenced by the culture in which conflict occurs, and this suggests some further explanations as to why toleration and avoidance are so common. In many organizations, a vision of harmony and integration is promulgated (Martin, Kolb). When this is the case, the expression of conflict is often viewed as antisocial (Greenhouse 1986). Only those who can demonstrate the ability to keep personal conflict in check and who exhibit self-control are able to get along with and earn the respect of their peers and others in the organization.

When avoidance and toleration dominate the ways individuals and groups deal with differences, existing structures and systems are likely to go unchallenged (Martin). Disputes over the same organizational issues continue to surface but are never definitively resolved (Bartunek and Reid). Conflicts surface over and over again: over coordination and autonomy at the school, over funding priorities at the biotechnology firm, over discipline and conduct in the CID, and over client management at the accounting firm. But this process of repetition and redundancy also reinforces existing structures of authority and influences the ways conflict is handled (by avoidance, toleration, and passive resistance). Informal efforts by peacemakers and other boundary spanners to resolve the conflicts are also more likely to facilitate the status quo of conflict processes than to challenge it (Friedman, Kolb). Thus it appears that the avoidance and toleration modes of handling disputes may also reinforce the current power/status system of an organization—an outcome that may be satisfactory to the power holders but not to those who challenge its legitimacy, authority, or effectiveness.

Personal attributions. Within the organizations studied, conflicts arise for many reasons. Many are inevitable, due to the interdependent structures in which people work. What is so interesting, however, is the tendency for those involved to frame and interpret the disputes as "personal" rather than structural in cause. That is, there is a tendency to personalize conflict and to blame the people who are currently on stage during the times when conflict dramas are played out (Pettigrew 1973). This occurred in most of the settings studied here; people in certain positions became lightening rods for blame and censure, regardless of other explanations for the dispute (Bartunek and Reid, Dubinskas, Friedman, Van Maanen).

Critics who have identified this problem point out that, in defining the causes of conflict, overemphasis is given to interpersonal and group conflict to the neglect of the structural and societal bases in which these interpersonal and group differences are embedded (Collins 1975; Kriesberg 1973; Mouzelis 1967). The studies in this book begin to explain this dynamic by suggesting that participants in conflict are likely to focus on personal issues to the neglect of structural ones. That may be why models of interpersonal conflict management (Thomas 1976; Pruitt 1981) are so much more popular than discussions of the structural bases of conflict. But, to the degree that disputes are personalized, their organizational and societal origins are minimized or ignored, and so serious challenge to existing systems and structures is unlikely (Abel 1982).

The Relationship Between Conflict and Change

The manner in which disputes are addressed has implications for organizational change. To the degree that conflict avoidance and toleration predominate as modes of conflict handling, they lead to reinforcement and replication of existing modes of operating rather than to evaluation, modification, or replacement of those structures. Bartunek and Reid argue, for example, that passive resistance at the school undercut the planned change effort. In a slightly different vein, Martin points out how difficult it is to change gender relations in the workplace when the conflict is obscured by a veneer of humanitarianism. The off-line activities described by Van Maanen and Kolb provide opportunities for people to deal with differences within the system in a way that reinforces the system.

In particular, conflicts tend to reinforce already established power and authority relationships. For example, Sheppard, Lewicki, and Minton (1992) point out that many challenges to justice, fairness, and impartiality in organizations are resolved in a way that deals with the specific problem but leaves unaffected the underlying systemic causes of the unfairness. In this volume, Kolb stresses in her study that the ways the women mediated conflicts were structurally very similar to the already established hierarchy of their organizations. In Martin's case, the conflict patterns also duplicated the already established hierarchy, with the CEO appearing to make the final decision. In both of these studies, the gendered structure of organizational relationships is reinforced. Morrill indicated that, when authority relationships were present, conflict tended to be resolved unilaterally. Finally, in Dubinskas's study, the more powerful CEO was able to impose her will on the less powerful scientists, forcing them to work on "doggie-doo dipsticks" rather than "magic bullet" cancer cures.

In at least one of the cases, conflict-handling behavior *did* lead to large-scale system change. By ignoring the private and informal dimensions of collective bargaining, the new management at International Harvester almost destroyed the company (Friedman); however, this was no doubt not the change they intended. More frequently, the previously existing conflict patterns served as a force for the status quo, supporting the already established formal structure and diffusion of power.

It is not necessary that conflict have this relatively conservative effect; other studies (Bartunek 1984; Child and Smith 1987) have described ways the conduct of conflict in an organization can foster major change rather than retarding it. It may be, however, that conflict that stimulates change is fairly rare. We argue here that change is particularly unlikely to occur if the conduct of conflict is primarily private and informal, leading to modes of conflict handling that emphasize avoidance, toleration, and private grievances. By keeping these disputes out of sight and managing them off-line, social relations and norms of the workplace may be subtly redefined (Morrill) but in ways that support existing structural arrangements.

The studies in this volume indicate that change is not always part of the agenda for disputants. Some of the conflict-handling patterns described here appeared satisfactory to virtually all of the participants. These include the time-outs described by Van Maanen, many of the more private grievances illustrated by Morrill, and the mediation strategies described by Kolb. Patterns presented in some of the other chapters led to satisfactory outcomes for some, but not all, of the participants. For example, the patterns described by Martin and Dubinskas were satisfactory to those already wielding hierarchical power, and the passive resistance described by Bartunek and Reid was satisfactory to those who are able to resist change. There were also some clear "losers," however, in each of these chapters. Finally, the Friedman chapter illustrated an outcome that was unsatisfactory to virtually everyone involved. Thus the chapters indicate a clear relationship between the degree of satisfaction with conflict handling and the amount of change being attempted. In the situations in which no major change was being sought (e.g., during the time-outs), the participants were quite satisfied. When significant change was being attempted (e.g.,

Friedman, Bartunek and Reid), however, the conflict and its outcomes were far less satisfactory to some of the key parties in the dispute.

The conservative effects of conflict have implications for the way diversity plays out in organizations. If the studies presented here are indicative of broader organizational dynamics, diversity of class, race, and gender as well as ideological differences are likely in most organizations to be translated into daily work problems, personalized and avoided publicly, and managed primarily in the private spheres. In the process, these important social issues are likely to be transformed from group to individual issues, from social concerns to matters of task, and from public interest to private venting (Friedman, Kolb, Martin). These tendencies make it less likely that, without another kind of intervention, most diversity-related conflicts will lead to any significant changes in the way organizations adapt to a work force that is becoming increasingly diverse.

Returning to the UIC Chancellor Decision

It is useful to return briefly to the UIC chancellor decision and to consider how the concepts developed in this chapter help us understand the outcome. The basketball game (although taking place within a huge public gathering) permitted a safe, private environment in which President Ikenberry, Governor Edgar, and the board members who were present could share data and feelings, informally test their individual decision preferences, and develop a collective agreement on a course of action. But the decision-making process considered as a whole, beginning with Ikenberry's description of characteristics needed for the chancellor position and ending with the basketball game, reinforced the status quo with regard to characteristics of the chancellor. While there was a public and formal call for diversity among candidates, the private, informal activities that took place—such as the job description Ikenberry provided—supported sameness. Government officials apparently sought publicly to emphasize diversity by lobbying for Paula Wolff, a woman. They didn't take into account, however, the emotional impacts their lobbying would have on academics who experienced their academic freedom being challenged. The combination of events led to a decision regarding the chancellor position that was very similar to previous decisions, not one that fostered the diversity that was a public aim of the search process.

Conclusion: Next Steps for the
Study of Conflict in Organizations

There is a strong call for organizational studies to be "useful," to produce work that has direct application to specific problems in organizations (Beyer 1982; McKelvey and Aldrich 1983; Thomas and Tyman 1982). The call for prescription is particularly strong in the conflict field, where people have an interest in learning how to deal with differences better (Fisher and Ury 1981).

Recently, Brief and Dukerich (1991) have challenged the idea that prescription is the appropriate end of organizational research. They argue that current research in organizational studies is better suited to provide practitioners with diverse explanations about phenomena than with specific applied steps. Research should aim to help practitioners act from a more knowledgeable base.

The approach we have taken in this book is consistent with this challenge. We have not attempted to propose specific action steps based on our analysis. Rather, we have attempted to broaden the understanding of conflict and conflict handling in organizations beyond its implicit boundaries of public, formal, and rational approaches. The chapters have consciously taken an antithetical approach to this predominant focus by addressing private, informal, and nonrational means of conflict handling. Ignoring these dimensions creates a one-sided approach that is likely to be detrimental in the long run to full understanding of means of conflict handling. Even more important, ignorance of the crucial roles played by private, informal, and nonrational approaches is likely to retard the ability to "see" these activities and their positive and negative effects, their ability to facilitate or block crossing interpretive divides, and their tendency to reproduce current organizational systems rather than change them. If conflict is to foster social change, it is necessary that private and informal dimensions of conflict management be brought out into the open, to be on stage to be viewed and understood.

By highlighting the understudied dimensions of conflict, we hope to stimulate study that explores in more depth the relationship between public and private, formal and informal, and rational and nonrational dimensions of conflict. We noted that private, informal, and nonrational

conflict handling make sense only in light of public, formal, and rational manifestations of conflict (and that, conversely, public, formal, and
rational manifestations often depend on them to succeed; see Goffman
1959). The work in this book primarily takes one pole in a dialectical
approach, an emphasis on the understudied dimensions of conflict, to
increase the attention given them. In a sense, the book is conflict-based
itself, aimed at fostering a different perspective than the current dominant one. But the presentation of a different perspective is not adequate in itself; on the basis of the conflict it may help to create, we hope
the book will lead to a more complex understanding.

In sum, in this book, we have brought behind-the-scenes conflicts out
into the open next to their public, formal, and rational counterparts. The
next step is to bring the interplay of these types of conflicts to front-
stage attention.

References

Abel, R. 1982. *The politics of informal justice*. New York: Academic Press.
Allison, G. 1971. *Essence of decision: Explaining the Cuban missile crisis*. Boston: Lit-
tle, Brown.
Bartunek, J. M. 1984. Changing interpretive schemes and organizational restructuring:
The example of a religious order. *Administrative Science Quarterly* 29:355-72.
Baumgartner, M. P. 1988. Social control in suburbia. In *Toward a general theory of social
control*. Vol. 2, ed. D. Black, 72-103. New York: Academic Press.
Beyer, J. M. 1982. Introduction. *Administrative Science Quarterly* 27:588-90.
Black, D. 1990. The elementary forms of conflict management. In *New directions in the
study of justice, law, and social control*, ed. Arizona School of Justice Studies, Arizona
State University, 43-69. New York: Plenum.
Brief, A. P., and J. M. Dukerich. 1991. Theory in organizational behavior: Can it be use-
ful? In *Research in organizational behavior*. Vol. 13, ed. L. L. Cummings and B. M.
Staw, 327-52. Greenwich, Conn.: JAI.
Child, J., and C. Smith. 1987. The context and process of organizational transformation:
Cadbury Limited in its sector. *Journal of Management Studies* 24:565-93.
Collins, R. 1975. *Conflict sociology*. New York: Academic Press.
Cyert, R. M., and J. G. March. 1963. *A behavioral theory of the firm*. Englewood Cliffs,
N.J.: Prentice-Hall.
Felstiner, W. L. F., R. L. Abel, and A. Sarat. 1981. The emergence and transformation of
disputes: Naming, blaming and claiming. *Law and Society Review* 15:631-54.
Fisher, R., and W. Ury. 1981. *Getting to yes*. New York: Houghton Mifflin.
Gioia, D. A., and P. P. Poole. 1984. Scripts in organizational behavior. *Academy of Man-
agement Review* 9:449-59.
Gluckman, M. 1955. *Custom and conflict in Africa*. Oxford, England: Basil Blackwell.
Goffman, E. 1959. *The presentation of self in everyday life*. Garden City, N.Y.: Dou-
bleday.

Granovetter, M. 1973. The strength of weak ties. *American Journal of Sociology* 78:1360-80.

Greenhouse, C. 1986. *Praying for justice: Faith, order and community in an American town.* Ithaca, N.Y.: Cornell University Press.

Janis, I. 1989. *Crucial decisions.* New York: Free Press.

Kriesberg, L. 1973. *The sociology of social conflict.* Englewood Cliffs, N.J.: Prentice-Hall.

March, J. G., and H. Simon. 1958. *Organizations.* New York: John Wiley.

McKelvey, G., and H. Aldrich. 1983. Populations, natural selection, and applied organization science. *Administrative Science Quarterly* 28:101-28.

Miles, R. 1980. *Macro organizational behavior.* Santa Monica, Cal.: Goodyear.

Mintzberg, H. 1979. *The structuring of organizations.* Englewood Cliffs, N.J.: Prentice-Hall.

Moch, M. K., and J. M. Bartunek. 1990. *Creating alternative realities at work: The quality of work life experiment at FoodCom.* New York: Harper Business.

Mouzelis, N. P. 1967. *Organization and bureaucracy.* Chicago: Aldine.

Pettigrew, A. 1973. *The politics of organizational decision-making.* London: Tavistock.

Pruitt, D. 1981. *Negotiation behavior.* New York: Academic Press.

Sheppard, B. H., R. J. Lewicki, and J. Minton. 1992. *Organizational justice.* Lexington, Mass.: Lexington.

Simmel, G. 1908. *Conflict and the web of group affiliations.* New York: Free Press.

Thomas, K. W. 1976. Conflict and conflict management. In *Handbook of industrial and organizational psychology,* ed. J. D. Dunnette, 889-935. New York: Rand McNally.

Thomas, K. W., and W. G. Tyman, Jr. 1982. Necessary properties of relevant research: Lessons from recent criticisms of the organizational sciences. *Academy of Management Review* 7:345-52.

Author Index

Subject Index

About the Authors

Jean M. Bartunek is Professor of Organizational Studies in the Carroll School of Management at Boston College. She received a Ph.D. in social and organizational psychology from the University of Illinois at Chicago and has served as Visiting Assistant Professor at the University of Illinois at Urbana-Champaign and Visiting Scholar at the University of Illinois at Chicago. She is coauthor of *Creating Alternative Realities at Work: The Quality of Work Life Experiment at FoodCom* (1990) and has written numerous journal articles and book chapters. She is a member of the editorial boards of five journals and was chairperson of the Organization Development and Change Division of the Academy of Management. Her research interests focus on the intersection of social cognition, conflict, and organizational change.

Frank A. Dubinskas is Assistant Professor in the Carroll School of Management at Boston College, where he teaches Organizational Studies and Management of Technology. As an anthropologist (Ph.D., Stanford University) researching industrial organizations, he focuses on knowledge management and collaboration in complex organizations. He has studied cross-functional integration and conflict in various high-technology environments, including start-up biotechnology firms (published in his book *Making Time: Ethnographies of High-Technology Organizations,*

1988). Other field research includes the new product development process in the worldwide automobile industry (with Kim B. Clark of Harvard University) and the management of advanced manufacturing automation projects. As an NEH Fellow for 1991-1992 at the School of American Research, he is writing about his recent yearlong field project at Apple Computer, Inc., on a concurrent engineering project in computer assembly innovation involving a U.S.-Japanese collaboration.

Raymond A. Friedman is Assistant Professor of Business Administration at the Harvard Business School. He received his Ph.D. in Sociology from the University of Chicago and spent a year as a Research Fellow at the Harvard Business School. His areas of interest include organizational culture, organizational change, and labor relations. He is currently studying attempts to change labor-management negotiations. These studies have included direct observations of negotiations as well as joint training in "mutual gains" bargaining (with a team from Harvard's Program on Negotiation).

Deborah M. Kolb is Professor of Management at the Simmons College Graduate School of Management and Executive Director of the Program on Negotiation at Harvard Law School. She is the author of *The Mediators* (1983), an in-depth study of labor mediation, and the editor of *When Talk Works: Profiles of Master Mediators* (forthcoming), a collection of in-depth profiles. The book is based on a multiyear project that involved 12 mediation scholars in a comparative investigation of successful practice. She is currently carrying out field research on gender issues in negotiation and on informal dispute-handling processes in organizations. She received her B.A. from Vassar College, her M.B.A. from the University of Colorado, and her Ph.D. from Massachusetts Institute of Technology's Sloan School of Management. She is on the editorial boards of the *Negotiation Journal, Journal of Contemporary Ethnography, Journal of Conflict Resolution,* and the Jossey-Bass Conflict Resolution Series, and is 1992 chairperson of the Conflict Management Division of the Academy of Management

Roy J. Lewicki is Associate Dean for Graduate Business Programs and Executive Education and Professor of Business Administration at the College of Business, The Ohio State University. He received his Ph.D.in social psychology from Columbia University. Prior to joining the faculty of The Ohio State University, he held faculty and administrative positions at Yale University, Dartmouth College, and Duke University. His research interests include managerial bargaining and negotiation, mechanisms for the resolution of disputes, justice systems in organizations, and ethical decision making. He has coauthored and edited 11 books, including his most recent, *Justice in Organizations* (1992), and has written approximately 25 book chapters and articles. He has been chairperson of the Academy of Management Interest Group in Power, Negotiation, and Conflict Management and received the first David Bradford Outstanding Educator award from the Organizational Behavior Teaching Society for his contributions to pedagogy in the fields of negotiation and dispute resolution.

Joanne Martin is Professor of Organizational Behavior at the Graduate School of Business and, by courtesy, the Department of Sociology, Stanford University. She is currently the McNamara Faculty Fellow and Director of the Doctoral Programs at the Graduate School of Business. She received her Ph.D. in Social Psychology from the Department of Psychology and Social Relations, Harvard University, in 1977. Her research has focused on two topic areas: distributive justice and organizational culture. She is the author of numerous articles and four books, most recently *Cultures in Organizations: Three Perspectives* (in press) and *Reframing Organizational Cultures* (coedited by Frost, Moore, Louis, Lundberg, and Martin, 1991). She has served as an officer of the Academy of Management and as a member of the editorial boards of several journals, including *Administrative Science Quarterly* and the *Academy of Management Journal*. Her current research focuses on the effects of gender and race on organizations and organization theory.

Calvin Morrill is Assistant Professor of Communication and Sociology at the University of Arizona. He received his Ph.D. in Sociology from Harvard University and also spent a year as a Junior Fellow at the Center for Criminal Justice, Harvard Law School. He is completing a book-length manuscript on conflict management in corporations and is also conducting research on social structure and the labeling of unethical behavior among corporate managers. His current work includes a methodological study of the disputing process, investigations of conflict management in complex, high-risk organizations, and studies of language and culture in different dispute settlement institutions.

Linda L. Putnam, who received her Ph.D. from the University of Minnesota, is Professor of Communication at Purdue University. Her current research interests include communication strategies in negotiation, organizational conflict, contradictory and paradoxical messages, and language analysis in conflict. She serves on the editorial boards of seven journals and has edited special issues on dispute resolution for *Communication Research* and *Management Communication Quarterly*. She is he coeditor of four books, including *Communication and Organization: An Interpretive Approach, Handbook of Organizational Communication,* and *Communication Perspectives on Negotiation,* a volume in the Sage Annual Reviews of Communication Research. Three of her articles and books have received best publication awards from the Organizational Communication Division of the Speech Communication Association.

Robin D. Reid works as an Organization Development Consultant for a small human resources consulting firm, Cook Ross Associates, in Chevy Chase, Maryland. Prior to her current position, she was a Management and Organization Development Specialist for Data General Corporation in Westboro, Massachusetts. She received her M.B.A. with a concentration in organizational consulting from the Boston College Graduate School of Management in 1988. Her consulting work focuses on helping organizations and their leaders manage effectively in times of rapid change.

John Van Maanen is the Erwin Schell Professor of Organization Studies in the Sloan School of Management, Massachusetts Institute of Technology. He received his Ph.D. from the University of California, Irvine, in 1972. He has been a visiting professor at Yale University, the University of Surrey (United Kingdom), and INSEAD (France). He is the author of numerous articles and books, including *Essays in Interpersonal Relations, Organizational Careers,* and, most recently, *Tales of the Field* (1988). He is on the editorial boards of several journals, including *Administrative Science Quarterly, Human Organization,* and *Journal of Contemporary Ethnography.* He is also the General Editor of the MIT Press series on Organization Studies and the Sage Publications Series on Qualitative Methods. His teaching and research interests include organization theory, organizational sociology, cultural processes in organizations, management of public and private institutions, and organization behavior.